Praise for Chrissie Hynde's

RECKLESS

"A love letter to rock 'n' roll. . . . Honest and distinctive. . . . [*Reckless*] gives an accurate sense of what it's like to sit down with Chrissie Hynde. . . . Acerbic, clever, confrontational."
—*The New York Times Book Review*

"Rich and ragged. . . . Engaging. . . . [Hynde] writes just like she lives, and just like she makes music. She does it her way, which is an inimitable multiplicity of things: impulsive, untamed, ragged, proud." —*The Daily Beast*

"Chrissie Hynde's autobiography, *Reckless*, out-rocks them all."
—*The Washington Post*

"Rebellious, fierce. . . . Full of engaging stories, dry wit and revelations." —*The Guardian*

"Fascinating. . . . A portrait of an era." —Vogue.com

"Entertaining. . . . Sarcasm and dry humor shine through. . . . One can almost hear her deep, sneering vibrato."
—*Pittsburgh Post-Gazette*

"[A] fascinating memoir." —*Financial Times*

"A stirring tale of rock, regret and redemption. . . . Unflinching. . . . *Reckless* is a survivor's tale, a portrait of a woman bolstered by conviction and buoyed by extreme fortitude."
—*The Buffalo News*

"This long-awaited memoir tells [Hynde's] life story in full and utterly fascinating detail. . . . She brings a fantastic eye for detail, a withering and sardonic sense of humor, and a fearless emotional honesty." —*Library Journal*

Chrissie Hynde

RECKLESS

Chrissie Hynde is a singer, songwriter, and guitarist, best known as the lead singer and songwriter of the enduring rock band the Pretenders. Hynde released nine studio albums with the Pretenders, beginning with 1980's *Pretenders*, which *Rolling Stone* called the #13 Best Debut Album of All Time. Most recently, she released her first solo album, *Stockholm*, in 2014. She lives in London.

www.chrissiehynde.com

RECKLESS

My Life as a Pretender

CHRISSIE HYNDE

ANCHOR BOOKS

A Division of Penguin Random House LLC

New York

FIRST ANCHOR BOOKS EDITION, AUGUST 2016

Copyright © 2015 by Chrissie Hynde

All rights reserved. Published in the United States by Anchor Books,
a division of Penguin Random House LLC, New York. Originally published
in hardcover simultaneously in Great Britain by Ebury Press, a division of
Penguin Random House Ltd., London, and in the United States by Doubleday,
a division of Penguin Random House LLC, New York, in 2015.

Anchor Books and colophon are registered trademarks of
Penguin Random House LLC.

The Library of Congress has cataloged the Doubleday edition as follows:
Hynde, Chrissie, author.
Reckless : my life as a Pretender / by Chrissie Hynde.
pages cm
1. Hynde, Chrissie.   2. Pretenders (Musical group).
3. Rock musicians—United States—Biography.   I. Title.
ML420.H9976A3 2015   782.42166092—dc23   [B]   2015027449

Anchor Books Trade Paperback ISBN: 978-1-101-91223-2
eBook ISBN: 978-0-385-54062-9

Book design by Maria Carella

www.anchorbooks.com

Printed in the United States of America
10 9 8 7 6 5

To Natalie and Yasmin

"Life teaches you how to live it,
if you live long enough."
TONY BENNETT

CONTENTS

PROLOGUE

I was twenty-seven by the time I finally met him. I'd been on a mission but the truth is, I didn't even know it was him at first although the signposts trailed as if in marquee lights behind me. Then by his alchemy one day I changed from being an ugly duckling into a swan and flew off taking him with me. Along with Pete and Martin, we sailed into the setting sun with its light bouncing off us.

So this is my story, our story. Me and Jimmy and all the rest of them. All my crazy friends (many now departed).

I couldn't have told this when my parents were alive, I would have had to leave out the bad language and tell a lot of lies about what I'd been doing all that time I was gone. I'm so sorry for that, Mom and Dad, I know you were proud of me. I regret half of this story and the other half is the sound you heard.

Here it is then girls, my reckless life.

Chrissie Hynde
London, June 2015

RECKLESS

1
BEAUTIFUL TREES

The first thing I think of isn't the rubber tires or cars or factories—it's the trees, and they will always be my lasting impression of it.

The first one I saw was the cherry tree. It was expecting me. Trees have personalities, subtle but a baby can tell. The house on Hillcrest Street stood on the crest of a hill paved with red bricks. When a car drove up it made a distinctive sound like a Spaniard rolling his Rs. I loved that sound and I loved that house painted blue, the color of choice for an Akron house, with its covered porch you could sit on when it rained. And I loved the pond in Uncle Harry's backyard next door. But mostly I loved the cherry tree.

Melville and Dolores; Bud and Dee; Mr. and Mrs. M. G. Hynde. Akron, Ohio; Rubber City; Tire Town. Those were the different names of my three parents: father, mother, hometown.

Father: blue eyes, Marine Corps uniform, playing a harmonica. He held me aloft so high I could have touched the ceiling. Mother: perfect nails, Elizabeth Taylor hair, red-and-white striped dress, impeccable. Hometown: streets, trees, streams, the Ohio seasons. I learned everything I needed to know from the three of you.

My mother was from Summit Lake. Her dad, Jack Roberts, was an Akron cop. Her mother, Irene, a seamstress, played piano in the church, Margaret Park Presbyterian. It was to her house on Hillcrest Street where they took me from People's Hospital that day in September 1951.

Summit Lake was Akron's Coney Island, the place for boats and rides and summer pastimes—and that's where Bud and Dolores starting seeing each other. They were bound to meet because his sister Ruth had married her brother Gene.

In later years, my dad spent many hours researching the Hynde family tree. He even trawled through the family records in Edinburgh's town hall after I married a Scotsman. (Yes, there's my dad wearing a fishing hat, Bermuda shorts and Hush Puppies, wandering the cobbled streets, always looking up.) "Scotland—Home of Golf," as said on the tea towel I gave him that he displayed above his workbench in the garage where he crafted his own golf clubs, listening to the police band on his radio.

"Oh, Bud, why are you listening to that?" My mother, critical of any hillbillyish behavior.

"Now, Christy, do your neighbors know you're Scots?" he asked loudly, every time he came to London. "They don't care, Dad. They're Greek."

The family heritage fad for families started in the seventies. Before that, if you weren't part of an ethnic minority like African, Italian or Jewish, you were simply American. There were no Hispanics or Asians around, not up north. We looked and sounded like the characters in cowboy shows on TV: *Have Gun—Will Travel*; *Tombstone Territory*; *The Rifleman*. (I knew all the theme songs.) White Europeans: we owned the joint. I must have been fifteen before it occurred to me to ask where the Hyndes came from. And the Craigs, the Roberts and Joneses. According to my father "they," as in "we," had come from Scotland via Nova Scotia. His theory:

"Now, Hynde was originally spelled H-Y-N-D—the E was added as a flourish!"

(Most of his sentences began with "now.") I think the "flourish" referred to the florid style of script they wrote in back then. I must have heard him say that fifty times.

My mother's people were from Caerphilly, and must have found jobs in the coal mines of southern Ohio, as Welsh coal miners would have. "Wales? Where the heck is that? Is that a country?" I asked. Her mother, Irene, had been adopted along with her brother and sisters, Edna, Glovina and Louie. I never knew why; I forgot to ask my mother when I had the chance.

My maternal grandparents, the cop and the seamstress, divorced. I never asked about that, either. It was uncommon to divorce back then. My mother wouldn't have talked about it anyway. There's a lot I never knew, I suppose, like with every family.

Before she married she went to New York City to work as a model. I never appreciated how bold that was for a girl back then. It was the "Land of Opportunity," but people like mine didn't get very many back then. Now I see that's where her sense of glamour came from. Always ultramodern. Then she became the wife and mother she was born to be, like every woman in her community.

When I was eight she went back to work, as a secretary, but she always made dinner and did the housework. I wasn't allowed to come to the table in bare feet. She ran a tight ship.

Grandma Roberts was living with us when she died. She moved in with us on Stabler Road, leaving the little apartment in North Hill where she'd been on her own since the Hillcrest days. I was ten when she had a heart attack at the dinner table. An ambulance came and took her away, and we never saw her again. The thing that shocked me most was my mother saying, "Oh, God. Oh, God." I'd never heard her talk like that before. Was that swearing? No, it couldn't have been. We weren't allowed to swear.

My grandma Hynde was the last one of their generation. She spent the end of her days in an old people's home playing bingo. We always went to her house in Tallmadge for Easter and would spend the day with Aunt Ruth and Uncle Gene and our double cousins, Dave, Dick and Marianne, all five of us sharing both sets of grandparents. No, that wasn't a hillbilly thing. Not if my mother had anything to do with it.

Grandma Hynde listened to the baseball game on the radio and did crossword puzzles as good as anyone. By then, Americans were starting a new trend: not to have aging parents live in the family home. It wasn't the modern way.

My brother, Terry, played clarinet. Kids in the neighborhood called him Benny after Benny Goodman. Then he moved on to the sax and became as fine a sax player as I've ever heard. He was the musician of the family, not me. The only time I ever saw Terry starstruck was when I introduced him to Neneh Cherry. "Her dad's Don Cherry!" Terry could hardly speak.

I had no concept of life beyond Akron's leafy borders—the warehouses, factories, valleys, streams and woodlands, with their dramatic transformations. For all I knew every town had red brick roads and every fourth house was painted blue.

That's when Akron was the center of the universe.

•

Thirty years earlier, Akron and Washington, DC, had been the fastest-growing cities in the nation. Akron was the rubber capital of the world and we had all the major factories—Goodyear, Goodrich,

Firestone, General, Mohawk, Ace—and Washington had the White House.

Almost everyone had a job in one of these factories, including my grandpa (Leonard) Hynde, who worked for Goodyear Tire & Rubber. Hundreds of West Virginians moved up to Akron to get jobs as rubber workers, so many that it was often referred to as the capital of West Virginia.

When you walked down Main Street in Akron you either caught the fragrant whiff of rolled oats from the silos at the Quaker Oats factory or the acrid smell from one of the rubber factories. The latter, the distinctive pong like you get patching out in a hot rod, will still conjure to an Akronite the days when the city was the famous Rubber Capital of the World. We were big and important, renowned for rubber and the Soap Box Derby, which took place every year, kids from across the nation submitting their custom-built racers, one of which would soar downhill faster than the others and claim the trophy to national acclaim.

We had industry and abundant, rolling farmland for hundreds of miles to the south, east and west. (See how proud I am?) The Seneca Indians named it "Ohi-yo," meaning, "It is beautiful, beautiful river." Yes, Ohio: so beautiful.

My dad kept a collection of Indian arrowheads in a cigar box. Boy Scouts in his day were encouraged to collect arrowheads—it was in the handbook. My dad's were carefully labeled to tell precisely where each had been plucked from along the banks of the Cuyahoga Valley that the Eries, Seneca and other bands of Ohio Indians (I know they aren't referred to as "Indians" these days, but c'mon— they were the Indians to us) traveled through, portaging their canoes across what by the time of my father were their burial grounds.

The Amish and Mennonites settled there, their farms extending across Pennsylvania, so that they were often referred to as the Pennsylvania Dutch, although they were actually of German origin. They never used electricity or anything technology-driven. The men wore beards but never a mustache, as that would be reminiscent of the military and they were devout pacifists. Even buttons were prohibited because buttons evoked military connotations. They were a familiar sight in their somber black buggies drawn by somber bay horses that also pulled their plows, everything done by real horsepower. It was thrilling to see an Amish buggy when our family took a customary drive into the country for tomatoes, apples or corn, according to the seasons.

How strange it seemed, me in the convertible with my modern parents and the Amish in their old-fashioned clothes—women and girls in long dresses, puffy sleeves and white bonnets, the men and boys in suspenders holding up their rough cotton trousers—dressed like extras in a film featuring the pioneers.

They never changed. It's still just as common a sight to see a buggy nowadays, antlike atop a bridge traversing a twelve-lane highway as trucks and cars roar beneath them. They continue to go about their business the same as they did when the countryside was a sanctuary in which they could live out their austere lives undisturbed. With their steady, unchanging commitment to family and community, they remain a testament to their beliefs and values. They can put up a barn in one day; ordinary citizens can hire them to construct outbuildings. Ohio wouldn't be Ohio without the Amish.

Frank Seiberling, the founder of the Goodyear Tire & Rubber Company, built an English Tudor country estate on seventy acres of wooded land in 1912 in West Akron—the twelfth-largest house in America—and called it Stan Hywet Hall. It inspired the many mock Tudor mansions that still line Portage Path, named after the trail where the Indians once portaged their canoes, and elegant Merriman Avenue and all the surrounding areas with English street names—Mayfair, Hereford, Wye, Eton, Edgerton, Dorset, Hampshire, Wiltshire—names I only recognized as English when I returned years later.

Every city in Ohio had a train depot: Cleveland, Columbus, Cincinnati, Dayton, Toledo, Sandusky and Youngstown, even the smaller towns, Seneca, Barberton, Lodi, Lorain and the rest.

At one time America had the best train system in the world, probably because most of the men who built it were chained to other dedicated workers and not given time off. Along with the tracks that soon spanned America came a lot of music because, as well as picking up the heavy chain that bound them, they sang. The slaves gave us tracks of many kinds.

By the end of the fifties the extensive passenger-train system was, like the Indian Nation, history, so if it wasn't for the music there would be little else to show for all that hard work.

·

Ohio seasons were the ones pictured in calendars. Summers, hot and lazy, buzzing with life, pungent and green. Autumn, hesitant at first, slate-colored skies and leaves of scarlet and gold that dropped off the trees and covered the ground like an Indian blanket. Winters, harsh, the first snowfall like a fresh sheet thrown over the houses, storing them away until spring. We'd always have a white Christmas. Then came the spring, all blossoms, birdsong and fragrant breezes. Geese in formations of military precision came and went throughout. "Canada geese," my dad regularly reminded us. "People always say 'Canadian geese.' It's not Canadian geese, it's Canada geese!"

Aunt Binny, Grandma Robert's sister, and Uncle Harry lived next door on Hillcrest Street. Uncle Harry tended his tomato plants in the dappled sunlight while I watched the fish swim and glitter in his pond. Aunt Binny made us hand puppets out of socks, elaborate works of art they were too. I loved going to their house because I knew where they kept their stash of Beeman's Gum, just inside the top drawer of the sideboard in their dining room.

Akron houses smelled of wood polish and ironing and rhubarb pie, and seemed like the foundation of civilization itself. But it was a foundation about to shift. Our houses were in the way of progress. We had to move.

But we didn't have to move *from* our houses; we had to move our houses. All those homes standing in the way of the expressway, which was planning its nationwide takeover, were hoisted onto logs and rolled out of the way. Out of the way of the coming of a new America.

It was essentially the beginning of the end of Akron as a city. There were ditches where the houses had been, and wet clay got churned up to the surface where you could see and smell it. Even as a three-year-old, it seemed all wrong to me to be exposed like that.

The pond and the cherry tree were left behind to be dealt with by the bulldozers. My cherry tree.

Red bricks were hacked out and the streets abruptly dropped off at metal barriers prohibiting entry into the inner belt. Every street becoming a dead end. Across the swath of concrete, its other half could be found, spliced like a worm, still wriggling. The streets, houses, people and neighborhoods were simply in the way of this "urban improvement," insignificant next to the endless expanse of highway that would soon swallow America.

2

CUYAHOGA FALLS . . .
TERRY! CHRISTY!

When my dad got out of the Marines, after we'd moved to North Carolina and Florida to be with him, we moved to 8th Street in Cuyahoga Falls, a stone's throw from Akron. He would forevermore talk proudly of his time serving his country when he'd had malaria three times. While serving on Guadalcanal in the Pacific he'd had a glimpse of the mythical "others"—but for the rest of us, well, it would be some years before we paused to consider life beyond our borders: life outside of Ohio; life outside of the pages of *Life* magazine. We were the norm, the mean, the gold standard.

He got a job with the Ohio Bell Telephone company and would be a loyal employee for the rest of his working life. He had a "Yellow Pages" badge permanently pinned to his golf hat or fishing hat. "Oh, Bud, take that silly hat off!" was a plea oft heard around Hynde House.

The family went where the job took the primary breadwinner and never thought for one moment to question it. A pronouncement like "Cleveland? I'm not moving there—you can go on your own" had not yet found its way into the American consciousness. My generation would see to that. I would practically take it up single-handedly.

Terry had new friends, and they'd play in the backyards making tree forts, wearing raccoon-tailed Davy Crockett hats. Everybody had lasso designs on their bedspreads and maybe an Indian headdress along with their cowboy hats, six-shooters and holsters. If asked, I said I wanted to be a cowgirl when I grew up.

One bath time, my mother found a necklace in my pocket which wasn't mine. When questioned I admitted it was Patty Bordeman's, who lived behind us. I was made to understand that I had stolen it and would have to return it the next day. I didn't know what stealing was, but it sounded like I was in trouble.

The Bordemans' back door was on the side of their house, so with my mother watching I walked across the backyards, knowing that she wouldn't be able to see if someone came to the door or not. I was pretty sure I didn't want to tell Mrs. Bordeman about my "stealing," so I pretended to knock, waited a few seconds, mimed returning the necklace and walked back.

That might have been the only time I pulled a fast one on my mother.

Other than that, life was trauma-free, other than one major bummer that I wasn't dealing with very well: the furnace in the basement. It had a face and scared me to death. My dad would take me down, stand me in front of it and shout, "OKAY, DEE!" She'd switch the thermostat on and we'd watch the interior ignite. It didn't matter how many times they talked me through it, I was terrified of the one I called Furnace the Burnace.

I had my first nightmare about it—of it walking into the room where Terry and Dad and I were watching TV with white-and-pink icing all over its face. After that I would never go down to the TV room on my own. If I wanted to watch *Captain Penny* when Terry was outside, Dad was at work and Mom upstairs, I'd belt down the stairs, turn it on and scramble back up to the top of the landing and crouch in a sprint position.

Like everyone else who got earaches and sore throats as a child, I was taken to have my tonsils out. The nurse told my mother that I wouldn't go to the bathroom, so I waited for her to leave the room, climbed over the bars of the crib and showed my mother the route I took down the hall to "Go toidy." She snuck in my clothes in a paper bag the next day and smuggled me out before I had to get the operation, which was on hold on account of my getting tonsillitis again. I got a Dumbo the Elephant toy and a little dog for my Ginny doll—gifts for being sick. I never did get my tonsils out.

I discovered that if I bit hard enough I could break a glass with my teeth. "Bud—come quick. She did it again" was an ongoing commotion for a while. Pencils weren't safe around me either, when I discovered that if I bent them far enough they would snap.

I understand that, as children, serial killers torture animals. If Wendy O. Williams and I are anything to go by, rock singers like to break things when they're young.

I'd go next door to Timmy Porter's house, and we'd sneak into his dad's garage and pee in the gravel in the corner. Our parents seemed to know everything no matter how stealthy we were and we got found out but didn't get into big trouble, which surprised me. Maybe they thought we didn't know it was wrong, as we were only three. We knew all right, but we liked peeing there.

I heard years later that Timmy Porter got killed in Vietnam.

One thing about the Hynde household: it was never old-fashioned. You wouldn't find a doily or an Early American motif. No chance. It was wire sculptures, Miró-like motifs, and hold the lace, for Dolores Hynde.

So our next house, after my dad's transfer to Cleveland with Ohio Bell, was a bungalow on Sherborn Road in Parma Heights, characteristically new and modern with stained-wood siding, golf-course green lawn, matching shrubs, red geraniums and a black Ford Fairlane convertible with gold lightning bolts down the sides, gleaming with Hollywood glamour, in the driveway.

It was 1958 and everyone was home. No feature in *Life* magazine had America coursing through its veins more than the Hynde household: Marine Corps mementos, bowling trophies, Coty lipstick, Steve Allen and Jackie Gleason. This was Ohio. This was the heart of the nation, looking forward with opportunity, possibility and flair.

My parents had been the archetypal newlyweds, both from generations of Akronites; no higher education, no time or money for that sort of thing, they took their lead from the lifestyles presented in *Life*, *Saturday Evening Post* or *Look* magazines. My dad's job at the phone company meant that we could have a telephone in the basement and the garage. Nobody else had that.

The United States led the West, and the citizens of the world all wanted to be like us. We had Frank Sinatra and Elvis. We had Marilyn Monroe and James Dean. Everyone wanted to stand with us as we took our place in the sun. They knew all about us, but we didn't know about them.

The day we arrived in Parma Heights, as boxes were unloaded from the Mayflower van, I wandered next door into the garage of

Colleen McMonagle—a girl my age who shared my interests, which at that time were pretty basic.

Drawing horses was our favorite pastime. Sprawled across the floor, we improvised theme songs to accompany the furious coloring-in of stampeding horses . . . DUN dun, DUN dun, DUN dun, DUN dun, DUN dun, DUN dun, DUUUUUNNNN!

We drew horses grazing, horses resting—their legs folded under them with muzzles on delicate knees—horses rearing, horses galloping, horses trotting, horses jumping. But mainly horses rearing.

The best thing next to drawing and making tree forts was playing "lost girls," a game I devised in which I would convince a friend to join me in wandering as far back to the edge of the housing development and into the woods as we could go until we couldn't find our way back—followed by a blood-pumping rush of fear and mild panic.

We lived in a world where fearing for our safety was an unknown, as likely an idea as a flying saucer landing in the front yard. We were safe, fed, warm and provided for. We were the last of a dying breed.

We played baseball, no rules or catching, not for the girls, anyway, as we whacked the ball and watched it soar over the backyards. The boys had rules and took the game seriously.

We rode our bikes, accompanied by the constant sputtering of lawnmowers and the humming sound of heat and insects. I stuck baseball cards between the spokes of my bike, which made a loud thwacking sound as I got up to speed. In the ponds, we caught guppies, minnows and frogs.

The approaching bells of the ice-cream man set our hearts aflutter. The sharpening of popsicle sticks on the sidewalk to make spears was ongoing.

We wore striped T-shirts and corduroy trousers with elastic waistbands; never dresses or anything girly except to church or school. It was still a few years before the entire nation would start wearing blue jeans. Before the hippies came along they were only for farmers. Even beatniks wore slacks with their turtleneck sweaters, not jeans. Jazz musicians wore chinos. Marilyn Monroe once wore jeans in a film, as did James Dean and Marlon Brando. I would never have been allowed.

The world was full of promise and choice and no one was trying to hurt us. Feeling safe came as naturally as swatting a mosquito. I pranced between the houses on my colt legs, the ground awash with dew and crabapple blossoms. Life smelled good.

Every fifth house was the same, all up the block and around the corner. Things were newly built with good intentions. Mom called out across the backyards, "Terry! Christy! Christy! Terry!"

Then the Ohio Bell transferred my dad again—back to Akron.

3

AKRON

I started Fairlawn Elementary School, aged eight, with my first day as "new kid" ruined by the certainty that I would never be able to spell "people" or "Wednesday."

During recess, Lolly Reyant and Sally Bittaker, my fellow horse-loving compatriots, and I would wail! After drawing pictures of our alternative identities in class, we would assume our "horse" personas on the playground, galloping at full pelt, then sailing over hedge and fence. We were "The Herd."

Lolly was Tan Topper, a bay stallion with one white front stocking and a blaze from forelock to muzzle; Sally was Don Juan Ed, a dappled gray gelding; and I was Royal Miss, a chestnut mare with two white stockings and a star on my forehead. We trotted, galloped, snorted and pawed, reared and sidestepped, cantered and jumped, cleared bush and wall, never balking or shying; we crossed the length of the playground, carefully avoiding the area where the rest of the girls in our class were watching the boys play kickball.

One day in the summer, when our parents were out bowling, I saw some of Terry's friends coming up Stabler Road and thought up a plan to scare him. I liked to scare people.

I snuck out, intercepted his friends and asked them to surround the house and wait while I went back in, then, when they heard me scream, they were to bang on the screened-in windows as hard as they could for one minute. When I knew his friends were in position, I let rip with an almighty howl, triggering a house-shaking assault, not unlike an episode of *The Twilight Zone*.

Another time, I spied Terry sitting against the wall of the garage under the milk chute, reading *Mad* magazine. I went in, opened the chute and dropped a rock on his head. That time I was bang out of order and he was actually hurt. I was sorry. I'm not a violent person, but I couldn't resist a perfect setup.

I held my plastic "Jesus Saves" cross near a lightbulb before going to bed so it would glow in the dark. I didn't think I was religious and didn't think about whether I believed or not. Having said that, I could never understand how anyone with a modicum of rebelliousness or sense of fair play couldn't appreciate He who hung with lowlifes and healed the sick. I especially liked the story about Him driving those merchants out of the temple. Even Jesus could lose it if pressed.

I spent so much time in the woods that it went without saying that something transcendental was at work. Even a child could see that things didn't just appear out of nowhere. One afternoon, while staring into the sky intent on grooming, tacking up and jumping the horse I would one day have, an unfamiliar terror jolted me from my imaginings: I was beginning to love horses more than I loved God. I knew, even at the age of eight, to keep it in check.

•

Dianne Athey was a grade behind me at school. We met at Faith Lutheran Church and spent many a sermon choking on silent, painful laughter in the choir box. In summer, we swung on the trapeze she had rigged up in her backyard, me playing the supporting role in anything athletic but being a total bully when it came to harmonies and parts for our musical repertoire—on a cappella versions of the Kool-Aid theme song and "Foolish Little Girl."

Our bid for show business would have to wait a few years, but started when I got a baritone ukulele and the Mel Bay book of chords for an Easter present. Dianne already had a guitar, and we soon had a little thing going, nothing too exciting—"Four Strong Winds," and *Barnaby*'s theme song—a kids show on Channel 3. Stuff like that. Pretty crap really.

My dad played his chromatic harmonica and had an ocarina, aka a "sweet potato," which I would sneak down from the shelf and have a go on myself. (When "Wild Thing" stormed the charts years later, I could knock out that closing solo, no problem, me and a couple-of-dozen freckled West Virginians.) I copied Bob Dylan's harmonica holder out of a coat hanger so I could play my uke at the same time.

The new discount houses like Clarkins where my parents did their grocery shopping also had a record department. It was there that I first saw "I Want to Hold Your Hand." I stared in amazement for half an hour. I'd heard it on the radio but the long hair and Pierre Cardin suits threw me. I'd never seen a band that looked like them. In fact, I'd never seen an English band. This was a huge turning point. I abandoned my baritone uke and got a big-necked nylon-stringed acoustic guitar that said Zim Gar on the headstock. I couldn't play along to records as I wasn't good enough, but found with three chords I would make up my own tunes and sing along. I put to music a wistful message of love to Paul McCartney and found that singing came naturally when I was strumming my stuff.

4

WALK, DON'T RUN

met Nita Lee while doing time at Litchfield Junior High School. She was willowy, long of limb, and wore her platinum-blonde hair parted just enough to reveal her sorrowful face and the dark circles under her sad eyes. She was beautiful, delicate and nothing like the rest of the Litchfield Argonauts who stalked the corridors. She spoke other languages that only she understood.

Neither of us was interested in what the "popular" kids were interested in, like getting good or even passable grades, dating guys or wearing penny loafers, or whatever else they were doing. We didn't want to be like them. Our music was better than theirs and that was what defined us.

We weren't yet aware of what "nonconformity" was, but soon it would be the hallmark of our generation. We were well outside the margin of conformity already. My parents might have thought that Nita came from the wrong side of the tracks. They weren't snobs, but they had that keeping-up-with-the-Joneses mentality that characterized middle America.

Music was becoming the only important thing in our world. We sewed Empire-waist dresses, paisley-trimmed bell-bottoms and Nehru-collared shirts. Nita had recordings of old Hollywood theme songs and went into raptures at the sound of a violin as I did at the sound of an electric guitar. But what really set us apart, aside from our love of sewing, was that we were walkers. Our favorite pastime was walking to downtown Akron. It took a couple of hours from Litchfield, but we were in our element since there was nothing else to do, having rejected all things academic. We walked, rambling and philosophizing; our journeys up West Market Street were adventures. We studied every house and red-brick road, speculating about their histories while discussing the world and what might be out there beyond Akron—like English bands and girls who looked like Jean Shrimpton. Then, when reaching our destination, the intersection of Market and Main, we would make our way over to Polsky's or O'Neil's, the two department stores still presiding over what had once been the heart of a bustling urban community, and perch like two panting sparrows at the luncheon counter in Polsky's basement, sharing a grilled cheese. It felt like running away from home.

One day, I got on a bus at the terminal on South Main and rode all the way to the nearby town of Barberton. Taking a bus almost felt like a subversive act, given that most (white) Americans living in the suburbs were required to have at least one car per family. Only "poor people" got buses in the new world. Well, you couldn't walk to a bus stop out there—it was too far. You'd have to get a lift to catch the bus, so why bother taking the bus if you were driving anyway? Part of the "progress" process was to shun public transport. It was dead or dying.

I felt like I was on a secret mission, watching people milling around the bus terminal in Barberton. How old world it seemed, a public gathering in a public place. I came back to Akron aglow with the thrill of seeing another town, but I kept it from my parents, like my walks downtown. My secrets were starting to mount up. I was almost fifteen and my private world was gaining ground. I had no future plan, but I already knew I wanted to see everything. I wanted to see the world.

The downtown and its department stores were on their last legs, but we didn't know it yet. Akron was our world, downtown our playground. Like Nita was enthralled by those old music-hall songs, I was enthralled by the city. My city. My town. But the city was dying and I was clinging to it. I wanted its glamour, its past, recorded in black and white; I wanted to touch it, to feel it. We hardly noticed that it was largely abandoned already. We were still reveling in childhood memories of getting dressed up to go downtown.

Shopping malls and discount houses, warehouses stacked with price-slashed goods surrounded by acres of parking lots accessible only by expressway had taken over from the city's heart. But I clung to the downtown like a rubber tire bobbing hopelessly in an oily pond of urban demise.

One afternoon in Polsky's basement, an Akron pervert attracted to Nita's *Lolita*-like beauty sidled up to her; she was wearing one of her whimsical fairytale creations and girly sandals. He leaned over and whispered, "Mmmmm, what pretty toes. If I pretended to drop something now I could lean over and kiss those toes, and nobody would see." We weren't sure what to make of that but it was a big story for us and we referred to it often.

There was another Akronite we saw wandering the streets around there occasionally, known as Coats because he always wore seven or eight, even in summer. Other than Coats and the pervert, there wasn't much human interaction downtown by the late sixties.

A suffocating cloak of isolation was enveloping America. Only the destination places, cultural centers you'd visit or pass through like Chicago, New York, Boston, Philadelphia, San Francisco or Seattle, still functioned, with thriving downtowns, defying the seclusion that was spreading like molten lava. With the interstate highway system, nobody passed through places like Akron anymore—they drove around them.

Akron was now just one of tens of thousands of cities being subsumed into metroplexes, a sinister alchemy at play. The creed was "every man for himself." Even verandas, the front porches where people used to gather to commune with their neighbors, were replaced by backyard patios in the new prefab bungalows. You drove your car right into the garage and entered the house without having to see anyone. Everyone wanted to be lord of their own Ponderosa.

There were still a few nightspots downtown like the Black Cat— jazz clubs that were jumping in the fifties; now those too were dying. North Howard Street had been Jazz Central at one time. All the big names came to play there. Akron had been on the circuit and acts would pulled into town on the train and stay the night in one of the many hotels along Main Street. But not anymore.

My friends and I ran up and down the defunct platform, imagining what it must have been like to ride on a train back in the "olden days." Those times seemed so far away by the mid-sixties. None of us had ever been on a train. Eventually, the disused station and platform disappeared altogether, and all the hotels closed.

◦

Having transferred my father from Cleveland back to Akron, the phone company sent him back to Cleveland. This time, rather than move us again he decided to commute, along with millions of others—one man to a car.

The heavy traffic regularly came to a standstill at rush hour, and it would be sweltering in the summer and brutally cold in the winter. The cars battled the elements with special snow tires (good news for

Rubber City). Personally, I would have preferred to sit on a train and read the paper, but that wasn't the American way. No one wanted to share their space with strangers. Heaven forbid they might not even be white. Although no one would have openly admitted it, racial mixing, which was inevitable, was a cultural conundrum, to put it politely.

Everybody had to own and maintain a car. It was the biggest con in the Land of the Free. Well, along with the tobacco and alcohol industries, which also pumped out poison and had the nation in their grip. Pharmaceuticals and firearms would join the party in due course. Through advertising—both explicitly and stealthily—these "necessities" would corral us. We were setting our own ambush. And don't forget factory farming. Yeah, we were digging our own graves. We'd thought the Amish were the odd ones out, regarding them as out of step with the times for decades, but it was increasingly obvious that it was us: self-destructing and taking everything with which we came into contact down with us.

American households had no room for Grandma, but the car's needs were paramount. Every new house had a built-in garage or two. The countryside was being enveloped by concrete, and the tracks that had once been used to ferry passengers were now the sole preserve of freight trains.

Jack Kerouac described romantic characters who jumped into those empty cars and headed out west—hobos. I wanted to be a hobo. I was alarmed by the trend, but more alarmed by the fact that no one else seemed bothered.

Nita and I looked in the window of the Old Gold Store, the last of the pawnshops on South Howard Street. Old things. We wanted to touch artifacts in a world where everything old was cast aside. Soon South Howard would be bulldozed out of the way for another inner belt that led to nowhere, the Martin Luther King freeway.

There were only a few shops left struggling to stay alive along West Market Street as it approached the decaying downtown. Gilbert's Mexican shop was an oddity but beloved to Nita and me. Why Akronites would want to buy Mexican goods was anybody's guess, but when hippie fashion became de rigueur the fringed moccasins and jackets at Gilbert's were like gold dust to the five or six of us in town who had Moby Grape, Buffalo Springfield and Steppenwolf albums.

Walking was outmoded but walking was where I did all my thinking, and I thought nothing of setting out in any weather. I walked to school with icicles in my hair, which I washed like Cher did every morning (according to *16* magazine). I crashed over on frozen sidewalks, my knees like crushed walnuts, but kept walking. I slipped in the slush, ruined my boots in the salt, ripped my stockings in snowdrifts, but kept walking. I marched to Barb Martin's house through sleet and rain to listen to Kinks records. I trudged in the suffocating heat to Manners Big Boy for hot fudge sundaes, Amy Joy Donuts at Wallhaven for glazed crullers, Woolworth's for 3 Musketeers bars and *16* magazines, where I first saw a picture of Jane Asher and got the idea to cut my bangs. I journeyed down into the metropolitan park, ambling along the wooded paths and up to Debbie Smith's house, knowing Selma, her mother, would have a cheesecake waiting. "Chris! Eat! Don't you know Jews equate food with love?" I loved going over there.

I hiked to Dianne's on Waldorf Drive, swung on the trapeze, then dove into a bowl of chocolate marshmallow ice cream. (It's a miracle I'm not diabetic.) I walked along the tracks that ran beside

Nita's house with wonder and longing, imagining how far into the distance they stretched. Where did they go? I wanted to find out.

But I never saw anyone else walking on my adventure tours because there was no longer anything within walking distance. The corner shops that used to service every neighborhood were boarded up. You'd have to allow an hour to get to the nearest shopping plaza on foot, and not mind trucks and cars thundering along next to you as they negotiated their way around drive-through banks, drive-through diners, drive-through liquor stores and drive-in theaters.

When I started to realize that the days of walking were numbered, I subconsciously began to plan my getaway. Was I going to have to buy a car so I could get to work so I could pay for my car? Everyone around me was rushing towards the trap, and I was getting nervous. There was a meter running in me like a cab's, and although I'd never been in a cab I could feel it ticking over.

·

American cities boast about "urban renewal," but Akron's trajectory was essentially urban removal. Controlled climate, Muzak, uniformity and a parking space replaced the event of going downtown. Chances were, you wouldn't be getting out of your car, so why bother about personal deportment? Ordinary people lost all sense of glamour in any kind of daily context. People were becoming "slobs." You didn't see any of that in those black-and-white pictures of the forties.

English bands were amazed when they got to a hotel in the Midwest and asked at the front desk where the nearest shop was. "Yes, would you like me to call you a taxi?" They could see the mall from the lobby but couldn't walk to it. There'd be no place to cross the eight lanes of traffic between the hotel and smoke shop. They'd have to get a car. Traditionally, touring would leave them looking shipwrecked and scrawny. Six weeks on tour in America and they'd go home fattened-up like penned hogs.

The soullessness of mall culture eventually drove a huge portion of the youth population out of town altogether, as moving out of the parental house and getting an apartment downtown was no longer something to aspire to. If you wanted to move to an urban environment you'd have to go to New York City.

In Akron, urban life no longer existed. I found that diehard Akronites like my parents had no problem with the changes. They thought everything was just great. Any change in America was fine by them as they fiercely defended the American Way. To criticize was regarded by them as "anti-American." And they were particularly proud because the party they resolutely voted for usually won the election.

I maintained that the majority was always wrong, but learned not to voice anything like that at the dinner table. If I were to suggest, say, that cutting down millions of trees every Christmas seemed unnecessary, my dad would get exasperated because he thought it was a criticism of America.

"Oh, Christy—those trees *want* to be cut down!"

When I told them I wasn't going to eat meat anymore, it all kicked off.

"You're going to eat meat and you're going to be normal!"

They thought I was going out of my way to be different. I didn't dare say that I was having a moral dilemma. This was the generation gap in its formative stages.

These things combined with what was happening in Vietnam

meant that I and most of my peers were accusing our own parents of racism and bigotry. I see now that that was unfair and basically untrue. But they'd voted for the president who'd sanctioned the war in Vietnam, and they'd all joined the White Flight brigade moving out to the suburbs.

They and their fathers had fought two world wars to defend America, and they didn't see the need for change. They didn't want anything to rock the boat. We, on the other hand, were only interested in rocking the boat. We wanted to rock.

·

The sixties were exploding with great bands, and not everything in rock had been explored. A bit of tape played backwards was innovative and wildly exciting—we were a rapt audience. We were explorers. We wanted to nurture our consciousness, and we had a new world of mind-expanding aids to help us on our way. Pot and LSD would see us right on our journey of self-discovery.

Nobody drank alcohol unless they were "straight." You were either a "straight" or a "head." We were heads. It was our own youth culture, a little like England's mods and rockers but less style-driven. It was all about your allegiance and state of mind. Our state of mind was smoking pot (if we could get any); our allegiance, to Jim Morrison and whoever else was living on Love Street.

I didn't know it was LSD the first time I dropped it. Someone gave me a pill and I swallowed it when my parents were out playing bridge. I walked around the house on my own, looking at my shoes for a few hours, utterly transfixed. Shoes are remarkable things and I'd never noticed that before. Oh, it was acid, all right.

Anything that lifted us out of the mental haze that school

induced was invited in with open arms. School was a kind of torture and I couldn't force myself to be good at it. I lived in dread of taking my report card home—a domestic upset which traumatized the Hynde house every six weeks. I surrendered to the inevitability of failure and got used to the idea. And then I didn't care. Neither did Nita. We were willing losers. We stood up to face defeat with defensive arrogance. We had a band mentality.

We were starting to lose respect for the older generation, as we became obsessed with things that they clearly had never thought about. We were pretty sure we had the answers. We made a point of making a point of it.

By the time I was sixteen, words like "fascist" or worse entered my head as soon as my dad reeled off a demeaning retort to one of my "socially conscious" observations. My arguing with him enraged my mother, who regularly reminded me that I was the cause of her high blood pressure.

Identical scenarios to ours were being enacted in millions of American households. Teenagers collectively started to dislike their own parents because of these shifting value systems. We became an army of parent-hating pot smokers.

Thus my dismay and deep sorrow at the boarding-up of the downtown was something I kept to myself. Anyway, parents like mine had stopped going downtown in the sixties. They didn't want to be around "a lower class of people"—poor people, in other words; down and outs.

I didn't think so at the time, but now I see that they were just ordinary hardworking supporters of the American Dream who had seen off two world wars and upheld their idea of American values in Akron, Ohio, for generations. If I even so much as mentioned my misgivings about the car culture, my dad would counter me with "Gol darn it, Christy! Americans are in love with their cars, don't you know that?"

I found that, in order not to provoke an argument, it was better to avoid any form of conversation. My trying to be different was, to their minds, intended as antagonism towards them. It was better to say nothing. Having a conversation was out of the question.

Eventually, I'd have to walk.

5

WHLO APPRECIATION DAY

It was another fine summer's day when my friends and I set out for Chippewa Lake Park for WHLO Appreciation Day. WHLO was the local Akron radio station and radio was the beacon of light guiding our destinies; this day in particular would put me on my course.

Not everybody was as governed by the music on the radio as I was. I hung out with those who were. We were elitists, my girl gang. We didn't run with the guys, and we didn't flirt or think of having boyfriends. The "popular" kids did stuff like "go steady." We didn't feature it ourselves. It was all about the music. Sex? Not on the agenda at all. We had better things to do.

Debbie and Sue and Chons and Esta were in a band called the Poor Girls. I guess their parents didn't see it as the threat that mine would have. In fact, my folks had bought me a guitar. But set me up professionally? That really would have been a step too far. They would never do anything that might put me in the company of guys with long hair.

The Poor Girls even got a gig supporting Cream at the Akron Civic Theatre. I made Debbie a crushed-velvet vest/waistcoat with pearls sewn on to wear for their big night. And I waited by the back-stage door as Cream left the building and poked my rolled-up poster of them through the throng of fans for the band to sign, which they did! I even stole the courage to tell Eric Clapton about a great guitar player to look out for, B.B. King. I'd heard him on WLAC, out of Nashville, and didn't know if English guys would have known about him. (That's what total dumbbells us kids in the Midwest were.)

I hung out with Debbie, the bass player, a lot. She had the best collection of R&B records and we would go to a little shop downtown called Edfred's to buy singles. Debbie had a poster in her room that said "God Save the Kinks"; I didn't know it was a reference to "God Save the Queen"—the royal family and the English national anthem were unknown to me. Debbie had the coolest shoes, flat suede jobs, like desert boots but slinkier.

Sue, the lead guitarist and singer, and I were born three days apart—our mothers were in the hospital together so I'd known her all my life. She got me a Bob Dylan record for my birthday once—a friend for life. She was blonde and Germanic-looking like Marlene Dietrich.

Chons, on rhythm guitar, had long black hair and blue eyes and was the first person I ever met who said she never ate meat, and when she told me that, I never ate it again either. Best thing that ever happened to me. All it took was the mere suggestion. Nobody else was vegetarian that I knew of, but I started to think of meat-eating as a very weird practice and secretly regarded meat-eaters with distaste, almost contempt. Why would anyone kill an animal if they didn't need to? I learned to live and associate with "the majority," but never respected them. I got used to having this lack of regard for 97 percent of the population.

Esta Kerr had a harder time. She was the drummer, and I think she had some problems and ended up in a mental hospital for life. LSD wasn't a good idea for some of us.

Becky Keene, who would later change her name to Meg, was from an intellectual family. She played jazz piano and there were lots of books all over her house. She wrote the song "Hymn to Her" years later that I did with the Pretenders. Becky was the most individual of all of us. She would go to Litchfield wearing an enormous Mexican skirt and cowboy boots, and a crowd would gather round her like she was in a freak show. She didn't mind attracting that kind of attention; she was truly oblivious to criticism, almost arrogant in her defense.

Angela was more of a space cadet than the rest of us. We smoked opium together and her insane laughter was unforgettable. I don't remember how we got our hands on that shit. We were mad keen on smoking anything. She would get her kit off at the slightest suggestion and went on to be a stripper.

Nita was still my closest ally. Her brother collected guns and her dad kept a rifle next to the front door. Her sister never left the attic, where she read books and stayed with her cats.

Mary was from another intellectual family. She was good at art—we both liked to draw—and I think she made something of a career out of it later. Her dad had the '56 Plymouth that we went to Cleveland to see gigs in.

Shelly came from Holocaust survivors. Barb had tons of records. Her parents had a family-run Italian restaurant, Martini's. We listened to the Beatles endlessly. I would call her up at seven after scrambling to "red up" the dishes when they played the Beatles countdown on WHLO—the Top 10 Beatles records of that day— and we would listen together in silence, phones to our ears, on our knees next to the family hi-fis. She had the first Kinks album, with "Stop Your Sobbing" on it. (Years later I heard a Scottish roadie say "red up" and learned it meant "rid"—"rid the table of dishes.")

Of all the parents, mine were the straightest. Everybody was surprised to come to my house; it was so modern and clean. I didn't take my friends there often—preferring to go over to their houses, where I could relax and say what I wanted—but when I did bring them to mine they would remark, "I can't believe those are your and Terry's parents!"

My mother, ever-stylish and impeccable, was dismayed and certainly disappointed at having a hippie daughter and beatnik son. Parental disapproval meant I had to be stealthy in my behavior. It bugged me at the time, but had it not been for their total refusal to accept my need to rock, I might have stayed in Ohio and married a biker and be reaching under the sofa for my teeth now.

The day at Chippewa Lake Park was, in some ways, the beginning of this story. Never mind the rides and watching fairground workers, the "fine guys," who looked dangerous and worldly, there was something even better happening on that auspicious day. Mitch Ryder & the Detroit Wheels were playing and, for me, life was about to change forever.

Guitarist Jim McCarty, within the space of two songs, dismantled, rebuilt and changed my entire outlook on the world. He was a true guitar hero—the first I'd seen in the flesh. I felt what every teenage boy did when getting the bug. From that day on I regarded rock guitar as the pinnacle of life on earth. The fact that I was just a girl was irrelevant; the notion of being like McCarty was about a million miles out of my league anyway.

Mitch Ryder himself was a superlative singer in the then new mode of "white soul." He was a mesmerizing showman in his blousy pirate shirt and dress pants, his belt buckle slung to the side, resting provocatively on his hip bone. Slinky. He looked as sleazy as the guys working the bumper cars but had a voice implying lots of experience—experience I didn't have. These guys were men.

I was utterly entranced watching them when suddenly, mid-song, confusion derailed the performance and a fight broke out. A fight between band members! It was an out-and-out punch-up, the likes of which I'd only seen in barroom brawls on *Have Gun—Will Travel*. I was shocked, but found the fisticuffs as compelling as the music. Everything about the show was raw and dangerous and real. The music was manly and tough, the fight was the cherry on top.

I begged my friends to stay for the evening performance, so we goofed around the fairground looking at guys and greaser girls who we admiringly called "Rips," until it was time for the second show.

The sun went down and fairground rides lit up the sky in what remains surely the most perfect of all backdrops for any rock show as the band took the stage. The band didn't disappoint the second time around, but then, halfway through the set, things got tense. Another fight was about to . . . hang on a minute . . . what the . . . ? It was staged!

I'd been totally duped. The fight was staged! How cool—how totally cool! Oh, how I loved a good con. That sealed it. There would be no turning back for me. I didn't really imagine that I would ever get in a band, but I was now eternally devoted to the idea.

Now that I'd left Litchfield and was going to Firestone High School, time in the art room was my only sojourn away from academia. I had no use for history or learning stuff about the past—it was the past! Math terrified me. A dog had a better chance of understanding algebra. I just couldn't concentrate on anything I wasn't interested in. I was out of my depth in every class except art. I was good at painting and drawing and making things. My grades in art kept me from flunking out altogether. At least in the art room I knew my ass from my elbow. Just about.

One Saturday afternoon, on one of our long-ass walks downtown, Nita and I wandered into some store that had probably been closed down and taken over by a church group. The sign in the window said "The Outpost," and it was a down-and-outs' refuge where two guys, older than us, unshaven and with long hair, were loitering. Hippies were still a new thing—a rarity on the streets of Akron.

The good-looking one handed Nita a flower and asked if we'd like to go to a love-in. He was the first guy I'd ever thought of as beautiful. His dark eyes, long black hair, the flower, his talk of a love-in—I was smitten.

His name was Greg Burnett. I would hang out in Summit Mall on Saturdays near Disc Records in the hope that he would show up. He did. He had a chopper and was an amateur magician who could pull a rabbit out of the top hat he sometimes wore. He made posters of bands, wore fringed moccasins and a fringed suede jacket like the kind they sold at Gilbert's. He had his hair biker-style, brushed back, and had broad shoulders and slim hips; when sitting on his pretty motorcycle he looked like my idea of an angel. He was twenty—four years older than me. He was, in my eyes, perfect. He'd even been kicked out of a Catholic school, making him literally "too cool for school."

He'd pull up outside Firestone and rev his bike so that I, along with the rest of the student body, could hear it. I loved that sound and I loved him. It didn't last long, though. I was to find out that love never would.

The songs that were on the radio at the time can still bring a lump to my throat.

Richard Harris singing "MacArthur Park."

Jesse Colin Young, "Four in the Morning."

Tim Hardin, "If I Were a Carpenter."

A voice like Hardin's spoke for muted hearts, and I was finding out that only music could ease the pain of a broken one.

The far-reaching AM frequency meant I could get Nashville, Chicago, Detroit and beyond on my Westinghouse transistor radio at night. John R. from Nashville played B.B. King, "Don't Answer the Door," and the Mighty Hannibal, "Hymn No. 5," a gospel song about a young black soldier bleeding in a trench hole in Vietnam. Radio was a lot more educational than school for me and my generation of dropouts.

In the late sixties FM stations started going "underground." The shorter-range FM frequency had better sound quality and had traditionally played what we called "dentist-office music," the stuff our parents listened to. But when they went underground, radio really did become the voice of our generation. Commercial AM stations would never have played "Sister Ray" by the Velvet Underground, so we were finding out about shooting dope and alternative sexualities and all the stuff the adults didn't want us to know about.

Cleveland had WMMS—one of the nation's first underground stations, with the best music and disc jockeys. Cleveland always led the way in rock—the name "rock and roll" was coined in the city by disc-jockey Alan Freed, and English bands used Cleveland as a testing ground. If anyone was going to "get it," Clevelanders would. One thing you could say about backwater places that didn't have much of a scene was that we had nothing to do except listen to the radio. We were all music experts.

Billy Bass on WMMS was our guru and had free rein; if it was raining he'd play "Rainy Day, Dream Away" by Jimi Hendrix followed by "Rain" by the Beatles. There was no format.

Every Saturday, I'd go to Disc Records at the Summit Mall and trawl through the album bins (and keep an eye out for my guy with the motorcycle). That's when I first saw *Freak Out!* by the Mothers of Invention.

I looked at the gatefold cover for twenty minutes—it was a lot to take in. "Freak Out!" was not an expression I'd heard before. What did it mean? Probably a surfing term like "bummer"—coming off your surfboard. I knew that one. *Freak Out!* I took the album to Danny Smoot, who worked behind the counter, and he played a track, "Help, I'm a Rock."

I leaned up to the speaker. What was going on? This was like some kind of Beat poetry put to rock music. Even Terry, the jazz purist, would dig this. Rock meets jazz on psychedelics. It was something I'd never heard before. I had to take it home and call all my friends and tell them. The only way you'd hear about anything was by searching it out, because none of it was available to those who didn't have the ears for it. The underground scene was fertile and rich, exploding with experimentation and antiestablishment sentiment, and it spoke to us, not our parents.

You could only see a movie at the theater when it came out, and then you would never see it again. Sometimes a horror or sci-fi film was on TV, but that was about it. Ghoulardi, the alternative persona of Cleveland newscaster Ernie Anderson, was our other guru, who showed all the cool films on his TV show every Friday night. He had his own language and we idolized him, a Beat version of a ghoul. (One day his son Paul Thomas Anderson would be a big-shot film director.)

Rock stars were more important to us than actors. Actors were from an elite world, distant to us, but rock and roll was everywhere we went. Rock stars spoke our language.

Firestone was an ongoing torment, but only two more years with good behavior and I'd be out. I could *not* fail and get held back, but I still flunked Algebra 1 three times, including summer school. Summer school? Talk about punishment! What child-hater dreamed that one up? They eventually "waived" the course and let me graduate.

Vietnam was hanging over our heads. Guys were making a mad scramble to get accepted into college so they would be exempt from the draft. If they had brought in conscription instead of that elitist "draft" system (which the privileged could dodge easily), the sons of politicians would have had to go and things might have been different. If rich kids had been conscripted, the war would have been less divisive. Only the poor had no choice and got sent over. Some volunteers were from affluent backgrounds, no doubt, but no one we ever met—except for Bob Mosley from Moby Grape. When we heard he volunteered we were all shocked.

Every parent who wasn't living under the poverty line had spent their entire life saving up for their children's college education. That was what all American parents did if they could. My "mandatory conscription" theory is one I hold in retrospect only. None of us thought that way at the time. We believed there was never an excuse for war and objecting was the only reasonable response.

Nobody got a scholarship unless they were a real little straight-A student, and they weren't common. I never met one. Government grants like in England? Nobody had ever heard of that—it would be like socialism! "Christy—you don't get something for nothing," as my dad would so often declare.

Terry enrolled in Kent State University (KSU) and stayed there until the possibility of going to Vietnam passed. All we could do, other than stage protests, was to stand back helplessly as those who did get drafted, average age of nineteen, got sent over to drop napalm, bomb villages, ride around in helicopters and get killed in what we saw as an insane war that absolutely none of us understood the objective of. The entire youth population was polarized because of it, and it led us away from our childhoods and our parents. The generation gap became untraversable.

We watched the bomb strikes on television and it got worse every day—and even worse on acid. You had to be careful not to watch the news if you were tripping, and we all were. And so were the soldiers over in Vietnam. No surprise some of them came back so traumatized they're still holding out in chicken sheds.

Our resolutely antiwar sentiments were reflected by thousands of bands across the nation—bar bands who switched overnight from playing stuff like "Farmer John" and "Louie Louie" to psychedelic desert music while we danced frenzied under strobe lights. Every song on the radio had an antiestablishment message that only we could decipher. Our parents had no idea what it was we were doing, and we saw them as one with the enemy.

When we weren't out watching local bands, of which there were at least a few in every city in America, we congregated in hippie pads, dorm rooms or biker hangouts to smoke pot, surrounded by antiwar slogans, "Hallelujah the Pill!" free-love posters and psychedelic multi-band concert announcements from places like the Fillmore West and the Avalon Ballroom. Posters that promised spiritual healing, poetry and rock music:

KRISHNA CONSCIOUSNESS COMES WEST
SWAMI BHAKTIVEDANTA * ALLEN GINSBERG
THE GRATEFUL DEAD * MOBY GRAPE
BIG BROTHER & THE HOLDING COMPANY
MANTRA * ROCK DANCE
SUNDAY JAN. 29 AVALON BALLROOM 8 PM

Even posters were a new thing, formerly the domain of Hollywood, show business and the circus. Now, any bedroom could be transformed into a hippie palace with a few posters, lava lamps and a radio. Black light optional.

Zap Comix enlightened us with satirical insights and pornographic images that we regarded as liberating. Anything that was socially taboo was "right on" to us. We relished anything or anyone defying boundaries and generally being obnoxious with a capital "O."

"Free love" was more a state of mind than "sex" to little virgins like us, and we thought the main objective, "to be free," was to be free from inhibition and love your fellow man. But the so-called sexual revolution was upon us, and in the spirit of non-conformity we would conform to it. With the aid of the Pill, sex was to leave the discreet place where it had been having a relatively quiet life and become something akin to sport—losing its mystery in the pharmaceutical takeover.

The most potent factor in the sixties' descent into chaos was the birth-control pill. Never mind LSD—a passing fad—the Pill was king, and like Cher it needed no second name. The Pill was changing society beyond recognition, with the entire family structure about to alter unrecognizably. Sex was becoming a recreational lifestyle choice. If you were to mention the word "procreation" you'd probably get thrown out of any protest, commune or crash pad for being a bummer. Only a straight person would think like that.

In the name of women's lib, women were becoming like men, and that was good news for me because I wanted what the boys had. In thinking we were in charge of our own sexuality, now we could say "yes" instead of "no." Now we could fuck and run like they did, even if it didn't really suit our nature.

Did being like men liberate us? Of course not, but to hell with the finer points, we were having our cake and eating it! We could now have it away with total strangers and not worry about getting knocked up or ostracized, just like the guys. Words like "whore," "slut" or " loose" were replaced with "free," "hip" and "groovy." Clap clinics burst at the seams from coast to coast, while pharmaceutical companies rubbed their hands together and raked in the profits of free love.

There were books written on whether women had vaginal orgasms or not; orgasms were becoming an industry in themselves. Porn seemed like an underground joke and hadn't yet overtaken every art form ever invented. We weren't serious about anything except getting high and being free. (The tab was running, though.)

Me, I still just wanted to listen to bands, play records with my friends and smoke pot. I thought sex was, like becoming "a woman," something to put off for as long as possible.

Vietnam raged on. It tore through the collective psyche like Zorro's sword signing his "Z." The whole country was reeling.

As for you, Akron, the center of the universe; your axis was tilting.

6

TESTING, TESTING . . .
ONE TWO, ONE TWO

Cleveland, Ohio, was a testing ground for new products. I guess if a "new improved" toothpaste didn't fly, it wouldn't be the dent in a company's reputation in "the Mistake on the Lake" that it would be in the Big Apple.

Bands would do warm-up shows in northeastern Ohio to try out underrehearsed new material on hayseeds, who they thought wouldn't know if they crapped out or not. But although we weren't a major city like New York or San Francisco, we had the best radio in the land, so we were at the ready when someone like Todd Rundgren came to town, or Jethro Tull or Lindisfarne. Billy Bass, our resident disc jockey at WMMS, played "In-A-Gadda-Da-Vida" on heavy rotation while the rest of the nation was still pottering about to "Cherry, Cherry."

A band thought they were safe to roll into town jet-lagged and hungover, get a few rooms at Swingos, run through a set and start a course of antibiotics while working up to the important major cities, trying out the lights and running order on us, who didn't know any better. But that "us" included me and my girlfriends. We made it happen. We willed them to be great. We blew them like dandelions back out to take their seed around the nation.

When I was fourteen we got a ride from a benevolent parent

to Cleveland to see the Rolling Stones. Bill was wearing a yellow blazer and royal blue trousers and Keith, yellow trousers and royal blue jacket. They'd swapped the suits around. Did they think we wouldn't notice? Think again, you skinny, pockmarked, would-be R&B artists parading about in your exotic English threads in front of us in our homemade bell-bottoms wanting desperately to look like you—we noticed!

Puffy-eyed Brian with his tartan boots and Vox Teardrop guitar. How could anyone forget that? Mick bowing, a sweeping gesture, at the end of "Lady Jane." Mid-song, Bill plucked a note out of the air that had been launched at the stage by some screaming hairdresser, neatly put it in his breast pocket and resumed playing, without missing a beat. I bet she got a call later.

I sat embryo-like in the balcony, unable to scream, talk or budge—utterly mesmerized. I walked up as close to the stage as I could after the house lights went up, and ripped a little hole in the staging so I would have a fragment of the show to keep. I saw some folded notes that hadn't made it to the stage, like confetti on the floor, and pocketed them too. I saved them, and I would often take them out of my jewelry box and wonder who the girls were that had scribbled their phone numbers, hoping the band would intercept them. The underground sisterhood.

Standing in the foyer, looking at the others who had come from all corners of northeastern Ohio was an integral part of the experience. It was like a secret society. Not everyone needed to see the Rolling Stones in the mid-sixties, but you could spot those who did a mile off in their modified clothes and carefully studied haircuts. For us elitists it was a chance to catch a rare glimpse of the few who shared our passion: guys who'd got their girlfriends to undo the outside seams of their jeans and sew industrial-sized zippers up to the knees; chicks who'd been up all night sewing paisley inserts into their jeans, making them wide enough to sweep the ground. Everyone wore "hip-hugger" dropped waists, which was a new look that anybody who was a servant of rock had to feature.

Fifteen minutes before arriving at a gig, in the backseat of whoever's car I was in, I would pull out my makeup bag and open a trial-sized bottle of Bonne Bell, an astringent cleanser which took all the oil off a face like paint-stripper. I'd have some cotton balls in my kit to aid the process, then, with a face like a freshly sawn log, reapply a pale foundation and take extra care to cover my lips in it. Having lips wasn't the look. Then I'd get some more eyeliner on and blot it all with powder. The thought of any shine seeping through the thick mask was abhorrent bordering on phobic, and I checked a mirror every ten minutes to make sure I still looked like I'd been dead for the last five hours. I thought I looked cool, too cool for school. My bangs strategically hid any acne threating to appear but there was no need to fret, as it was immediately eradicated by the constant scouring of Bonne Bell, probably the closest thing to a DIY face peel there ever was. The word "pimple" still makes me shudder, and I thought the mark of civilization was when I heard the English refer to "spots"—much, much better.

The Akron Civic Theatre was one of those classic grandes dames that still graced every self-respecting city in the USA. Even urban-renewal planners hadn't the heart to tear them down. Gloria Mays and I went there to see a soul review when we were fifteen. Gloria had come in to Litchfield from another school and was a soul fan like no one else I knew. On the bill was Peg Leg Moffett, Gorgeous George and a long list of other acts, but the big draw was Jackie Wilson.

Gloria and I got there first and went right up front, in the middle, best seats in the house. By the end of Wilson's set, girls were in a state of ecstasy. Maybe soul audiences always got worked up like that, but it was definitely more nuts than any rock show I'd been to—more of a baptismal kind of thing.

Being the only two white people in the audience didn't faze us, but near the end of the show I got a frightening premonition as one of Wilson's crew came out into the front row, grabbed a girl from her seat and took her to the lip of the stage, where the notice-ably drunken singer was lying facedown, one leg dangling over the side, crooning into a drenched microphone. The stagehand then delivered her to Wilson (a former boxer who'd switched vocations after discovering he was a lover, not a fighter), who took her head in his hands and planted a big wet kiss firmly on her mouth, holding the position long enough to incite hysteria throughout the entire hall. The sound was deafening and not unlike the soundtrack of a "dinosaurs rampaging damsels" type sci-fi/horror film. But instead of fleeing for the exits, these damsels were throwing themselves at the stagehand, screaming: "Me next, baby! Me next!"

My premonition had "foregone conclusion" written all over it as I sank back in my seat and tried to hide like a naughty dog who'd been caught with a shoe in its mouth. I wasn't even wearing anything cool: a polyester dress, the top half blue-and-red stripes, divided at hip level with a plastic belt graduating into a blue A-line skirt; just awful, something my mother had got me at Lowry's Chil-dren's Clothes at Wallhaven, the XX size—the last thing I could fit into from there. I'd completed the hideous look with a pair of black penny loafers. Just a shame, really. Gloria, on the other hand, was far more mature-looking than me—blonde, certainly more of a goer and probably up for it. But for Gloria it wasn't meant to be. I prayed to be passed over, but instead was lifted from my seat like a rag doll, the muscular arms of Jackie's man raising me to the stage like a sacrificial lamb too paralyzed with embarrassment to protest. A hush fell over the audience, the collective intake of breath nearly pulling me back into my seat. I guess that was my first kiss, although there might have been one poorly aimed Juicy Fruit–flavored peck at a fun fair courtesy of a friend's older cousin, but no match for the salty, experienced lips of Jackie Wilson.

I also saw Sam the Sham & the Pharaohs on that same hallowed stage. Tons of shows had our attention as long as we could get someone's parents' car for the night. Usually the Plymmy, courtesy of Mary's dad.

La Cave in Cleveland was particularly good for blues bands, usually of the popular white variety like the Blues Project, which featured Danny Kalb, Steve Katz, Al Kooper, Tommy Flanders and Roy Blumenfeld. I had their album and played it over and over, and tried to learn the whimsical "Steve's Song" on the guitar. Every guitar player in America was onto it if they had an acoustic guitar, and "Flute Thing" was a classic of its time, kind of an anthem for those of us still in the thrall of the waning jazz scene that had been hijacked by tinkly bells and incense.

The Castle was a barn in Medina, out in the sticks, that the Brambles, Akron's own bar band, played regularly, and featured light shows of slides and strobes—a new medium, and just what the doctor ordered if you were tripping or smoking pot.

Head shops were thriving and every city in America had one. They were the only place you could get rolling papers. Pipes, hookahs and bongs were very popular, mandatory even. Everyone under thirty in the United States smoked a bong. Everyone. And who didn't have a roach holder?

Guys wearing love beads were hippie code for "hop on." When

Blossom Music Center opened, one of the first outdoor pavilions of its kind (the "sheds"), we especially loved going because you could always find a variety of dealers at every entrance and score, drop, then park yourself on a grassy hill and wait to get off.

Before Janis Joplin even hit the stage I was remarking to my friends how incredible the light show was. "Chris, the show hasn't started yet," they replied. But on three different tabs of acid, guess what, the show HAD started.

We went to see Canned Heat but they didn't show, so only the support band, the Velvet Underground, played that night. New York bands were more "arty" than the Midwest and West Coast bands (who were drenched in psychedelics), but the Velvet Underground had one of the first trippy light shows anyone ever saw. And singer Lou Reed was bookish-looking but pulled it off by being sexy as hell. Those onstage were automatically ten times sexier than anyone in the audience. Drummer Moe Tucker had a unique style of playing and, as she was a girl, well, that was always a welcome change. There weren't so many chicks in bands. The new "not having children" thing hadn't quite sunk in yet. Grace Slick, Cynthia Robinson (Sly's trumpet player), Janis and Joni—you could count them on one hand.

Sly and the Family Stone were big favorites, but becoming as famous for not showing up as for their music. Cancellations all the time, the drugs starting to work against the interests of the artist, which would be universal in a few years—Sly always ahead of the curve . . .

The Alice Cooper band played rough outdoor stages in fields and eventually in theaters. They played all the time. They were one of the more musically astute bands, and singer Alice was into a theatrical Gothic horror show thing that we adored. He'd have a guillotine onstage, and when they played the Akron Rubber Bowl a helicopter dropped paper underpants on the audience, which fell like rain next to my eyes where I lay facedown in the dirt, too stoned to stand up. Glen Buxton, the guitar player, was from Akron. We were all so proud of that.

A folk trio called the New Journeymen played for a fair at Litchfield Junior High School. They had a beautiful girl singer and I was impressed by a joke the guy singer made about existentialism. How cool was that? They got another girl in and changed their name a year later to the Mamas & the Papas.

I saw Tim Buckley play in a bowling alley. My friend and I waited in the parking lot afterwards so we could get a glimpse as the band left. I managed to awkwardly tell Buckley, "You were great." I wanted to say so much more. He in turn slapped the hood of the station wagon they were loading and said, "What do you think of the paint job?" (He must have found compliments in the parking lot as embarrassing as I would myself one day.)

I patrolled the underground parking deck for an hour after Led Zeppelin's Cleveland Arena concert, calling, "Jimmy . . . Jimmy," just in case he might wander through.

Becky Keene almost stole the show from the Who at the Music Hall in Cleveland when she started spinning and flailing her arms in a weird version of what Townshend was doing onstage. She was up and down the aisles, and it was obvious that no one in the audience had seen *that* dance before. She was a bit of a hero that night.

Janis walked back out onstage at Blossom after the lights went up, the band having long since finished the show, and invited any Heavy Bikers who might be present to go backstage. To see her with the lights up like that as the crowd was leaving, me out in the field still tripping, felt like a personal one-on-one encounter, even though she didn't see me, a mile away.

Every band I saw took a piece of me with them back into the night. Bands were everything; nothing else mattered.

7

WANTING THE WORLD

We were looking for adventure. We lingered long on Love Street. We had too much to dream last night. We wanted the world and we wanted it now. We were born to be wild. We were stone free.

We were stoned.

We didn't think of ourselves as "innocent." We read books; we devoured music; we smoked everything and dropped anything. Technically speaking, we were virgins, but we'd been around the world a few times by now, if only in our heads.

We'd seen them around Cleveland's Coventry and Akron's underbelly, the Portage Lakes, in *Life* magazine and in the pot-smoker's bible, *Zap Comix*. Those who looked like hippies on motorcycles with their outlaw colors, one percent badges, leathers, beards, engineer boots and dirty hair flattened under German helmets. Those of the loose swagger and commanding demeanor of . . . of . . . well, we didn't know of what exactly, but we wanted to find out.

At a glance, we could see they had experience; more than we did—a whole lot more. And that's what we wanted more than anything. When Jimi Hendrix sang "Are You Experienced?" we wanted to be able to say, "Yes Jimi—we are. WE ARE!"

The Heavy Bikers looked like an entirely different species from the buttoned-down-collared Firestone Falcons blushing under virulent swathes of acne in class every morning. No, our greasy-faced student body had nothing on them. From a purely aesthetic point of view, you couldn't come up with a better look than the bikers had. But they weren't hippies with motorcycles like I'd assumed they were. Hippies didn't slug chicks in the side of the head, forcing them to suck-off a whole colony of gorillas before throwing them down stairwells. But what difference did that make to us in Boredsville, USA? We just didn't care. These were the characters S. Clay Wilson portrayed, marauding through his pages, fighting and plundering and tripping their brains out while drinking Tree Frog Beer, wrestling demons and defiling witches. Plus, they rode great big fuck-off Harley-Davidsons and listened to Moby Grape. Well, surely they listened to Moby Grape. We all did. We all listened to the same music.

We were explorers. We read the *Tao Te Ching* and books on Zen Buddhism. We ate brown rice, George Ohsawa style. We learned about Eastern mysticism, like the beatniks, and read poetry. The poet Gregory Corso was the kind of guy to get a crush on, with his unruly hair and manly forearms. Poetry, beat-style, made the notion of growing up and joining the adult world seem noble and brave.

And Lawrence Ferlinghetti, writing about reality in "Dog." We thought we had a different view of reality than everyone who came before us. We thought we invented it. Allen Ginsberg serving *Reality Sandwiches*. Yeah, we definitely understood reality in a way that our parents didn't. But then, our parents weren't dropping acid.

It said right on the cover of Alan Watts's book *Psychotherapy East and West*, "Now is eternity." C'mon! Who didn't want eternity? And anything with the word "psych"—it, like "reality," was ours too.

Dolores Roberts, my mother, the model

My parents, Dolores and Bud, the Marine, on a date

The blue house
on Hillcrest Street

On holiday in the
Pocono Mountains

A family snap when Dad was stationed in Florida

My dad gives a lift

Dressing up with Patty, whose necklace I stole

Terry *(far left)* with neighborhood kids. That's Timmy Porter in the center.

Dee Hynde, a secretary

Christmas with the Hyndes

Our new house on
Stabler Road in the snow

All dressed up and
ready for church

Sewing. A little homemaker in the making . . .

Terry wailing under his painting of a drum kit

Me and Dianne. Still innocent. (But not for long . . .)

Nita Lee, class of '69

Chris Hynde, class of '69

Psychology, psychotherapy, psychedelics, psychosis and, yes—why not? Psychopath.

We read *Ramparts* magazine, which felt subversive. I subscribed under a pseudonym, feeling like an undercover agent when I retrieved it from the mailbox.

The Black Panthers were prowling the political landscape to the sound of the Last Poets. LeRoi Jones, forerunner of rap, spoke what sounded like true prophecy. Sly Stone really was taking us higher with his interracial band of virtuoso loonies dispelling just about every stereotype going while getting the nation to stand up and dance to the music. We were all in on it—it was a family affair. Even Miles Davis was going psychedelic.

James Brown? Okay, maybe that's pushing it. I don't think anyone actually wanted to imagine the Godfather on acid. But even he was flying the freak flag and lost the conk to an afro.

It was a rite of passage to get close to our people, whatever it took, by taking whatever they took. We were game. We were naïve, though. Come and get us, boys! Guys like Cincinnati's own Charlie Manson must have thought it was Christmas.

We had no sexual experience but we had Robert Plant. Anyway, why would anyone want to get it on with some schlub at school if it meant taking time out from listening to a skinny guy in a string vest who played guitar in an English band. Or a West Coast band. Or any band!

It was all about the music. If the drugs took us to the music then it was about the drugs en route to the music. Anyway, that part was nothing new. Contemporary music was defined by drugs and always had been. Dean Martin without a drink? Johnny Cash without amphetamines? Billie Holiday without a fix? Or Chet Baker? Judy Garland without a script? (Prescription, that is.) The lineup was endless. They might call it self-medication. They might call it a way to endure oppression, discrimination, cruelty or domestic abuse. But never mind the whys and wherefores—we wanted the drugs.

We were natural-born followers, copying whoever seemed the most rebellious. The Pill created a virtual smorgasbord of post-pubescent girls offering themselves up to anyone with a length of tool at the ready. The most studious professor, unsuspecting gas-station attendant, farmhand, shopkeeper or civil-rights activist wasn't going to turn down the entire student body of America offering themselves up to get experience.

We thought being "inhibited" was the opposite of being free. We wanted to be card-carrying members of the revolution. But we were too stoned to get serious about sex and, even if we wanted to, the mechanics of it were nigh-on impossible when you opened the bathroom door and faced a 200-foot drop through clouds, a dazzling rainbow, and had no feeling in your hands.

We were taking up philosophies from what we could interpret of the musings of twenty-three-year-old guitar players. We were the new generation of guitar worshippers. Electric guitar was the Holy Grail, the pinnacle of our culture; we thought anyone who could play like Rick Derringer or Johnny Winter was touched by divinity.

Drugs were the glue that stuck us to the same page. Musicians led our consciousness. Freedom was the thing to aspire to. Hendrix was always on about it: "Freedom!" Martin Luther King: "Free at last!" The Stones, too: "I'm free to do what I want any old time."

Never once did money or material gain enter a conversation. Hendrix articulated the way we felt better than anyone: "White collar conservative flashin' down the street . . . you can't dress like me." Nobody wanted to be part of the establishment.

Our parents had never considered all this "otherworldly" stuff.

They were preoccupied with mundane concerns like providing for their families. Suckers! We didn't have to do that now. We didn't have to do anything we didn't want to do for the first time in history now and eat it with lashings of extra cream. We were the Love Generation—especially if an English accent was incorporated. "Have a go on this, luv," would be received by a frenzied scrum from all quarters. This was, of course, all still conjecture to us little stinkers in the suburbs.

The first time I heard the term "groupie" was from Monti Rock III, with his band Disco-Tex and the Sex-O-Lettes on an afternoon talk show on television. The smooth-talking Puerto Rican showman with his irrepressible dance anthems—disco was still an underground and curious phenomenon—talked about "groupies," and though we weren't quite sure what he meant we planned on finding out.

Groupies were a new social category. Girls were now counting their number of conquests, just like guys. Leon Russell wrote "Superstar," a big hit for the Carpenters, but its original title was "Groupie Superstar." It described a groupie's love for a musician who had moved on. The problem was that groupies really did fall in love with guys who came to town, played a show, got lucky and then cleared off like a flock of Canada geese. There are women around the globe who still hold a candle for sex god Jim Morrison. That was the problem with thinking we were like guys. We were falling in love before they even had time to rinse it off and make their excuses for the rest of the week.

So-called women's lib was rather misled by the Pill. Women weren't in control of their bodies; the drug was. Taking procreation out of the equation was turning women into sex toys. No one seemed to mind. I know I didn't.

A common addition to our book lists was *The Physician's Desk Reference*, which was a thick textbook listing every pill going, including full descriptions of effects, side effects and illustrations of the pills or capsules. On pot you could read it and check off the ones you'd tried for hours.

We were hippie versions of Alfred E. Neuman, with "What—me worry?" philosophies, long-haired, freckle-faced and goofy, having grown up on *Mad* magazine, Dobie Gillis and Maynard G. Krebs. But, indeed, what did we have to worry about, as long as we could stay in school and not get drafted and find something to smoke?

Self-anointed gurus—charismatic, intelligent, power-hungry, narcissistic, twisted and egocentric—intercepted runaways by the bushel basket and were moving out west. It was good work if you could get it—raise hell while getting your knob sucked.

The whole nation was becoming a melting pot of music, experimentation, belligerence and sloppy sex. The drugs were going to get serious once the profits started rolling in. It was going to take more than a few decades to get fumigated.

.

A guy from Cuyahoga Falls, Mark Mothersbaugh, was putting a band together. My brother knew his brother. He was a bespectacled oddball, but then Ohio was a breeding ground for oddballs. I was asked if I wanted to be the singer. I guess I had that kind of personality, or maybe I just looked the type. The band was called Sat Sun Mat.

I couldn't practice in the same room as the rest of them, though. I couldn't let them see me—no confidence, insecure, shy, all the standard stuff every lead singer bigs up in interviews years later—so I shut myself in the laundry room with a cord stretched under the door in his parents' basement, and sang from atop the dryer. We learned "40,000 Headmen" by Traffic and "You Shook Me" by the Jeff Beck Group, favorite album tracks of the day kind of stuff. We got one gig in a church hall in Cuyahoga Falls. I was unnaturally unnerved with stage fright—I just hated the whole thing. Terrible experience. Greg Burnett, my chopper-riding magician, showed up after a well-meaning friend informed him about my big debut. I died a death. The band was good though.

8

PAUL BUTTERFIELD
AND THE SECURITY GUARDS

The Paul Butterfield Blues Band was playing in Cleveland. There was no possibility whatsoever that we weren't going to be there. We lied to our parents and piled into Plymmy. We loved Plymmy like a family pet.

Off to Cleveland we went. We were going to wail! We hoped we'd find someone hitchhiking who had pot, and could squeeze them into our own Merry Pranksters' bus while listening to the radio and singing along to every song.

Music was now written in a subterranean language only comprehensible to the initiated. The charts were laden with drug references and we spoke the native tongue. In traditional rhythm & blues, which was where all our music came from, drug references were hidden, coded in love songs.

"My love is growing stronger, as you become a habit to me," sang Otis. Drug or love? Who knew for sure? That's the beauty of a song—the meaning is defined by the listener. But by the time of flower power the guesswork was taken out of the equation: "Excuse me while I kiss the sky." Jimi saw and queried the difference between tomorrow and the end of time. Eternity was now everywhere.

Every day was another day to get high. Going to Cleveland to see the Paul Butterfield Blues Band was all the incentive we needed to search out the necessaries. And, as an added bonus to our magical mystery tour, we were about to have our first encounter with the world-famous Heavy Bikers, they of the famous patch, they of the fear-inducing winged-skull motif, they of the red-and-white colors. Ohio was second only to California in terms of motorcycle registration. We had the open roads and a "Bikers Are Us" mentality. The Heavy Bikers acted as security guards for all the coolest bands. They got to stand in front of the stage, see the show up close and ensure that no one so much as placed a finger on the band or the stage, and then escort the whole crew back to their clubhouse to party. It was part of the backdrop of the sixties—the Heavy Bikers and the best bands. And they had the drugs. Well, c'mon, if anyone had drugs, it was them.

We'd heard all sorts of crazy shit about them, like the Red Wings badge was suppose to mean eating a girl out on her period. Did people really do stuff like that? My girlfriends and I had absolutely no firsthand experience or any idea.

I would have taken a ride on a Harley any day over overseeing an altercation in some thug's jeans, but we just followed whatever *Zap Comix* had in its pages. Written by sex obsessives Robert Crumb and S. Clay Wilson, *Zap* offered very little for even the most twisted imagination to speculate on. If Crumb or Wilson hadn't drawn it, it probably hadn't happened to a human. We didn't know what the "missionary" position was, but the idea of injecting cum straight into a vein and growing a bulging wanger seemed pretty doable, according to Wilson.

Oh yeah and the Heavy Bikers had a rule about heroin: they weren't allowed to use it. I read that too, somewhere. Well, they could sell it but not take it. Not officially. That's always been the deal with dealers. Heroin wasn't on our agenda anyway. Not yet.

Bikers drank beer. But these guys were nothing like the football-toting, beer-swilling jocks at Firestone. Booze and tobacco were legal, so not considered drugs. We bought it hook, line and sinker, as you do once you get addicted. "Those aren't drugs!"

(Heh heh—yeah, they are.)

The Heavy Bikers were vying for control of the drug trade from coast to coast—trying to wrest it from the domain of the Mafia, who ran Cleveland like a racehorse on steroids. This would prove to be a deadly pursuit. The big money that flooded the drug trade would further corrupt the already corrupted, to whom murder was literally just a walk in the park.

The RICO Act, a law brought in to tackle organized crime, would eventually subdue the Heavy Bikers, and they would no longer be seen roaring through cities, brandishing their patches; they would have to go underground or legitimate. But the sixties was their heyday.

In my gang, I was the most impressed by them. A great big "Fuck Off" was their message as far as I could tell, and I liked it. They were more antiestablishment than anyone we knew. I loved the bikes and I loved the way they talked about honor and loyalty and brotherhood—and I loved the fact that they knew all the cool bands. I would have been happy to polish chrome all day long if only I'd been asked. (And one day I would get my shot at it—and much, much more.)

Butterfield. My friends and I inadvertently wandered into the backstage area while looking for our balcony seats—and straight into Paul Butterfield himself. That was my first time rubbing elbows with a real star. I shyly asked for his autograph. What to say in a moment like that? How much I had listened to *East–West*? We'd even snuck a portable record player into the girls' lav next to the art room and listened to it there. I had one other autograph on a rubber baseball—Bubba Phillips, star of the Cleveland Indians. Someone had got me that, though. I'd never met a famous person before myself.

We watched some of the band mime a game of ping-pong (like a scene out of *Blow-Up*)—how cool! We didn't even know what backstage was. We were still looking for our seats when someone in the entourage must have thought we were cute, because we were taken right up and seated next to the stage. Fantastic—we could watch the band up close! And the band could watch us.

I can see with hindsight how they must have found it amusing that their dirty brand of Chicago blues had reached the pubescent flower children of northeastern Ohio. My gang and I were too naïve to be groupies for the Butterfield band. Not to mention we were underage, which must have been apparent up close to them and their "security guards." It wasn't worth the trouble to mess with jailbait. Only a dumb-ass high school teacher would make a mistake like that.

Paul Butterfield had one of the great bands of the sixties, taking traditional Chicago blues and "whitening" it up a notch by adding scorching electric guitar with a white singer who was a blues-harp virtuoso, Mr. Paul Butterfield. For white kids this lightening of black music made it more relatable. After all, we weren't from the Delta and we weren't mature men, impoverished and dealing with adult problems. Even black kids weren't listening to the blues in the sixties. If there was a gig by one of the real-deal bluesmen, the audience would be predominately, if not totally, white.

The Rolling Stones almost single-handedly turned millions of white kids into blues aficionados. We listened to the Stones and then went on to explore the roots. That was the beauty of rock—it was one big exploratory carousel. You fell in love with a record and it opened the door to all its influences. All the English bands—the Moody Blues, Procol Harum, Cream, the Beatles, Manfred Mann, the Dave Clark Five and Dusty Springfield too—had roots in black American blues. When the likes of Otis Redding first went to play in England they were stupefied by the reaction they got. They were treated like kings. It wasn't like that back home, where they often still couldn't get rooms in segregated hotels.

I dreamed of playing harmonica like Butterfield, as did Cleveland's own Bill Miller, who played with aplomb in his own Mr. Stress Blues Band. Blues had overtaken jazz now and was the biggest influence on bands on both sides of the Atlantic.

Mose Allison, Mississippi's jazz-based, boogie-woogie piano-playing songwriter, practically wrote the "how to" song guide for the Who and the Kinks. Without Allison there would be no "My Generation" or "You Really Got Me."

John Hammond and Johnny Winter were making blues sexy to teenagers like yours truly. None of it was making chart positions, but that didn't matter anymore. We bought albums and studied them like early explorers studied maps. More white guys were playing blues now than anybody. It was a mixed bag—multiracial. Sly Stone spelled it out loud and clear: "It doesn't matter if you're black or white." Not in his band. Not in any band. Music was colorless.

Jimi Hendrix obscured and even transcended racial categorization more than anyone. Never once did you hear Hendrix referred to as a "black" musician. His expression, influence and virtuosity were so great that his color was overlooked altogether. Like Charles Mingus described in his autobiography, *Beneath the Underdog*, musicians lived on a "colorless island." When the Chambers Brothers had their massive hit "Time Has Come Today," nobody batted an eyelid at a black gospel group who played rock and roll dressed as cavalry soldiers singing, "And my soul has been psychedelicized!" And the Staple Singers, the groundbreaking gospel group and voice of black pride, were socking it to white audiences. Marvin Gaye was writing the book on how to live as a human: forget racial distinction. Otis and the Stones—who actually did write "Satisfaction"? Nobody knew or cared. Janis Joplin was another white singer who took her influences from black soul. Although she was big pals with the Heavy Bikers.

The Heavy Bikers were the only ones among us who were steadfastly racist, but they kept that quiet when partying with the kids who bought the drugs. American code numero uno: the customer is always right.

But back to Butterfield: we watched the band; the "security guards" watched the band; we watched the security guards; they watched us. After the show the band invited us to a party. A party with the Paul Butterfield Blues Band at the security guards' clubhouse? Yes, please!

I never equated not feeling threatened with the fact that we were jailbait. No one came too close to us and we thought nothing of it. It was peace and love, so we assumed. We were hanging out with my favorite band and the world-famous bikers, and they had some killer weed. Except it wasn't weed. We'd smoked hash before, but this wasn't hash.

"They can't hold their mud!" chortled one of the pill-mashers as Angela, Becky, Nita, and Mary did some weird free-form and, frankly, pretty frightening dance around the Cleveland HQ—fueled on what we later realized was opium.

But not me. I left them to their twirly "Go Ask Alice" dancing because I'd been invited upstairs by Buzzy Feiten, Butterfield's teenage hotshot guitar player. Intuition must have told him that I worshipped at the altar of rock guitar more than the others. (The others including the rest of the girls in the whole country, that is.) Feiten handed me a bottle of beer, not normally my tipple but I accepted graciously. I was on a learning curve.

We were ushered into a room adorned with crossbows, nunchaku, swords, bullwhips, brass knuckle-dusters and all sorts of pain-inflicting knickknacks, along with some Nazi paraphernalia and an antique pistol or two. But a framed "Wanted" poster claimed pride of place. The handsome, albeit psychotic, stare featured on the poster was on the face of the Heavy Biker now sitting on the bed across from me. According to the poster he was wanted in some Southern state for the rape of the governor's daughter. Evidently an accolade worth framing.

"I got reds, blues, yellows, uppers, downers—whatever you want," said he of the devilishly dark, authoritatively good-looking, jaw-grinding grimace who wore an oddly pointed leather hat that nodded to the sartorial sensibility of a warlock. He was one fine example of a governor's daughter's rapist, like a brooding mix of every member of Steppenwolf montaged into one police sketch of a sex offender.

He wasn't talking to me, though. All comments were directed at Paul Butterfield exclusively. I was to understand, even with my lack of experience, that women in that neighborhood did not speak unless spoken to.

It would prove to be a lesson hard-learned. Perhaps you can imagine how that didn't work out in my favor at first. It took me awhile. Maybe not on this underage jaunt, which I didn't realize at the time afforded a certain amnesty from getting covered in a variety-pack of jism.

Every "brother" had a position and was decorated with the corresponding badge, kind of like Boy Scouts for psychopaths, but I'm glad I was too overwhelmed and high at the time to articulate that thought or I doubt I'd be writing this now.

While Butterfield and his hosts were busying themselves with pleasantries concerning the volume of uppers and downers they could shift, Feiten and I were oblivious to all else but the radio, which was tuned to WMMS. When the last chord of Buffalo Springfield's epic "Bluebird" ricocheted around the room we had one of those mutual hallucinogenic experiences so common in the mid- to late sixties and were splayed in ecstasy at the sound of the chord by the light of a lava lamp in a haze of marijuana, strawberry incense and smoke swirling around and intermingling with the unfamiliar but soon to be run-of-the-mill odor of manly B.O. Then, abruptly, we were jolted back to reality—bliss terminated.

"TIME TO GO!" yelled the scar-faced keeper of the keys manning the door. It turned out that Angela had tried to come up the stairs, enticed by the acrid smell of weed, and got yanked off the bannister and hurtled back down, her dazed, not-quite-fully-knowing-what-was-going-on look (which on anyone else would be attributed to the drugs, but in her case was always like that) changing not one iota.

The clock on the wall was talking.

9

KENT STATE UNIVERSITY

It was 1969. I would have loved to do a runner the minute I was released from Firestone, but at seventeen I was still under the mental and financial control of my parents, maybe legal too. We couldn't even vote till we were twenty-one.

I didn't pay much attention to the way it worked, but I knew it would be too much grief not to play along with them on this one. I'd just have to get into a university and bide my time until I figured out what I was going to do for the rest of my life. What an ingrate I was! We all were.

I had no sense of trying to better myself by getting a degree in anything. The whole idea of having a career was anti-antiestablishment. Even the word "goal" was a kind of treason. I just wanted to listen to music and smoke pot. It was already obvious to me that I'd never stick it in any kind of establishment.

I was a forerunner to what would one day be loosely referred to as "an underachiever." White kids who have nothing to prove and can't be bothered to prove it. This dropping out was something I took seriously. But none of us knew what we were dropping out into. It didn't take a degree in psychology to work out that this general apathy was inherent to dope smoking. I was already a cliché.

I'd been browsing for colleges through a stack of catalogues that my folks had sent off for. Some had horse riding—out of state. How cool would that be, to finally learn to ride and jump and all the stuff I'd imagined back at Fairlawn? Funny how it seemed so important back then, but now . . . I was changing.

The truth was, with my flunky grades no schools were going to take me. I guess my folks thought it might give me some incentive to look, or maybe they were still delusional enough to think I might turn out to be who they wanted me to be. No doubt they had higher hopes for me than I did. My only incentive was to get out of their house.

Kent State University, being a state school, was obliged, despite my poor academic record, to take me as I was a full-fledged Buckeye. (That's what we were called: Buckeyes from the Buckeye state, after the Ohio buckeye tree. Every state had a tree representative.)

That was fine by me. Kent was a cool university, famously bohemian, known for its art and cinematography departments and anti–Vietnam War stance—and fifteen miles away from Akron. Far enough for now.

I started as soon as I could, two weeks out of Firestone. It was the summer term, three months shy of my eighteenth birthday. My parents dropped me off at my assigned dormitory, Fletcher Hall. I was going to be sharing a room with an Italian girl (they called themselves Italians then, not Italian-Americans) from Cleveland. She had big bouffant hair, which she set in those rollers that I'd stopped using way back when I went "Beatle chick." She looked like a singer out of a group like the Shangri-Las; she wasn't flying her freak flag in army fatigues like me.

I waved goodbye to my folks, never for a moment stopping to wonder how they felt about it all. Terry had moved out a few years earlier and was also at Kent. Was it a sad day for them? It never occurred to me to think about it. My relationship with them was now on permanent disconnect. I was only interested in getting serious about the one thing I was good at: goofing off.

I had my little corncob pipe and, as soon as Miss Italy went out, I flared it up. First things first, then I went to the record store on Water Street in downtown Kent.

Kent was charming and old and had a train that ran right through the middle behind the bars on Water Street. It looked just like any town out of a cowboy film. The only thing missing was horses tied up outside. The sound of the train whistle always had an underlying feeling of promise to it: "Come away." There is no other sound like it, haunting and imploring and mysterious. Come away.

I'd just got Neil Young's solo album and was about to invest in *Happy Sad*, the latest by Tim Buckley. And I do mean invest. I looked at the back cover for half an hour in the shop, unable to unlock my eyes from his doleful gaze. Tim! He was looking right into me, *Mona Lisa* of the day. Then I forked out and took that baby back to my room, where I listened to it over and over and over again.

Our heroes, like Young and Buckley, did not court attention outside of the underground arena. They did not seek publicity or fame. They did not want to be discussed, be controversial or have anything to do with the general population. We had to go out of our way to find them. And we did.

Buckley had a unique voice, which could soar like a bird—my favorite singer of all time. He wrote about things I'd never done, but I thought I knew how he felt anyway. I knew exactly how he felt. A good singer can do that. Longing. He expressed a lot of longing. He was a soul singer.

Young was the other one. After "Helpless" came out, the whole underground nation was in love with him. Now, Young's first solo album was never off our turntables. It had to be heard several times a day.

It was a perfect summer. Music was everywhere. I had my little pipe and would walk to downtown Kent every night after toking up, my head full of songs. Led Zeppelin would be releasing their second album soon. I'd be getting that, fresh off the press. Jeff Beck's was out. Tim Hardin. Richie Havens. Johnny Winter. Pacific Gas & Electric. Cream. The Velvets. Captain Beefheart.

The Beatles had seen us through the last eight years, guiding and uniting us. *Abbey Road* soon. Janis had left Big Brother and gone solo, so we weren't worried about her leaving us. Jefferson Airplane were getting more and more political—still tripped-out, though. You could always rely on the Airplane to be musically inventive and crazy as fuck at the same time. Well, with Grace Slick leading the charge you knew you were in for a ride through the funhouse.

Hendrix remained as steady as the third stone from the sun, and the Stones were now super-powers. *Let It Bleed.* We felt cosseted in the camaraderie of the best our generation had to offer, articulating every feeling we had. We thought it would never end.

I loved being in Kent. There were people walking the streets like in a real town. This was human pageantry on display where it should be. Being vegetarian was to inform everything, the course of my destiny. I was baffled that the entire hippie nation hadn't become vegetarian en masse. It made no sense as eating meat went against the whole dialogue. Were the hippies just as hypocritical as the rest of them? I couldn't admit that but I understood why I loved songs like "The Loner" so much. I didn't want to be like the majority anyway. The majority were always wrong.

As for school, I knew it was just a matter of time before I'd drop out. If I finished and got a fine and professional arts degree, what could I do with it anyway? Become a teacher? That wasn't going to happen. I didn't need a degree to be a painter; I didn't see that getting a degree would have any value at all. But I needed time to work out where I was going to jump. I didn't have a clue.

All I knew for sure was that I wanted to see the world. How was I going to go about it? Well, I didn't know. But I thought if I kept not doing what I didn't want to do, I would naturally get closer to what I did want. Common sense. Never mind intentions. Everybody had good intentions, but they usually crapped out anyway. I didn't want intentions; I wanted the facts.

I walked downtown to Water Street every night and sat on a doorstep with a slice of pizza outside one of the twenty-seven bars that attracted all the dregs from northeastern Ohio every weekend: assorted strays, bikers and fuckups, the people I wanted to know.

Everything at my parents' had been so unforgiving, conservative and unwelcoming of anything out of the norm. Now I could dive in—sit in a doorway eating pizza and not have to tell anyone where I was or when I'd be home. No reporting back to headquarters; no "Aye, aye, commander!" Oh, yeah. This was, as my dad would say, "the nuts!"

I'd walk up North Main Street to my new friend Monkey Bill's place. The houses in Kent were big old wooden Ohio houses with verandas. A gaggle of nonstudents—giggling, stoned goofies—would pile into the back of Bill's pickup truck and we'd bomb out to Brady Lake, pick cherries, then jump into the lake for a swim.

One afternoon, I spent an hour scrubbing out the stains in the ancient porcelain sink in Bill's kitchen until it gleamed brilliant white. I was always good at making things or cleaning—good with my hands—and I couldn't wait for him to see it. But his reaction was scathing.

"It took a year to get it like that!" he snarled, revealing a glimpse of something at odds with pacifism and his usual laid-back demeanor. Well, everyone has boundaries.

I had real hippies for friends now. It was even better than I'd hoped for. There was a guy who lived in Ravenna, eight miles up the road, who we called "the Tim Buckley guy" because he had the hair, work shirt, beads and was slight and poetic-looking. Probably every town had a Tim Buckley guy. And now I had a work shirt, beads and was trying to be poetic-looking.

I didn't have a care in the world, except for my concern that I was going to blow it and get thrown out if I flunked out. It was kind of a foregone conclusion, so I just tried not to think about it. I could get a job and a room somewhere, surely.

My parents had never hit me or come home drunk or done anything abusive, but I was still scared of them. That's how it was. Parents were the law. Nothing was negotiable. I tiptoed around them. It didn't stop me doing stuff behind their back that would have horrified them, though. I think I just didn't have much self-discipline—I was always average.

I'd hang out in Orville's or JB's or the Pirate's Alley, the main bars on Water Street. You could shoot pool in Orville's and it had a vending machine that had pistachio nuts. I loved to get the red dye from them all over my fingers. I'd never had pistachio nuts before; I was getting worldly.

By September, the fall term, I'd passed and was still enrolled. I'd moved up in the world, out of Fletcher Hall, and had my own box room with a single bed and desk in Leebrick Hall. I was very pleased with the arrangement, just getting settled in, stretching out with my desert boots up on the bed, contemplating how I'd get through this next term when . . . a knock at the door.

"Hi, I'm Debbie—in the room next door. I wondered if you'd like to go out and get a hamburger with me."

"Debbie," her hair in pigtails, was wearing a V-neck sweater and pleated skirt. I winced and declined, but within a week she too had become psychedelicized, her hair returning to its natural frizz, almost an afro. It turned out that she loved rock music as much as I did. Ditto a joint and a tab. I renamed her Stella, after Star-eyed Stella, S. Clay Wilson's dyke-pirate heroine. (You couldn't call someone "Debbie" on acid, it just wasn't right.)

I now had a pal to get fucked up with. Dianne had gone to Ohio State in Columbus, so I couldn't make her do stuff with me, but it was a great setup with Stella in the next room. (She never ate a hamburger again, either. Well, who could on acid?)

A willing student, history-major Stella would smoke weed all night while studying, then pass out listening to side one of *Neil Young* so that everybody else on our floor would eventually have to listen to the record on heavy rotation as it got to the end of "The Old Laughing Lady" and the needle rose and dropped back to the first track—over and over and on into the next morning at full blast, Stella oblivious to the phone ringing next to her head and fists pounding on her door. She could listen to Hendrix on head-phones while brushing up on Shakespeare. Nothing could impair her academic prowess. Not even hanging out with Stupid here could compromise her good habits. She was my opposite. You know, yin and yang.

But dorm life didn't suit me. My nomadic inclinations becoming manifest, I started a long-lasting habit of uprooting and moving every three months.

My calligraphy professor (Kent offered some good alternative courses for dummies), Doug Unger, must have noticed my general uninterest but gave me A's—the only A's I'd ever got in my life outside of art. I couldn't relate to an authority figure, though, even if he was only in his twenties. Stories about students getting it on with teachers seemed far-fetched to me. "Naw—who would do that?"

He presumably saw some kind of potential in me because he kept on giving me A's, I guess to encourage me. Maybe he, playing the good teacher and all, could see I was miserable and thought he could get through to me. Of course, there's an outside chance that I was actually good at calligraphy, but I doubt that. I could hardly even write. Good with pen and ink though. Who knows?

Then he offered me the one place available per semester in his instrument-making class. I hadn't even asked for it; he just offered it to me, such a thoughtful man he was. Great! A class of one. And this was something I could actually use. I loved dulcimers and owned one already. Joni Mitchell!

I took a long time selecting the perfect rosewood—dark and fragrant, a pungent, sexy wood—and began planing and carving and gluing and steaming and bending it into shape. I glued many layers together to form a block and proceeded to carve the headstock, all that whittling I'd done as a kid paying off. I was on my way to making a beautiful dulcimer. And so I found out that there really are good teachers who want to go out of their way to help problem students. Unger had entirely too much faith in me in thinking I'd finish it, though.

I met Hoover at KSU too. She was friendly with the "get-down boys"—the few guys on campus who dressed like the Faces and liked

English bands. There were about seven of them, all told, out of a student body of ten thousand. And, like me, Hoover was good at giving get-down haircuts. She had a VW Beetle and would drive to wherever we needed to go to see a band. So, apart from classes, school was starting to shape up very nicely indeed.

10

FOUR DAYS IN MAY

I got through the autumn quarter and was hanging in, barely. That is, I hadn't flunked out yet, an achievement in itself. I went to a few art-history classes, but not many. I got a job modeling for the sculpture department so I had enough spare change to get me through the weekends.

The winter term was unremarkable. It's too cold in Ohio in the winter to do much. Well, I guess I could have gone to classes. I did go half the time but resented assignments. I thought I should be more spontaneous than that if I was supposed to be an artist. Lazy, really. I balked at any kind of instruction.

I discovered an off-campus horseback riding class, to my joy, which accredited points so it counted as part of the curriculum. Even that didn't go well for me when I went to the stable one morning to "tack up," having not been to bed after a night of experimentation. It became obvious that I was still tripping when I tried to get the harness on my horse. He was gigantic and getting bigger. With only the two of us in the stall, he could tell, sure as shit, I was off my head. You know it's bad when a horse is eyeballing you like something's wrong. He tried to back up but there was nowhere for the freaked-out animal to go. I could see getting the bit in his mouth would be impossible in the state I was in, so I mumbled an apology, frantically wrestling with the sliding bolt on the door and got out of there before one of us got hurt.

After all my aspirations to be a great horsewoman, I counted that as a personal tragedy and was ashamed. I never told anyone about that day. (Presumably neither did he. Hard to know for sure on acid. Mr. Ed.) My definitive failure.

I had to offer myself up to the psychology department, as they needed humans to run some experiments on. It was a way to earn the credits I needed to pass, and it was starting to look like I'd need more of these extra credits than most. Art students had to do shit like that, I guess, so that we did something other than just noodle around. In the "experiment" I was instructed to press a button every time a certain image came up on a screen. The guy conducting the test raised his eyebrows and told me that I had the fastest reaction times of any woman they'd tested on campus. Like a man, I guess. What good was that going to do me?

That was about it for my life of academia. Sometimes there'd be a gig on and Hoover would drive us. One night, we went to Pittsburgh, a hundred miles through a terrible blizzard to see the Kinks. Every time a truck passed, the little Beetle pulled to the left and almost came off the road, but we finally made it. Hoover was one helluva driver. After the show we were sitting on the curb outside the venue, getting our heads around the drive back to Kent, when Ray Davies himself walked right past. He dropped a towel, bent over to pick it up and saw me sitting there. Eye contact. That was the only memorable thing that happened during the winter term.

Spring arrived. I was by then an old hand at going downtown, wandering from bar to bar, finding pot and watching Terry's band, 15-60-75, and the James Gang. I'd moved out of Leebrick Hall as

soon as the winter term ended, and got a room in a house on Depeyster Street, two streets from Water Street.

I was eighteen and enjoying my life, but I had to figure out a way
to get out of going to school altogether. My wage from Poots' Snack
Shop, where I made ice-cream sundaes and deep-fried donut holes,
wouldn't cover independent living. Anyway, I was about to get fired
from Poots. A good-looking guy from Akron, Bob Smith, would
circle the pop stand on his sportster, nod to me to jump on and I'd
sneak out for a spin. My boss caught me dismounting and gave me
the chop. Slave driver!

I didn't have a boyfriend and was pretty backward in that
department—still a virgin but not too bothered about it. It did occur
to me that maybe I wasn't normal. That worried me a little. I had
no way of knowing and wasn't sure what being normal was anyway.
I'd never even seen a naked guy. I suspected that that in itself wasn't
normal. But I was happy with my relationship with guys on records,
in bands.

We were proud that KSU was a recognized "antiwar" university
like Berkeley in California. There was a group of political students
on campus, Students for a Democratic Society (SDS), who were
radicals. I didn't know much about it, but I wanted to be a radical. I
knew I was against Vietnam, like everybody else.

One night, on acid, we encountered some Vietnam vets in a bar
and got into a conversation, unintelligible to them and regrettable to
us. It was grim. Nobody showed the vets coming back from 'Nam
any respect. We thought they shouldn't have gone in the first place.

The war was a terrible blight on our certainty that we were making the world a better place—more conscious, more inclusive, more free. With the war raging, our optimism just spelled "more bullshit." We were completely helpless to stop it. What could we do? The real problem was that none of us understood why we were actually in Vietnam. No one seemed to be able to offer a clear explanation. The spread of communism was the reason given. So, if the commies got Vietnam, they were coming for us next? Seemed a little abstract to us pot-smoking peaceniks.

The draft system was devised in such a way that the offspring of the affluent would never have to go to war. It was the one thing we didn't argue with. Are you kidding? Would any self-respecting hippie agree with the idea of conscription? Absolutely not. Like the Amish, hippies maintained a stance of unconditional pacifism. The only song I remember that addressed this omission was "Fortunate Son" by Creedence Clearwater Revival. (A song I dug out many years later and passed on to Paul McGuinness, who managed me for two weeks, to pass along to his main band, U2, to cover.)

Other campuses voiced dissent. Right on! And the radio was spilling over with antiwar songs like Barry McGuire's hit "Eve of Destruction," which noted that communism wasn't as much our problem as racism was. But what could we do about the war in Kent, Ohio?

FRIDAY NIGHT, MAY 1

Our charming president, Richard Nixon, who my parents, as far as I was concerned, had single-handedly put in the White House, was reported to have sent troops into Cambodia. It was a red rag to a bull, to us weekend revelers.

What a liar Nixon was! He said he wouldn't do that!

We had to show support for our side. As usual, the street was packed with crazies on Friday night, so there was no shortage of manpower, and we were, to a man, off our faces as we rolled garbage cans into the middle of Water Street and set the contents on fire. It made for quite a display, what with the smoke and flames shooting up. If anyone dared try to drive through our blockade, they'd get their windows smashed out. Someone tried; it felt good. Smashing the windows out of a car is a great feeling.

Flag burning was also a popular form of protest, and I admit that we didn't realize how privileged we were to live in a country where protest was allowed. We just assumed life was basically fair. After all, we'd grown up watching *Lassie*. Plus, there were a hundred thousand of us spread all across the country, so we had that safety-in-numbers sense-of-security thing. We felt impervious to danger.

We saw sickening images daily on television: Vietnamese families decimated, machine-gunned and napalmed—their homes burnt to the ground.

Fatuous slogans like "Give Peace a Chance" further frustrated things by giving the bogus impression that we were doing something about it. But rhetoric rang hollow as, indeed, rhetoric always does. Again, never mind intentions, what were the facts? We idolized the Beatles, but if they couldn't figure it out, who could? Talking about peace and love was airy-fairy while people were getting their limbs blown off. There was a lot of posturing in the name of protest, but like an art installation what did it mean? How much more thought-provoking could things get? Where was the solution?

We were confused, pissed off and had to be careful not to see the news while on acid.

Saturday morning rolled round to the news that a curfew had been imposed on the city of Kent. You weren't to leave your house after 10:00 p.m. unless you lived on campus, where the curfew was extended to 11:00.

Guess where everybody who lived off campus went that night? Correct. We were going to crash in someone's dorm room to take advantage of the extra hour. We wanted to listen to music and party as usual. And we were all fired up by our spectacle of a protest the night before.

The ROTC—Resident Officers' Training Corps—was a very unpopular presence on campus. Anything "military" was unwelcome, and its headquarters was in one of the old wooden buildings where a lot of the art classes were held. Obviously it had to go.

The campus was crammed with off-site visitors such as me, so a party atmosphere was in full effect. Every dorm room blasted music out: Hendrix; the Beatles; Crosby, Stills & Nash; Led Zeppelin; Steppenwolf; Richie Havens; Jefferson Airplane. The grassy common was like a festival site. Then the real party began.

As it got dark, an A-team of longhairs charged down the hill, hurling railroad flares through the windows of the wooden ROTC building. Old and rickety, it went up in flames within minutes, filling the sky with bright orange plumes—just the ticket for a thousand stoned students. All of our faces were lit up by the enormous bonfire, and people were dancing and cheering and waving bandannas in total jubilation.

What we'd failed to note was that the National Guard were stationed just a few miles up the road in Ravenna where they'd been called in because of a truckers' strike.

The crowd was raging with riot in our hearts, but in the distinct manner of a student party—a party with the flame-engulfed ROTC building as the centerpiece. Everybody was dazzled watching the greatest light show ever, but the party was about to end.

Seemingly out of nowhere, National Guard jeeps appeared, racing across the common while teargas canisters exploded all around. Within moments, the campus itself actually looked like an on-the-spot report from Vietnam. Everyone was running and shouting to get away from the ROTC building as it burned out of control, with the fleet of army jeeps moving in.

Fire engines bounded across the common. The firefighters did their best to quench the flames, but the building was already a goner. Students pulled the fire hoses out of the fire trucks, causing the water to shoot and spray everywhere except on the building.

Then there was the stampede. Everyone was panicking, trying to flee the teargas. Some used shirts dunked in puddles to cover their faces from the stinging, sticky gas, but there was nowhere to run because the common was enclosed by a chain-link fence. We were trapped. And when a few thousand panicking, freaked-out people running as fast as they could hit that fence, it was potential carnage.

Nobody teaches you how to behave in a panic situation like the ABC of emergency resuscitation—where is it when you need it? Why don't they teach *that* in school instead of algebra? When we were kids we used to have fire drills, and we were taught what to do in an "air raid" if they dropped the bomb. Put your head down on your desk and fold your hands behind your neck. Crowd control? Not a dicky-bird about that.

It was a no-way-out situation. If you fell over, good luck to you as you'd be trampled underfoot. The chain-link fence was getting closer by the second.

Suddenly, I heard a voice shout, "Waaaalk!"

I immediately came to a halt and shouted, "Waaaalk!"

Everyone who heard the word stopped running and in turn shouted, "Waaaalk!"

Guys charged the posts of the fence with what looked like karate kicks, bending them over so that the fence became like a springboard, with people taking running leaps and bouncing off trampoline-style into the darkness, away from the smoke and chaos. I still wonder who he was, the first guy to yell "Waaaalk!"

SUNDAY, MAY 3

We woke up to the news that there was a total curfew imposed on the whole of Kent. No one could leave any place of residence on or off campus. No matter, there was nothing to do on Sunday anyway.

I wanted to go back to the house on Depeyster Street, but there was the curfew. I snuck out anyway, ducked between houses and trees and made my way back, amazed to see armored vehicles positioned on the corners of the streets. Talk about overreacting!

MONDAY, MAY 4

I was back in my room on Depeyster Street. I told my friend Cindy Hino on the phone that I'd hook up with her later. Cindy almost seemed like a foreigner; not so much because her family was from Japan, but because she was from Pennsylvania. We'd gone to her parents' house for the weekend once and, to me, it felt like another world. She told me on the phone that there was going to be a "peaceful protest" early afternoon, so I'd see her on the common. Today was mid-term and assignments and portfolios were all due to be handed in, so everyone would be there anyway.

Anyone who lived in Kent was heading for the common. No one wanted to miss the protest, and we were all anxious to have a look at the scene of Saturday night's fire in the daylight. The atmosphere was charged. We felt good about making our view on the war known. Our voice mattered and we felt at one with our brothers and sisters across the nation. Right on!

The grassy, rolling common was teeming with students. I'd never seen it so packed. I couldn't even make out what was left of the burned-down ROTC building. I pushed my way through the crowd.

Then I heard the tatatatatatatatatat sound. I thought it was fireworks. An eerie silence fell over the common. Then a young man's voice: "They fucking killed somebody!"

The quiet felt like gravity pulling us to the ground. Everything slowed down and the silence got heavier. Minutes passed—and nothing. Then the sound of a siren. An ambulance was cutting its way through the crowd.

I could see it. The ROTC building, now nothing more than a few inches of charcoal, was surrounded by National Guardsmen. They were all on one knee and pointing their rifles at . . . us!

They looked freaked out. What happened? Angry students had been throwing stones at them and shouting, "Fuck off—get off our campus!" Then they fired.

By the time I made my way to where I could see them it was still unclear what was going on. The Guardsmen themselves looked stunned. They were still surrounding the burned-down building. What had they been guarding? There was nothing to protect; the ROTC building was gone now. Why were they there? Were they ordered to fire loaded rifles into the crowd? That couldn't be possible. No.

We looked at them and they looked at us. They were just kids, nineteen years old, like us. But in uniform. Like our boys in Vietnam.

There was a sense of incomprehension wherever you looked.

I sat down on the grass. Teachers were telling everybody to leave. I wasn't leaving. Some men picked me up. I sat, cross-legged and rigid, as they carried me away. I still didn't understand. But it was time to go. School was over.

Cindy Hino's boyfriend, Jeff Miller, was staying, though. He couldn't get up from where he was lying, facedown, the blood leaving his lifeless body and flowing into the nearby gutter.

11

NORTH OF THE BORDER

The KSU campus was totally evacuated within twenty-four hours. Students lined up at the entrance ramps of the interstates, hitch-hiking back to New York or Pennsylvania or wherever it was they were from.

There were investigations, but I don't think anybody ever discovered exactly why the Guardsmen were armed with loaded rifles. Or why they were guarding the charcoal remains of a building. Or why they fired into a crowd of civilians for throwing stones. It still remains a mystery, as far as I know.

A couple of weeks later on the radio, we heard a new song by Neil Young, "Ohio," about the horrible event. That made us feel better; we needed to be acknowledged. I knew Jeff had been a fan of his, so I was happy that Young had become our spokesman, our voice. It was a big element in easing us out of shock.

I'd moved back to my parents' house. The deal was that we were supposed to finish the spring term at home and send our assignments in. It was pretty safe to assume *that* arrangement wasn't going to work out for me. I couldn't get my assignments done at school, so I certainly wasn't going to on my own without someone standing over me with a stick.

I met up with the one guy I could hang out with from Firestone. Chris was an intellectual, straight-A type and dug all the same music as me. He was home from Urbana, where he was at college, but now it was summer so school was out for everybody. We listened to the Beatles and to John Lennon's new solo album a hundred times. Chris played guitar and was good at art.

We embarked on our own summer of love, smoking lots of pot, listening to music, and hanging out with Chris's older sister Pat and her boyfriend, Dick. They were all brainy psychology majors who talked endlessly about Freud. We smoked our brains out and I heard the phrase "In the final analysis . . ." a lot. It was the first time I'd ever hung out with people older than me. Pat and Dick must have been twenty-one. Adults! They were fun, and they liked having me and Chris around as sidekicks.

We got this idea to take off and hitch rides around Ontario, so I lied to my folks and said I was going up to see a friend whose family had a cottage in Port Carling. I hated lying to them but if I'd told them what the real plan was, well, let's just say it was better not to tell them. For a start, my hitchhiking habit would have pushed them over the edge. And Chris had long hair, so they didn't like me hanging out with him.

Pat and Dick gave us a ride to Cleveland Hopkins Airport. Exciting! As a going-away treat, Dick did a planche for us on a pillar right there in the airport. He was a gymnast too when he wasn't rolling joints and talking psychology.

We exited the airport in Toronto and stuck out our thumbs. Dharma bums! We got as far as we could before it got dark, then bought a loaf of brown bread and a round of Gouda cheese sealed in red wax. That was a new thing to me, like yogurt; I'd never seen these exotic foods growing up. Even whole-wheat bread was a relatively new thing. Then we pitched our little tent in a local park and crashed out.

We kept going, going nowhere. I liked the feeling of that. Someone on the road gave us a phone number to call if we got back down to Toronto. We hitched rides and it was easy, as we had practically nothing to carry. The tent just hooked onto Chris's or my belt. We had a Bunsen burner but that was about all.

I loved Canada, and I was especially happy to get back to Toronto to walk the city streets surrounded by other people doing likewise. It was everything I'd been missing in Akron. It wasn't a small college town like Kent, either; this really was a big cosmopolitan city.

We called the number we'd been given on the road. A woman answered the phone, and we asked if we could crash there. She sighed and said she was at the end of her tether with the constant people traffic in her place, but then she asked us what signs we were. When we told her we were both Virgos she changed her tune and asked us to come by, saying she needed some Virgo energy. Proper hippie.

Georgia Ambrose had dark skin, blonde hair and green eyes. She wasn't white but it was hard to tell which races she was mixed with. She was definitely the most exotic-looking person I'd ever seen— beautiful, in fact. She was a jazz singer and held regular Buddhist meetings in her big, rambling wooden house on Wellesley Street. A ton of people would arrive and chant "Nam-myoho-renge-kyo" while Chris and I sat in the kitchen, listening. It was all new to me. I thought it was the best place I'd ever been. But the thing that impressed us the most was that Georgia Ambrose was about to have a birthday. To our total disbelief she was over thirty!

My parents would have gone nuts if they knew I was hanging around all this Buddhist "malarkey," not to mention the rest of this "Port Carling" vacation I was on. But I wanted to stay.

We rented a little apartment. It was empty but for our two sleeping bags. We got a couple of mugs and plates, and we had the Bunsen burner, of course. There was no money left out of the hundred or so dollars we'd been living on, but I saw a "waitress wanted" sign in an Indian restaurant, went in and applied for the job. They offered to hire me! I'd never been to or eaten in an Indian restaurant before, so I was thrilled for an adventure. I was all ready to start my new life in Toronto.

Chris wasn't so keen, though. If he stayed in Canada he'd be a draft dodger and never allowed back into the States. I was pretty sure that if I were a guy I'd be going for the "conscientious objector" option—draft dodger, whatever you want to call it. But I wasn't a guy so it wasn't my call. Naw, my parents would have died of shame.

That was the only time in my life that a guy would make a decision for me, although I totally supported Chris so I guess it was mutual. We went back to Akron, the two Virgos, and then it was our turn to have our birthdays, both nineteen. Time was always running out.

·

The autumn quarter started and it was business as usual for everyone in Kent. Well, except for the four who got killed and the nine injured.

There was still one major problem that had to be addressed in my "any experience is better than no experience" theory. I had to get rid of my virginity.

I'd put it off so long that it was becoming a hassle to think about.

And even more than experience, not being hassled was consideration numero uno to a pothead.

It's not that I wasn't sexually motivated. I was a hot little number, but all the heat was in my head and focused primarily on a turntable. Still, I can't remember having sexual fantasies about actually getting it on with one of my rock-star heroes. I wanted to be them, not do them.

I think starting out with LSD and graduating to sex was a good way of approaching the subject. I'd already found that being in love wasn't dependent on receiving treats in the sack, or whatever went on in there. My love affairs had been loftier than that.

S. Clay Wilson's sordid fantasies in *Zap Comix* had rather dispelled any yearning to manifest lust in my search for eternity. Having a slathering demon ramming his engorged, vein-strangled four-foot-long tool up my nether regions wasn't the turn-on that listening to Robert Plant screaming down a mic was.

I had wanted to keep the whole process at bay, where it wouldn't get in the way of fine guys like John Hammond singing about it, but the time had come. It had to be dealt with sooner or later. And it was getting later.

Procreation was by now not part of the equation to us little nature lovers. We didn't even know we were confused. We were just trying to keep up with the illustrations of orgasmic ecstasy we saw on all those "Hallelujah the Pill!" posters: the naked, flowing-haired priestess of love on her knees, head thrown back, howling at the moon while straddling some scrawny, bearded eager-beaver who couldn't believe his luck. Variations of which found their way onto the walls of head shops coast to coast. It wasn't porn; it was free love. Hallelujah!

We'd been conditioned to think that multiple partners was a

form of liberation and that not getting attached to one person was freedom. The well-documented and historical notion that the heart wants exclusivity wasn't acknowledged at all. Marriage was considered as something arcane, a product of the establishment— something your parents did.

I'd been shy of bodily functions from the get-go. My first period had been a huge blow to my self-esteem. Becoming a woman was an obstacle that had horrified and dogged me throughout my teens, but I wasn't a guy and I was never going to be a guy, which I had to accept. That meant I'd probably never play guitar in a band, so the worst part was already taken care of.

Sex. In movies there was always a smoldering build-up until two bodies touched and the flame ignited. I'd seen it happen like that on film, but never like this.

My first encounter was a different cinematic animal altogether. In fact, forget the animal part. I accepted an arranged meeting via letter: "Do you have any objection to having sexual intercourse with me this Thursday?" It was clinical and just marginally more sexy than two chimps grooming each other.

The "union" was, in short, not very successful. And, although in the words of Iggy Pop, you could eventually "drive a truck through it," my unused birth canal couldn't really accommodate what the quota turned out to be. It was, however, a start. Now that I was released from the worry of how to ditch this last obstacle in the way of my hippie aspirations, I was free to roam.

I was still too shy to approach, seize, collar or consider a sexual conquest, though. I didn't know how to flirt or chat up and I wouldn't know if a guy was coming on to me if he had his cock out with a green flag tied to it. But not to worry. We had drugs for everything now; it was just a matter of finding the right one to assist me in my quest for sexual liberation, which would turn out to be more a form of enslavement in time, but, hey—we were so in love with drugs that we were about to turn sex into one of them.

I just needed to delve into my rudimentary knowledge of herbs and pharmaceuticals. Starting with the Pill. Well, yeah! This is what made it all possible. Keep poppin' those babies and don't you forget it!

Pot: the great enhancer that only made the mechanics of sex more abstract and unworkable as I froze in the hold of utter paranoia, wondering if my body was normal. Pass.

LSD: This rendered almost any physical endeavor impossible. Even changing a record on the turntable could take the better part of an hour, three-quarters of which might be spent marveling at the prismatic color arrangements dancing around the wave-like grooves of the LP as it melted, mutating into something breathing and slithering up the spindle of the turntable. That could take all day. I'd think twice before accepting the challenge of a flaccid dick taking off into full erection and disappearing up me in that state. Are you kidding me? Pass.

Cough syrup: not an aphrodisiac and left the user pretty goddamn happy to sit in a chair and watch dust drift and float around the room for entire afternoons. Pass.

Opium: Well, when you shut your eyes and find you're driving a nifty little sports car at high speed only to wake back to reality when a brick wall approaches, no, you're just too stoned. Pass.

Mad Dog 20/20, or MD 20/20 to us, the wino's tipple of choice: If you can approach a total stranger in a smoky bar at two in the morning who's having trouble lighting his own cigarette because he's trying to light the filter end he's so fucked up, and still find him attractive enough to say, "Hey, daddy—whatcha got in yer pants there—anything for me?" you know you've found the key.

It's alcohol, folks! Bingo!

And basically that's how we became champions of the universe, sexually speaking.

12

SOUTH OF THE BORDER

I can't say I was overjoyed to be back at Kent after the possibility of a life in Toronto, but I rolled with the punches.

I found a nifty little place to live in a tiny converted garage in the alley next to the A&P, Kent's main grocery store. I painted the walls, as always when I got to a new place. I did like painting; I loved holding a brush, just not for school. Maybe I'd become a painter like I always thought I would; a painter and decorator, at least.

I was back on Water Street hitting the bars, a little more jaded than the flower child who breezed through the year before. Everyone drank White Russians, Singapore Slings or Tequila Sunrises. Liquor was obviously easier to get than anything else so we were all becoming drunks. Bad system, but what could you do?

On the weekends Stella and I would get up on the tables in the Pirate's Alley and dance, waiting for some outsider, some sucker, to buy a round. Drinking was a new high for me, and I discovered that if I was drunk enough I could pick up a guy. I'd never be able to do that if I wasn't loaded. I was still shy, but nothing five shots couldn't fix. I'd wait till the end of the night and see who was left in the bar. Pretty rank, really. But I wanted to be sure I was normal, or at least try to find out. I didn't really care about the sex—more the adventure—but I was hopeful it might live up to its reputation. Still, who didn't agree that one-nighters were never very good? Men, that's who. Well, "any experience is better than no experience" was my motto.

By the time the booze allowed me to get "restless," I wouldn't remember much anyway: sloppy, not skillful; never any complaints, though. Oh, men didn't care about that, and I was getting my experience and I wanted more.

I had one friend who was an out-and-out sex fiend—she couldn't get enough and didn't need alcohol to drag anything with a schlong on it back home and into the sack. But I was in it more for the thrill of the unknown without being too bothered about the how or why or what. I guess I was a bit like her when I think about it. We were all still in "free love" mindset, but it was definitely starting to turn.

I liked getting stoned but you could get really fucked up on booze as I was finding out. Never mind cocktails, I was happier knocking back straight tequila; it was a lot more to the point, and I've never liked fuss of any kind. I wasn't very good at moderation, either. I'd trained myself to need the rush of the rollercoaster in everything. That was what we were all into: overdoing it. You think you love it but the truth is that it loves you. I was just getting wrecked, more than anything. There was nothing high about it as time went on. Booze. Just an addiction any way you cut it.

The James Gang played regularly in JB's, and I would sit on the floor at the feet of Joe Walsh and bask in our very own world-class guitar hero right there where I could reach over and touch his tennis shoes if I'd wanted to.

The Numbers Band—15-60-75—played there too. Their singer, Bob Kidney, used to do nights at the Berth in south Akron, another place I used to sneak out to when I lived at home. No more sneaking by this stage, but I was getting jaded.

I got a job in Jerry's Diner. It was pretty cool, I guess—converted trolley car, red bar stools all along the Formica luncheon counter—but I was a lousy waitress. My people skills weren't great. If someone ordered a hamburger I copped an attitude, and someone always ordered a hamburger. It was going to be a long haul, this "hating meat-eaters" road I'd embarked on. I'd never turn back, though. No way. I wasn't even sure what being a vegetarian was exactly—I was still figuring it out, treading a singular path that few seemed to be on. People asked me if I got special injections! Fools. That would change eventually when I'd start to meet my people—animal-rights activists and Krishna devotees, lifelong vegetarians all. I was making brown rice, George Ohsawa style, pretty regularly, but I had such a backlog of junk food in me that it would take more than that to clean up my garbage can of a system.

The days were getting shorter and it was getting cold. At school I was still slugging away like a prize-fighter, stunned, going through the motions, all the while knowing I was losing. It was becoming a blur like an endless bout. Was I still going to be trying to figure out what to do by the time I was twenty? When a fighter loses heart it's all over.

Our heroes were starting to drop off. The Beatles were breaking up. It was like a nightmare. It seemed like everything was on the brink of collapse.

It was over for Janis and Jimi. Brian Jones was gone. Jim Morrison was losing it, getting his cock out onstage, a drunken, belligerent mess like the rest of us. He wasn't long for this life either.

·

I saw the poster nailed to a tree: winter course in Mexico, *Universidad de las Américas*. I read it over a few times. Mexico, they did a course in Mexico? I wondered if it was expensive. Surely my folks would never let me do that.

My parents were cowed by our breakdown in communication. They'd even taken a course in graphology to try to understand Terry and me better. Sitting down and just talking about things seemed out of the question. But it wasn't just us; the whole nation was rocked by generational disconnect.

So how was I going to talk them into it? I'd hardly earned any privileges. Of course, they had no way of knowing what a fuck-up I was becoming. For all they knew, I was going to classes and studying.

I'd never heard of anyone in Ohio speaking Spanish—hardly something I would need. Nevertheless, I must have offered a convincing argument: "a unique opportunity, a once-in-a-lifetime deal." I never understood why they agreed to it, but they did. Maybe they were just relieved that I wasn't trying to drop out yet. Using the word "opportunity" was a good move. I'd have to remember that.

The university was in Cholula, a little town in the state of Puebla. On the bus ride in from the airport I wasn't chatterboxing away with the rest of the girls in that high-pitched frequency of females in groups. I was more intent on what I could see out the window: dusty roads, rugged terrain, mountains, scattered little towns with adobe buildings and guys in white with straw hats driving pickup trucks, old fifties models.

As we approached what looked like the university, the first thing I saw was an extensive barbed-wire fence circling it. I didn't like the look of that. The bus drove in and I already wanted out.

There were about thirty of us in line to get room assignments in the dormitories. Three rough-looking *muchachos* were sitting on a bench, watching us. They didn't look like students to me. I had to think quick because the line was getting shorter and I was in it. I left the queue.

"Do any of you live near here?"

They nodded in unison. Of course, they had just come to check out the new crop of girls.

"Can I stay with one of you?"

One of them—white, bushy mustache, looked a bit like Lee Marvin—picked up my little case and we made for the exit. It was one of those win-win deals. I got to live off-campus and he got a Midwestern girl who was curious as hell.

He had a cool setup, a room in a hacienda including a shower. Basic. A sink, mattress, everything you needed. I made myself at home like a stray dog trying not to take up too much space.

He was from Oregon. I'd never met anyone from that far away. He seemed to know his way around. He was an older guy—maybe twenty-two.

I didn't smoke any weed in Mexico. I know, that surprised me too—I thought that would be the first thing I'd get into—but I'd never experienced culture shock before. Maybe a little up in Canada, but nothing like this. The disorientation was like tripping in itself. I just wouldn't be able to handle any more. I never thought that could happen but, well, I was still on a learning curve.

I went onto the campus once or twice so I would have something to tell my parents. Naturally, I didn't inform them of my alternative arrangements. We had an unspoken rule that I didn't tell them anything they wouldn't want to hear. I think that was by mutual agreement, but I can't be sure as we never discussed things.

I tagged along with Jim—the Lee Marvin lookalike—and his Mexican buddy, who talked about soccer a lot. Americans only had baseball and football, and in my experience you either liked music or sports, not both. They were fanatical about soccer there. Bernie, the Mexican, called it football. Everything was different in Mexico.

I couldn't really go around on my own very well because I didn't want to get lost in Cholula. It was just a bunch of dirt roads and haciendas and guys who hissed at me if I was on my own—no street signs or anything.

All the men sat around in groups when it wasn't too hot out, drinking a gloopy sort of beer that they ladled up out of big tubs. My impression was that it was the women who ran everything and did the work, while the men drove around in those fifties pickup trucks and drank their beer. As much as I was a smartass in Ohio, in Mexico I was out of my depth all round.

I'd stand at a primitive little bar with the Lee Marvin guy. Even he drank that gruel, licking it off the corners of his mouth like all guys with mustaches do when they drink. I'd just wait there watching, fascinated by everything, especially the local women buying tortillas from tortilla factories—kiosks just about big enough for the two women who served out of the hatch. The señoras would line up to buy a stack of maybe seven or eight, freshly floured, wrap them in a piece of muslin they'd brought and put them in their basket. You didn't see that at the Acme.

One day, when we were out walking, a group of locals hissed at me: "Blondie! *Mamacita!*" I spun around, flipped them the bird and shouted, "Fuck off!" thinking nothing of it. But it really pissed my compadre from Oregon off. He was furious. "Don't you *ever* do that again!" he growled, and took off, leaving me in the dust to catch up. He ignored me for the rest of the day.

I was beginning to learn some life lessons, rules to take with me. For a start, don't ever mouth off if you're with a guy. In any culture you care to mention that's the rule. (Except in white suburban USA.) Nobody will respond to a skinny little nothing, even if she's an obnoxious big mouth, when there's the chance of a punch-up on offer. She doesn't exist—she only represents the guy she's with. They'll go for the dude every time.

Like a dog on a leash, ferocious and aggressive, you take it off the leash and it soon realizes it's out of its weight division and behaves itself. He didn't have to explain it. I figured it out and then he started talking to me again. I liked the way guys could hold their own like that, not talking if they didn't have to.

Although I wasn't smoking the killer weed on offer everywhere or drinking the white beer, I did get a taste for the other local brew, mescal. But it didn't really suit me. I didn't have the personality for it or maybe my chemistry was wrong or something. I would get pretty vicious, demonic even, after a few slugs; I couldn't stop myself wanting to go crazy before passing out.

My gracious host threw me into the courtyard naked one night, and I had to hide until he let me back in to get my clothes before he turfed me out for good. So I got a room on the other side of the hacienda.

I was happy to have my own little place in Mexico. I managed to find some music magazines in Spanish and decorated my room exactly like I did all my places, with pictures of bands taped up on the walls. In one magazine I found the words to a new Dylan song, "Watching the River Flow"; that went up on the wall.

Even though I pissed him off, the Lee Marvin guy still let me hang out with him. Well, there weren't that many chicks around, only those college girls. But I was more fun than those girls—

c'mon!—and always game. Yeah, guys liked me. I think I was more like a guy than a girl. Guys never felt like they had to look after me. So long as I could keep my mouth shut.

I was definitely getting an education, "going to school" in Mexico. Like what to do if you encounter a pack of wild dogs and they take an interest in you. You bend down, pick up a handful of stones, look like you mean business and lunge towards them. If there are no stones around, do it anyway. The dogs will take off.

That's kind of a good one to know metaphorically too. It's like looking confident onstage. Nobody needs to know how you shat your pants ten minutes before going on. No. No. No. That is not the ticket they paid for. Confidence is usually a bluff—if you're lucky you might have it, but frankly nobody will know the difference. There's enough fear in this world and people want to see the courage of conviction. That's showbiz. Mexico was a good primer.

Another handy tip I got living in Cholula was to always carry an empty Coke bottle, one in each hand, when going out alone at night. Nobody wants to get smashed in the head with a bottle.

There was this dusty little club halfway to the university, where Lee Marvin and the Mexican used to drink. One night, after a few myself, I borrowed someone's guitar and sang a song or two. That was my only public appearance so far. Oh yeah, apart from the one night I got onstage with Sat Sun Mat in Cuyahoga Falls.

I didn't think I had enough experience yet to write songs, but I wasn't really worried about it. By now I was getting too old to be in a band anyway, it looked like the moment had passed. I only got up and played in the bar that night because I was drunk, but it did remind me of certain aspirations. How could anything be better than singing and playing guitar? I must have written a couple of songs by then to play that audience of three, but I don't remember.

Mostly, I was taking second-class buses that only cost a few *centavos* (see, I was learning Spanish), and I didn't care where they were heading. I was seeing a new world and felt more relaxed when I was moving.

I was totally at ease sitting among farmers with their cages of chickens and sacks of grain and babies. I'd sit quietly at the back and copy the women with their arms folded tightly around their ribs to stop their tits getting trashed by the painful, violent jerking and bouncing of bus over rock and gravel. Even with my flat chest it hurt like hell if I didn't hold tight. Those ladies knew. I was with people I had nothing in common with other than basic human elements like pain and hunger, but I felt, for the first time maybe, at home. I think it just felt right to be moving.

The school term was almost over. I'd been in Mexico for six weeks and didn't want to go back to Ohio, not just yet. Brrrrr. Wait for spring. I told my parents some bullshit about private Spanish tuition if I stayed on a bit. I still don't know why they went along with such an obvious lie. Maybe I was more convincing than I remember, or maybe they really believed I was learning Spanish like I said. I got a reprieve and managed to stay on after the silly girls I'd come out with were long gone.

I had a couple of friends now. One was named Julie, who got a room in the same hacienda and had a little black bottle of expensive perfume—"Joy." I used to have one by Yardley called "Oh! de London" back in high school, which I loved, but this was more, you know, like real perfume. She let me wear some. I was getting sophisticated.

And I met another girl named Kaththee. I think she made up that spelling. They did stuff like that in California. She had a camera and took pictures all the time, including some of me naked in the rain in a paddock next to a horse. She told me to scream as loud as I could. I didn't want to scare the horse but she was the photographer, so I did it. The pictures were shit. Some good ones of the horse, though. I already didn't like having my picture taken.

I did like being with these new friends from far-reaching places. One thing that surprised me (apart from still not smoking pot) was how much more I knew about music than most of the people I met. I even met someone from California who hadn't heard of the Velvet Undergound. Imagine that! Ohio radio, the best.

Now that I didn't have to pretend to be in Cholula for school, it was time to see more of Mexico. I went to Cuernavaca. That's where Kaththee had a swanky apartment—a penthouse with lots of potted plants in it.

Somewhere or other I got sick and had to go into a little clinic for a few days. I don't remember what I came down with, just the cool white sheets on the cot and nurses in uniform who I couldn't understand.

It's amazing how much can happen in a few weeks on the road. This was going to become a habit to me; seeing new places would become like a drug. Better than drugs. And there was a whole world still to discover. I was as optimistic as a junkie in a poppy field.

Some travelers I met were going on an overnight bus ride to Acapulco and asked if I wanted to join them. Every hippie in America dreamed of going to Acapulco because of the famous Acapulco gold but when we arrived there in the middle of the night I wasn't feeling it, so I stayed on the bus and climbed out in the morning in a place called Zihuatanejo.

It was a paradisiacal beach town, unspoiled and primitive. I wandered along the pristine beach and met a Canadian guy, a nature boy from way up north in Ottawa. He went barefoot even on the scorching sand. He had Steve McQueenish blue eyes, hair bleached white from the sun and his body was burnt a reddish-brown color. Yes, like McQueen at the end of *Papillon*, the "Hey, you bastards, I'm still here" scene, but younger. He spoke quietly and slowly, with a peculiar accent. He told me how he used to ice skate for hundreds of miles on the lakes and rivers back home.

When you're alone and don't know anybody it's easy to meet people.

We found a shelter of some kind, a *palapa*, but it was so warm at night that we slept under the stars on the beach down by the rocks. He would steal food from the one tiny shop nearby and we would hang out in the *palapa* all day, drinking wine. He had real technique and could steal a bottle of wine like a magic trick.

Every morning we dove into a cove enclosed by perfectly formed round white rocks too big to get a grip on, too slippery and smooth. I couldn't get out once I was in, so he'd have to pull me out. Someone said there were sharks around there. "What about sharks?" I asked as he was leaning over, about to dive. He shrugged and smiled, so I jumped in after him. My time with him was a lovely way to round off my curriculum—I even got a suntan.

But I had to go back. My parents had been paying my "school" fees and I was beholden to them.

Every time I returned to my folks' place it was that little bit more weird. With me and Terry gone they'd moved from the house on Stabler Road to a new one on Olentangy Drive my friends and I referred to as the "*Clockwork Orange* house"—it was so angular and modern. I just sat in "my" room.

One day, a couple weeks after I got back, a telegram arrived. It was from the Canadian. Telegrams were usually only a couple of lines, but this was a three-page rambling monologue that I couldn't understand. I think it was meant to be a poem. All I could make out was that he wanted me to meet him in Toronto. T.O! I was happy to go back up there.

When I saw him again something had changed. Civilization did not suit him. He looked even more bedraggled in a city. He had shoes on now but they were beaten up and a few sizes too big. No socks. Clothes didn't fit. It looked as if it pained him to wear anything. He told me he'd been sleeping under the street in the sewer, on a hammock he'd strung up down there, or sometimes under parked cars.

We walked around Toronto all day. It was summer so it wasn't cold—not hot like Zihuatanejo, though. Being with him on the city streets felt all wrong, like salamanders dodging buses. When it started to get dark he led me up the side of a building—we climbed the fire escape to the roof—and then he sat down in a corner on the gravel, wrapped his arms around his knees and went to sleep. The cold wind off Lake Ontario whipped around the roof as the sun disappeared. I didn't think I was going to get to sleep up there, so I woke him up and persuaded him to climb back down, and we crashed out under some bushes on the lawn of an apartment building.

I had just about decided to stop thinking about rock music when I got back from Mexico, but then I heard Bowie. *Hunky Dory*. I tried to tell the Canadian about it, this great new music, but he just looked at me like he couldn't understand what I was talking about.

I wanted a wash so I climbed in through a window at what appeared to be some kind of college and found the locker room and showers. When I came out he looked at me with sad eyes and said, "Now I'm going to walk with you for one block and then I'm going to leave you." We walked for one block, me waiting for him to say something, but he didn't. Then he turned around and walked away.

I was going to have to find a place to stay the night, as my return plane ticket wouldn't be valid yet. I saw a guy walking a dog and took that as a sign of domesticity, so I asked him if he lived nearby and he took me back to where he was staying. It was an alternative community in a high-rise tower that had been taken over by "the people," called Rochdale. It had its own radio station and police force to warn if the police came. You needed a special pass to get past security. There was an independent population of freaks living there, presumably for free, and I guessed illegally, but with a sophisticated internal system: shops, drugs, cafés—everything you needed was in-house. I stayed with the guy and his dog, and in the morning went to the airport and got the flight back to Cleveland.

13

BEWITCHED AND BEDRAGGLED

So it was Bowie who got me into him: Iggy Stooge, aka Iggy Pop. Thanks, David—I loved you anyway but thanks again.

Before Bowie, the Stooges were just another local band as far as I was concerned. Local as in Detroit opposed to English as in Hull. I therefore paid them little notice. The grass is always greener (unless you're in Acapulco), or so I thought. Bowie started mentioning him in the rare interviews he gave. The term "mainstream" wasn't mainstream yet. Fans still enjoyed being part of the underground elite, of which Bowie was still an underground delight—and Iggy Pop was a step or two removed again.

Every cell in my body had become a receptor, transposing Englishness into something like a hormone or vitamin needed to stave off rickets. But Iggy Pop, aka "the world's forgotten boy," was right there in my own backyard, oozing testosterone—an oil spill's worth.

My Bowie obsession ambushed me just as I was having one of my rare but not entirely unknown moments of thinking, "Maybe it's time to grow up." I had two or three of these over the years. The first one was when I dumped my Beatles drawer. All the posters and magazines and paraphernalia, including my Beatles tennis shoes, went in the trash. By the age of sixteen I thought maybe it was a bit childish to keep poring over such mementos. Thus the purge followed by intense remorse.

Then, when I got back from Mexico. That time lasted for a week or two. Time to abandon these childish obsessions and unrealistic yearnings. *Hunky Dory* saw the back of that notion. I never lost my faith.

"Now, what do you want for your twenty-first birthday, Christy, a watch?"

"The Gibson Melody Maker I saw advertised in the *Beacon Journal* for $100."

They really were the best parents in the world. But I couldn't be a good daughter—not yet.

The Stooges' *Fun House* album became my after-work fix. "Dirt" soothed any mental or emotional aching and gave me the incentive to go back in to work the next day, so I could go home afterwards and listen to "Dirt" again.

I found a copy of the British music paper *New Musical Express* at Gray Drug at the Summit Mall. Whoever the buyer at Gray was at that time, I thank you a thousand times over, you humanitarian and visionary.

The picture on my wall showed Iggy astride a mic stand. He backflipped. He walked on outstretched hands. He healed the sick. The picture of him shirtless, wearing those silver strides, took pride of place next to a poster of Brigitte Bardot.

It was September 22, 1972, when I watched Bowie's unforgettable US debut as Ziggy Stardust in awe and wonder. I'd just turned twenty-one (and had no idea that I had less than a year to go before I would leave Ohio and America for good). Sue and I drove to Cleveland early to stand out in the cold and listen to the soundcheck. A gray day in Cleveland at its bleakest was the perfect setting to hear the band run through "Five Years." Pure magic.

Bowie emerged with his minders to walk back to the hotel. I had never been so close to anything that made me feel "Soul Love" like that before. But this was not the Veronica Lake lookalike I'd fallen in love with while listening to *Hunky Dory*. Ziggy sported a get-down boy haircut in orange, a short green denim jacket and pegged green jeans rolled up over platform boots. It walked a mere three feet beside me. Trick or treat!

He and his minders were keeping the pace next to us. They seemed to be watching us as if they weren't sure when to cross the street. Other side, big boy. The tall, good-looking one with the green eyes spoke. His name was Anton and it looked to me like he was black. (They had black people in England who spoke with English accents?) He invited us to join them. I'm pretty sure we didn't look like groupie material. I was wearing a cable-knit fisherman's cardigan. But there wasn't anybody else around.

We went to the band's suite at the hotel and I sat there. I was practically trembling and incapable of looking Stardust in the eye, but mumbled: "People in Cleveland will love it if you play that Velvet Underground song." They'd played "Waiting for My Man" at the soundcheck. Stardust replied, "Oh, maybe we will do that." I should have been an A&R man.

Anton asked if we knew a place to eat. Take David Bowie out to dinner? Let's go!

Ziggy waited for me to pull the seat forward and then climbed into the back of my mother's Oldsmobile Cutlass. "This is a nice car," he said politely. How embarrassing to be driving my mom's car! And the funny thing was, I can't remember even one other time my parents had gone away overnight. This must have been Providence intervening—I'd hijacked her car and now David Bowie was in it. That was just weird.

The show was one of those turning points in American culture, and now my fellow Stouffer Girls, who I'd fumbled trays alongside in a poorly executed waitress job—older, divorced Neil Diamond fans who'd laughed at my Bowie scrapbook—now they would know too. I liked being right for a change.

Debbie, Sue, Hoover and I drove to Detroit to see the show again. Witnessing Bowie onstage with Mick Ronson was life-changing I'm sure for everyone there. Ronson, a guitar giant of rare beauty with platinum-blond get-down boy hair, satin strides and muscular forearms giving it some on the Les Paul, was truly God-like. Oh, yes, let the children boogie!

As was my wont in those early years, I couldn't leave with the rest of the audience when the house lights went up. I needed to get closer to the stage as security cleared the hall. "C'mon, Chris, let's go—it's over!" As always, my girlfriends trying to urge me to the exit.

And then, there he was. He too was wandering around the emptying hall, glassy eyed—wandering like me. Iggy Pop. Kicking through the plastic cups, cigarette butts and litter, probably wondering why it hadn't been him and his band up there onstage enjoying the rapture of all, he was lost in thought, or maybe just stoned, oblivious to the fact that his number-one fan of all time was standing in front of him. With the lights up I could see him in all his glory—dirty blond hair and blue eyes turning green. He saw me—the only girl left in the empty hall—and looked into my eyes. I couldn't speak during the hundred-mile journey back to Akron.

I had a plan to get Dianne to leave Columbus, where she was going to Ohio State University, and come to Kent. Who cared what school it was? What difference did it make to a dropout? Stella and Dianne were different from me, though. They were going to get degrees and make something of their lives.

She was pretty miserable there so it didn't take much to talk her into it. Maybe she missed me bullying her. I know I missed driving from Dairy Queen to Dairy Queen, from Stow to Medina, and pigging out on chocolate-dipped frozen custards. Now the gorging would involve drugs and men. Well, they didn't have a Dairy Queen in downtown Kent.

I found us a basement apartment on West Main Street and waited for her to join me. The stalling-for-time-while-waiting-to-figure-out-what-to-do-with-my-life plan wasn't working. Now I was just stalling for time. The figuring-out part hadn't happened.

There were two truck drivers who came in for breakfast at Jerry's, where I was still holding down my job. Wearing something resembling a waitress outfit, an apron pulling the ensemble together, I served them. I guess I wasn't the humble servant I'd been aiming for when reading the *Tao Te Ching*. I was too arrogant to pull off these waitress gigs. I didn't mind the service part, but the clothes! Me, in a skirt? No.

Dianne arrived and we moved into the apartment. Every morning, I'd crawl down from my bunk (it must have been set up for multiple students—four showerheads in the bathroom and bunk beds) and drink a 16-ounce bottle of Royal Crown Diet Cola. I liked the synthetic chemical taste. It offset a hangover nicely, especially with so many other chemicals in the mix.

I wasn't delusional or thinking anything was going to happen for me in Kent. I was coasting on apathy, and that made me want to get off. Dianne used to bring out a miniature chest of drawers like something from a doll's house. Every drawer had different pills in it. I'd go to class (the final days of school), do badly, then work my shift waitressing at Jerry's, go back to the basement and get Dianne to get out the drawers. Then we'd go downtown and wait to see what kind of pill it was we'd dropped.

I'd had my eye on the truck drivers ever since they came to my attention at work. Dianne and I liked both of them, which was fine because they didn't seem to mind which one of us they got. They shared a house closer to Brimfield just up the road, which was often referred to by the locals as "Brimtucky"—a bit more like Kentucky than Kent.

Fine guys, as we used to say. I was getting a taste for something. I was hoping I was normal, that all the parts worked. They were older, twenty-two or twenty-three. They'd need to have experience because I didn't know what I was doing.

Between them they had a BSA and a Corvette, which they'd park next to the curb outside the diner where I could admire them. In Ohio that was known as "foreplay."

The '70 Corvette was a work of art: a custom paint-job to look like a shark; iridescent silver sides graduating from blue to gray then down into a yellow underbelly, and with its red interior it really did look like a shark. Ohio was good for shit like that. And the BSA, a nifty little English speed machine. Students didn't have that stuff.

I didn't mind a trucker—a dark one and a blond one. "Wrap 'em up—we'll take one of each."

All the drugs and alcohol were distorting our better judgment. I was in and out of the clap clinic more often than a syringe-wielding nurse could say, "You're just going to feel a little prick."

But it wasn't just me. That's the thing about the clap, it's contagious. Nobody minded because we were taking so many pills—what difference did a course of antibiotics make? Anything was curable. I even hitched a lift back from the clinic in Ravenna once and, by the time I got to Kent, discovered that everyone in the car must have come into contact with the same strain.

"Hang on a minute—you were with . . . what's his name? Oh, shit! That means . . ."

A car of total strangers united by one disease. Now that's brotherhood. Although it was around about now that the peace and love thing was on a downward spiral. Forget peace and love; we were just trying to get loaded.

I think it was mainly Dianne and the dark one, and me and the blond. Was I becoming partial to blonds? No, I'd have whoever would have me. But is that not a universal theme? (The philosopher in me is always trying to make things make sense.) Or maybe it was the other way around, me and the dark one? Oh, it didn't matter.

Mine would have a go, but he was usually too fucked up to deliver. I only realized looking back on it what the belt looped like a tourniquet dangling from the doorknob meant. I didn't know about all that at the time, the paraphernalia. Hard drugs were taking over from the psychedelic experimental "trying to improve our minds" stuff. The straight world didn't like hallucinogens anyway. But everybody liked to get high, and there was something for everyone in pharmaceuticals.

Those truckers weren't even hippies. Smack leveled the playing field—come one, come all. The dark one, after giving Dianne hers, would say, "C'mere, Chris, and I'll give you your dessert," as a favor to the pretty blond who had nodded off on the job. They were good buds like that, covering for each other. Kent was rife with dessert.

14

TATTOOED LOVE BOYS

The jig was almost up. A few more residences in Kent saw me the unwilling tenant in a badly enacted *Howard the Duck* rip-off: "Trapped in a world he never made." That was me. It was all going in the wrong direction and descending into a fug of alcohol and pills. I stalled for time and time ran out. Dianne stayed in Kent and continued working towards a degree. Why?

I'd get a place in Akron and a job, and get her to move in with me. Stella had dropped off the face of the earth—moved in with a boyfriend. Well, I think it was a boyfriend. It was hard to tell if it was a man or woman. Anyway, she was still at it to get her degree too. What was it with these people? C'mon!

I'd waited on tables at Stouffer's in a red polyester dress, hairnet and apron—"Would you like sour cream or butter on your baked potato, sir?"

I'd waited on tables in a white shirt, black skirt and apron in the restaurant of Blossom Music Center. "An extra strawberry shortcake and hold the steak!"

The plan now was to make picture frames for Ray Packard, Akron's premier gallery owner who kept art alive in Highland Square and beyond. I learned to measure, saw, cut, nail. The Packard Gallery was a bubble of consciousness where I could look at beautiful lithographs; Miró, Spain! (Someone, come and get me!)

Dennis Connelly framed pictures next to me in the basement, listening to a station that played opera as we measured, cut, nailed and X-Acto-knived. When I couldn't bear any more hard-to-handle arias, I went up for air and to admire the pair of Borzois, Russian wolfhounds, fenced in across Exchange Street.

"I bet those two can run like fuck," I thought.

(It would take me another forty years to understand what Connelly was listening to. When he sang an aria at my father's funeral, then I understood.)

I got Dianne to move into Marky Clayman's house on Crosby Street in Highland Square with me. Marky lived upstairs and we took the ground floor. I painted the walls with resignation; pictures of Keith Richards went up. Dianne and I posed for a photographer who had, ahem, "artistic flair." With the fee we bought a new cooker.

Marky Clayman was the entire soul of Akron channeled into one individual. He never changed himself or his surroundings. A Mark Duffet painting hung slightly crooked on the wall, year in, year out. *National Geographic*, *Ramparts*, *Down Beat*: every issue, dating back, far back. A ticket stub from Montrose Drive-in on the table, where it had lain since the night of the screening, seven years before.

Marky: baseball cap; can of Pepsi; bottle of Cheracol-X. (He had one hacking cough.) An employee of the City of Akron's water department, he would hold court at his kitchen table, the plaintive melodies of Miles Davis's protracted notes searching the room like beams of light illuminating the dancing dust almost imperceptibly. The soundtrack of changelessness. Codeine.

Cheracol-X, cough syrup of choice for the codeine aficionado, had to be signed for in a pharmacy (if you weren't underage), where the pharmacist kept records of visits so the user had to travel a wide-ranging circuit to satisfy his or her requirements. You could only hit the same pharmacy after a week, maybe two, so ensuring daily rations was a full-time enterprise. Who said a junkie couldn't hold down a job?

Annie was there the day I got the job at Halbert's doing mail-order coats of arms, with a bunch of unemployable types who could draw. The deal at Halbert's was that we "researched" family names and made up roughly what might look like a family crest for them.

Levine, Klonowsky,
Hivnor or Best,
If you have the cash,
We have the crest.

Something like that. We all had desks under fluorescent lights in a warehouse in what resembled a course in creative therapy for the mentally impaired.

Everybody has a family history. And if they didn't, well, they did when we got through with them. I could barely make my quota. (Dianne, the good student, took her commissions home to turn in at the end of the week. What discipline!)

I saw Annie across the table and right away I wanted to know her. She had something. Tough and self-assured, she had experience and it showed. Even her hands were gnarly and nimble. Those hands had been around.

When my name was shouted out at roll call on the second day, she looked up and said, her matter-of-fact voice always hinting at sarcasm, "You're Dolores Hynde's daughter? I used to do her hair." My mother had told me she was losing her hairdresser to the company I'd applied for. This was she?

By week two Annie invited me to live at her place. Her Copley Road apartment was one floor above a drugstore, the walls lined in circus posters. Little did my mother know that her hairdresser had been a mushroom-distilling freak; "Does she . . . or doesn't she? Only her hairdresser knows for sure!" was the claim on the Miss Clairol ad. We discussed the possibility of drilling a hole in the floor and liberating the jars of pills downstairs.

Annie thought nothing of disappearing for days, driving her Ford Falcon to Florida through man-eating Ohio blizzards, trekking for hours ankle-deep in mud through cow pastures, plucking mushrooms from piles of manure and driving back to Ohio with a couple of baggies full of the stinky magic buttons.

The word "organic" was just entering common vernacular, and how timely, too. After ingesting two or three of the purplish-gray mushrooms, every pore in our respective bodies would ooze as we melted into the living sofa while watching the chairs and walls breathing deeply. (I thought I saw Annie's cat Poppy hanging by the neck from a lamp, but it was only a black scarf. It still makes me shudder to think about it.) But, despite the distorted, lingering and often frightening effect on reality that the mushrooms had, we devoured them, and the road trips to Florida increased to "often."

Annie used to draw her psilocybin-inspired fantasies, and they went up on the walls next to the circus posters. (Stevie Nicks still draws those.)

We were entering the world of the "knock-on" effect. There was

My mother posing proudly in front of the *Clockwork Orange* house (looking rather *Clockwork Orange* herself)

Me in Dianne's bedroom on Waldorf Drive. Wearing one of the first in a long line of bad self-haircuts.

Jackie Wilson. My first kiss.

Mitch Ryder & the Detroit Wheels. Life changers.

Kent State band the James Gang

Jeff Beck is coming to town!

The Paul Butterfield Blues Band. That's Buzzy Feiten on the right.

Iggy Pop, platinum blond lunatic circa '73

The Poor Girls: Chons, Debbie, Esta and Sue

Becky Keene, aka Meg
Keene, who wrote
'Hymn to Her'

Dianne as the bass player in Nervus Rex

15-60-75, aka the Numbers Band. That's Terry, third from right.

Star-eyed Stella with strategically placed Iggy Pop sticker

Some "get-down boys" at KSU

Posing as a hard-ass for a student photographer in a KSU paper

GREAT MOMENTS

IN

REVOLUTIONARY

CULTURE

Glen Buxton, Alice Cooper's Akron-bred guitar player

Me, age fifteen, with Zim Gar guitar, Stones and Dylan

always something available to counteract the effects of whatever the drug *du jour* required for a smooth landing.

Valium was quickly becoming a comedown favorite. Doctors were writing scripts right, left and center. Any minor complaint would be rewarded with a prescription for valium during most of the seventies. "Doctor, my toe hurts." Presto! Yellows were 5 milligrams, and blues 10. It was a nasty addiction, often producing suicidal side effects. Annie herself threatened to stick her head in the oven one day until I rushed out to get her some fried chicken. (Against my principles, but a matter of life or death—the chicken got death but Annie lived another day.) She was always up for any kind of gratification, and was possessed of a fierce sensualism, which could even override the urge to commit suicide.

Alcohol was by far the cheapest and easiest to find "remedy." A bottle of MD 20/20 only cost a buck and a half. On the down side, alcohol, more than all the rest, was the gateway to destruction, darkness and depravity.

I would like to take a moment to acknowledge that I was now twenty-one and the drugs had worked their magic on me. I was well and truly fucked up most of the time, or at best, reeling from the effects of the day before. I don't like how much this story is influenced by them, but they were the defining characteristic of my generation. And all our heroes. And in the end, this story is a story of drug abuse.

•

Hoover had also left Kent and was renting a house on West Street, just off West Market in Akron. She seemed to know all the stragglers. She gave good haircuts, was very welcoming in an Italian mother sort of way, could cook and had good records, and that was the key.

It was there that I met Scotty, a fuck-up from Cleveland, but a good-looking fuck-up.

"So, you're a Scorpio," I said to his astonishment as we dusted ourselves off, getting up from the floor.

"How could you tell?" he asked, impressed with my astrological intuition as, indeed, a Scorpio he was.

"Because you have a scorpion tattooed on your forearm."

We weren't there for his intellect. We weren't looking for intelligent life on earth anymore. The thing about Scotty, on the plus side, was that he was as close as any of us were going to get to that standard of beauty we found so unobtainable. The skinny, androgynous English musician.

Apart from the English musician part, he had the look and was right there in northeastern Ohio, not an ocean away. And as he was the first to point out, "I'm not skinny where it counts." You get the picture.

On the down side, he was a petty larcenist and always in trouble, which was an attractive trait to me in theory, but a pain in the ass to deal with. Was it auto theft or dealing grass? I didn't know why he was doing time. I don't think I even asked. Who cared? It was always something.

Star-eyed Stella was back and enjoying the perks of Scotty; I'd had my run (he was very accommodating, benevolent, you could say), but I was happy to accompany her to visit him at the Cleveland Municipal Jail. That was the sort of place I got dressed up for. Lawbreakers—right on! A chance to get out of Akron for the day and have a look around inside the pound. Arf arf!

The Heavy Bikers, they were there too, visiting brothers loyal and true. It was in the elevator that we met again, the gallant security guards who'd held court that night with the Paul Butterfield Blues Band. They looked the same as I remembered them—larger than life—but I looked different. I wasn't jailbait anymore. We were reunited and going D – O – W – N.

The difference between being "illegal" and "there for the taking" was as clearly defined as, say, a broken collarbone to all present except your hapless narrator. But they were the time keepers, I wasn't really paying attention. I was more concerned with how many Quaaludes I could shove down my gullet while managing to find a bit of wall to brace myself on.

They looked tall and regal in their heavy chains and boots and beards and greasy jeans and rotting leathers. But I was hallucinating just that little bit extra. Come to think of it, so were they, in all probability.

It felt so intimate in the confined space of the elevator; they looked exaggerated, like the reflections you get in funhouse mirrors. Anyone within strangling distance could see I was off my face, so it was no surprise when they cornered me in the parking lot after my eyebrow-raising announcement in front of guards, brothers, old ladies and fellow inmates in the visiting room: "Hey, Scotty. If I'd known there was this little hole in the partition here I'd have brought you some 'ludes." I might as well have shouted it through a traffic cone.

Chaos and disorder were to be ongoing themes for me with a mouth that flapped like a rag nailed to a post in a windstorm. Thus my comeuppance shouldn't have come as a surprise. (Better that girls with big yaps learn when it's still only a foot in the mouth. But some don't learn.)

Truth be told, I was thrilled to find myself enveloped by the very same "friends of the band" I recalled so fondly from that romantic night of chord sequences with Buzzy Feiten. "I must have died and gone to heaven," I slurred, referring to their winged insignias.

Stella, who had not been party to that glorious night of yore, recoiled in horror at this invitation to an S. Clay Wilson–style act of sexual violence.

I continued my descent.
Okay—you start . . .
"Give us your drugs,"
was the growling demand
"No I will not!"
(barely audible dribble)
"Oh yeah? Why?"
came the curt reprimand.
"I need them they're mine"
(but let us not quibble)
"Why do you need them?"
my predators gaining
(I picked up the gauntlet
with no time remaining)
"You need a club,
I need to cop"
That's all she wrote,
Signed and sealed.
Full stop.

And that was, as the saying goes, my parting shot: game over; good night, Irene; sayonara; *bonne nuit*. By exceeding the dosage,

Quaaludes tend to make you do and say things you might later regret. It says it right on the packet.

The hairy horde looked at each other. It was their lucky day. "How 'bout youse come to our place for a party?"

A party? Sounded good to me. What a nice surprise! Who doesn't like a party?

"Follow us."

I got into Stella's car, surprised by her less-than-enthusiastic response: "I'm not going to a fucking party. I'm going home. If you want to go with them you can go on your own."

I was too loaded to argue with that. If she didn't want to have a good time then that was her problem. Whatever. She dropped me a block away from the clubhouse and patched out, leaving me in a cloud of gravel dust. Spoilsport!

But what neighborhood was this? I could see they'd moved from their Gothic mansion in Coventry to a modest little affair in a white slum that had "Jeffrey Dahmer" written all over it.

I started to twig that the proposed "party" was going to be hosted exclusively by yours truly, as the tattooed love boys methodically unchained a series of padlocks to reveal a dark and noticeably empty house, before shoving me into a dank den. I was led upstairs to another dark room with the smell of the dissection table. A party of one.

Garçon, make that five glasses.

Now, let me assure you that, technically speaking, however you want to look at it, this was all my doing and I take full responsibility. You can't fuck around with people, especially people who wear "I Heart Rape" and "On Your Knees" badges.

"GET YOUR FUCKIN' CLOTHES OFF!"

But, I . . .

"SHUT THE FUCK UP!"

Ah. Can I just . . .

"HURRY UP—WE GOT SHIT TO DO!"

Ahhhhh. I . . . do you guys . . .

"SHUT THE FUCK UP AND GET 'EM OFF, OR WE'LL TIE YOU UP IN THE ATTIC AND GET TO YOU LATER!"

But, you know, if you want . . .

"HIT HER IN THE BACK OF THE HEAD SO IT DON'T LEAVE NO MARKS!"

Oh, that's not really . . . do you think . . . ?

"YOU'RE TOO SKINNY, ROCK STAR—YOU OUGHTA EAT AT MCDONALD'S MORE!"

Hey, you know, I don't . . .

"SHUT UP OR YOU'RE GOING TO MAKE SOME PLASTIC SURGEON RICH!"

But . . . I can't . . .

"STOP TALKIN' AND START SUCKIN'!"

I considered their demand while sustaining a volley of lit matches, which bounced off my rib rack and underlit their stony expressions before dropping to the forensically soiled carpet, leaving little trails of blue smoke to struggle briefly and then disappear—like I wished I could.

The other thing, the good thing about Quaaludes: I wasn't duly perturbed. I was getting experience, and I was out of Akron.

Like I said, I'd never blame others for my transgressions. That would just be bad form. Painting oneself into a corner could pass as an art installation by any other name. So I humored them and gave them the Quaaludes.

Later that afternoon, I was drawing portraits on napkins at the kitchen table in their disappointingly downgraded HQ. You're welcome. And I found out something useful: bikers associate artistic ability with witchcraft or some kind of magic, and if you can commandeer the old pencil or brush reasonably well you might get a shot at airbrushing some goblins walking across a sand dune on the side of a van or maybe Satan himself coiled around a gas tank. You could even be kept on hand as resident artist. Career Opportunity!

The ugly blond one gave me a lift back to Akron after stopping by some nurse's house and grabbing a pack of Marlboros out of a carton in the fridge. Apparently, you could just walk in and have whatever you liked from any chick who had been touched by the club. It was no doubt her car too that he drove while Steely Dan's "Do It Again" played on the radio. Great song—one of my favorites.

It was winter and typically around zero degrees. Filthy snowbanks crusted with frozen slush and oil were piled up alongside the interstate's shoulder. On the way back to my apartment we stopped off at the Brown Derby in Akron and I bought dinner. Surf and turf for the gentleman and a selection of side orders for the lady; all part of the service.

As he saw me up the wooden staircase above the drugstore he affectionately belted me on the thigh and said, "You ain't a half bad chick."

At the time I didn't recognize that European turn of phrase but understood that there was something different about this lumbering outsider with the unpronounceable name. He offered to pick me up on his bike after work later that week. I drew my quota of coats of arms while looking forward to the ride, trying to imagine what his bike looked like.

He arrived on time (they always do at first) on a class bike, panhead, low to the ground, minimal chrome and a surprisingly cheerful yellow gas tank. The brooding chopper (like all their bikes) was a work of artistic perfection, a fair bit more glamorous than its owner.

He told me that "green" for a tank was bad luck. I was learning about luck and its assorted talismans. You get to understand superstition if you're an outlaw, junkie, fairground worker, hooker or biker.

Although I was now schooled in certain customs, I still thought I was only there for the ride. In fact, nobody was only there for the ride. Like a tattoo or a dog, the Heavy Bikers were for life.

For the next few weeks he'd pick me up when my working day was through and we'd roar onto 77, him saying, "Let's boogie through this traffic," as we sidled up between cars—kicking off them with his steel-toed boots, letting all motorists know to "fuck off out the way"—and boy did they ever fold when they heard the mighty growl of the Harley and saw us approaching in their rearview mirrors. We cruised along like that all the way to Cleveland, and everyone, bar none, deferred to the patch on the back of my Heavy Biker as we sailed right up to the front of the lights. I liked riding with an outlaw. I liked the feeling of moving fast—moving fast and moving away—and soon that's what I'd have to do. Move fast and move away.

Annie surprised me when I brought him home. I thought she'd be impressed with his bike. Turns out, like Stella, she wasn't into bikes. Annie was like Gloria in the Cassavetes film. She had her apartment and her cat, and she wasn't about to let some knownothing (me) fuck it all up.

I could see there were a few things that didn't add up about that guy. Like when he'd take me to his place—who was the chick sleeping on the couch? Who smoked Salems? Only chicks or black dudes smoked menthols, and black dudes did not feature with the Heavy Bikers, white supremacists that they were. Funny how much one will turn a blind eye to get at the drugs.

Chicks were a commodity to be exploited and "disposed of" when no longer useful. But chicks (present company guilty as charged) overlooked obvious shit when in the thrall of some muscle. To be fair, a lot of guys take advantage of girls like that. Well, except for the last part, the waste-disposal part. That was fairly unique. They lent a whole new meaning to the expression "dumped"—but I didn't know that yet.

"What's the matter? Don't you like women?" I said to the ugly blond's bro after he marched me up the stairs and started knocking me about, in what I was learning was a form of sexual foreplay.

KERPOW! A flash of white stars exploded, lighting up the room and leaving trails across the ceiling. What happened to the "hit her in the back of the head so it don't leave no marks" rule?

The only rule was to never be seen again if you did get out. A little story that a girlfriend (who I learned years later didn't get out) told me went like this. A chick, let's call her Hillbilly, decided she'd had enough, walked out on her "old man" and went back to West Virginia. A year later she showed up in Cleveland, gingerly testing the water.

After a few months of hanging out she started to relax, thinking maybe everything was fine, bygones forgotten. One day she saw her ex and he offered her a lift somewhere—an act of good will. She accepted. En route, he said, "I gotta make a stop, pick something up," and told her to "come in for a minute" rather than wait in the car. Everything seemed nice and friendly. She followed him into the house, where he told her, "Take off your clothes and stand on the sofa," pulled out a gun, then shot her in the leg, and said, "Now call an ambulance."

Stories like that were commonplace with the Heavy Bikers and they were getting worse. It was time to go. Still, I had a soft spot for my Heavy Biker, and wherever he is now (he's dead) I bid him an upward and onward journey.

15

THE FINAL COUNTDOWN

ike being in an elevator when you can't tell if its moving or not; I wondered when I was going to hear the "ding!" and see my floor light up. I was twenty-one and time was slipping away. In boxing terms it was time to punch or get out.

I was coming up to the final count.

In the mornings, when I'd walk to Packard's Gallery on Exchange and Jefferson, as was my custom, I'd take a different route every day so I could explore all the back lanes and passages, zigzagging through the tree-lined streets past the grand old houses along Oakdale to Portage Path: verandas, swings, trellises, squirrels and the red brick roads. I got to know the gardens, their snapdragons and rose bushes. The neighborhoods were run-down, worn out, but they had charm—something you couldn't find out in the suburbs.

Highland Square had been left to black families, gays and Akron university professors, or anyone who didn't mind sharing air with the under-aspiring; in other words, poor people or bohemian types who wouldn't join a country club even if they could. (May I point out how much I loathe the distinctions of black, gay or anything that implies anything.) I wanted to find that colorless Island that Charlie Mingus talked about. Like Lee Morgan, I was in search of a new land.

The streets in this neglected part of town were from a time when people sat out on their front porches in the evenings—or walked to the neighborhood deli or visited neighbors or looked after one another's kids—the Akron of my infancy, every fourth house painted blue like the one on Hillcrest Street, before the tractors and plows moved in. A lifetime ago.

Something was happening to me. Even the gigantic oak trees that had ushered in whole families and seen them right through to their endings seemed to be waving me past—past the Akron houses with their Akron stories. The winds off Lake Erie that swept over northeastern Ohio like searchlights announcing the grand opening of a new discount store seemed to be announcing my leaving. That way. You go that way. It's time.

Overhead, the leaves rotated like a paint-by-numbers picture of autumn, scarlet, magenta, gold, chartreuse, bidding me to dab in the last color. Farewell.

I'd always welcomed the sudden change in air, the signal for the advance of winter and retreat of summer, but c'mon! The hiss through the leaves sounded like smirking.

"How about everyone just backing off around here," I thought. I was lost. What was I going to do? The summer—buzzing with pond life and furious insects banging like missiles into screened windows and wavy lines of heat melting everything in the distance—seemed to be telling me to go, in a surrealistic delirium. I was all fucked up.

I walked on through the falling leaves. They seemed to change course, mid-descent, as if choosing the exact spot to land. Even a leaf had more direction than me. I clung to the heart of Akron. Down the valley and up the hill into Glendale. Oh, my cemetery, console me one more time. I wandered among the crypts and mausoleums containing the remains of Akron families, the little stone markers denoting the final resting places of children. Sad clusters. I'd read the inscriptions, some barely legible, so weathered were they by the harsh Ohio winters. There she is: "Isobel Falor—gone to sleep on this day 1876–1879." I know your name. When was the last time you heard anybody say it out loud? "Isobel."

How often I'd returned, kicking through the leaves. I didn't want to be faceless in the crowd. I wasn't meant to be here.

Just outside the city limits the whole country was bending over to take it up the backside. The green meadows of Montrose were being churned up and rolled away, concrete expanding over the hills of Ohio like molten lava.

Duane Verh called me from Cleveland. I agreed to an audition to sing in a band he was putting together. It was no secret that I had aspirations.

Bass players were all cool during the "Rescue Me"/ "Groove Me" days, but Duane was super cool—the coolest of the cool cats in the Cleveland music scene. Whatever he wore, he wore like a Jamaican: short-sleeved Italian shirt, open collar, gabardine trousers, thin belt, Italian shoes, ribbed socks, hair pushed back, jazz-musician style. And he had an imperial beard, the thumbnail-sized tuft between chin and bottom lip. With his dark Croatian eyes, he was exotic, for sure, and I wanted, would have loved, to be in his band.

I was going to need money and a passport.

I moved back into my parents' house: one last effort; let's get on with this thing. "Christy, I know you're going to do what you want to do, just don't let me see it!" The only request my mother made that I would take seriously.

I didn't realize then that my parents' out-and-out disapproval of everything I held sacred was a gift. I would have to find my destiny; as it said in the *Tao*, "Raise your children like birds to fly."

"You won't win on this one, Christy." I heard that often.

"I will when I'm gone," I thought.

Corn, tomatoes, apple cider and macaroni and cheese were the only things we agreed on. Oh, and Mom's apple crisp: "Yes, please."

It would still be dark as my dad drove me in his orange Carmen Ghia to Halbert's corrugated tin warehouse, with its overhead strip lights, me, first of the degenerates to arrive. He'd drop me and continue on to Cleveland through hail and downpour to the telephone company where he served a lifetime to maintain and put his two bright kids into college.

So they could drop out.

I was accepted into the Ontario College of Art in Toronto. I'd taken the day off work from Halbert's, flown up there and submitted my portfolio, a meager collection of half-finished junk I'd salvaged from my laughable efforts to get through the courses at KSU, including the unfinished dulcimer. They accepted me!

I must have thought my parents would pay the tuition fees. I didn't have the money. Had they known they were on the cusp of losing me forever, maybe they would have. But even I didn't know how close I was to the end.

The end of Akron.

My head was pounding, sticky with violence, idealism and visions of rock bands. I really was getting jaded. I had a hunch: a city could protect me, or I could learn how to airbrush gas tanks. I had one eye on an XLCH in a Harley-Davidson showroom. And the other eye covered in panstick to hide the purple and yellow bruise I'd left the Heavy Bikers' clubhouse with that last time. I didn't think I'd be going back there, but they probably had other ideas.

Leave *now*.

16

LET'S GET ON OUTTA HERE NOW—
LET'S GO!

It was now 1973. Bowie had revived my faith in rock. It had staggered and lost its balance, but only temporarily. And Lou: I saw him at the Akron Civic Theatre—one of his solo shows after leaving the Velvets. Going strong—there was still hope.

As long as Iggy was out there, there would always be hope, but it had been a bad few years if you were a rock star and twenty-seven. That feeling of immortality the sixties had imparted certainly took a hit.

In my personal story, like in a mining disaster, hope was running out as each day passed. I'd never seen a passport before, and I was going to need one. I'd need an accomplice too.

Cindy Smith, Debbie's older sister, had a '65 Corvette Stingray in racing green, with a white convertible top—the coolest car ever made. A few years back, when the Jeff Beck Group had played Cleveland I went with Cindy. It seemed so long ago: now.

The top was down as we zoomed under glittering turnpike lights, stars and clouds racing overhead while the heater blasted our go-go boots under the dashboard where we passed the joint low.

Cindy wore chunky silver rings that made a clunking sound every time she changed gears, thrusting the chrome ball forwards and sideways while the Stingray lurched and lunged, patchouli oil wafting from her wild hair.

She knew local WMMS disc jockey Doc Nemo. Cool, cool, cool—everything was cool. But nothing was as cool as the Jeff Beck Group, rock giants who towered over us grateful connoisseurs, reinforcing our belief. We were dazzled by Beck's virtuosity, the nancy-boy posturing of his cockerel cohorts and the sheer excellence of Rod Stewart discovering his mega talent in front of our very eyes.

Nemo invited us to meet the band after the show. I was wearing my houndstooth shirt with the label that said Trafalgar Square in it. That sounded English to me. Did we look English enough? The DJ had a baggie full of killer weed so we were ushered into their hotel room, no questions. Rod Stewart and Ron Wood showed Nemo the door straightaway but kept the bag of weed, and us.

Rod the Mod (he of the original get-down boy haircut!) and Woody with his black gypsy eyes (the first in a family of canal gypsies to be born on dry land) and me and Cin! Apart from getting that autograph from Paul Butterfield and sharing a beer with Buzzy Feiten, this was my only close encounter so far with the major league.

Clearly, the two fops were not unused to girls stripping off as soon as room service delivered the ice bucket and split. Are you kidding me? They "entertained" their way across America and back many times over. But nothing like that was on the cards during this outing, not with sixteen-year-old Chris Hynde in the mix. Good grief, no. Pot was one thing but, beyond that, well, I was still sewing outfits for my Midge doll.

Stewart grabbed a guitar off one of the twin beds, wielding it like a pool cue, and rammed the headstock into my bony rear end. But sexual innuendo was lost on me, even when instigated by the ultimate get-down boys: Ron "Wood if he could" in his tapestry strides and Rod "up for a prod" in his granddad's undershirt.

With we girls showing no signs of disrobing, the randy duo devised a game to amuse themselves. Stewart scribbled impossible-to-pronounce names—at least when very stoned—on the joints: "Corolleum," "Sleghegsstoose," "Ramsplano."

We'd reach for the roach and he'd snatch it back, waving a bony finger. "No! No! No! Not till you say it!"

Beck himself made a brief appearance, darting into the room, taking one look at us and leaving quickly with a couple of joints and Cindy's car keys. Jeff Beck was in Cindy's Corvette, tearing up the expressways of northeastern Ohio, and Cin and I were smoking pot with Rod Stewart and Ron Wood. Oh, what a perfect day.

I don't know how long I lay passed out on the bathroom floor, but the plan concocted in my absence was that I would stay with Wood and Cin would go off with Stewart. I put paid to that notion, telling them, "I can't stay here! I have my driver's training lesson in the morning!"

That kind of blew it for Cindy, and I reckon that night is what the song "Cindy's Lament" is about. But then, I'm the girl who thinks Bob Dylan wrote "Standing in the Doorway Crying" for her, so don't quote me on that.

Consequently, Cindy seemed like a good person to go to London with. I called Duane and canceled the audition. I didn't tell my parents what I was planning, but left my newly arrived passport out on the kitchen counter where they would see it.

England, finally, here we come!

17

LIMEYTOWN!

I stepped off the plane at Heathrow and onto English tarmac with "I-G-G-Y" on one lens of my wraparounds, and "P-O-P" on the other, written in Old English lettering, which I'd carefully applied in Halbert's white-out. I'd stitched "Bernice"—of "Cum Fix" fame (my S. Clay Wilson alias)—on the back of my denim jacket in snakeskin. Sartorially, I was a victim of the Summit Mall, but I was trying my best to look cool enough for London. "I'm here!"

It was 1973, the month of May, the best month of my life thus far. We exited Heathrow, got in a black cab and told the driver to "Take us to a hotel in London."

My first sightings of Victorian and Edwardian buildings, cobbled streets, red pillar postboxes and phone booths and the double-decker buses driving on the wrong side of the road were more beautiful than all my schoolgirl imaginings.

It wasn't the sixties, though. Former dolly birds in miniskirts now looked like tired versions of the teenage daughters they were with. (Those mother-and-daughter sets seemed to be everywhere.) Girls walked arm in arm with each other in a way I could never imagine doing with my pals. (Walk arm in arm with Annie down Copley Road? Good Lord, no. She'd think I'd gone crazy.)

We passed a hundred pubs, their amber lights ever-so inviting. I tried to peer in and get a good look at every traffic light. "Old boys," men in pubs, didn't seem to mind sharing the bar with people half their age. I would soon discover that they all bopped along to the same music on the jukebox like it was perfectly normal. It seemed kind of freaky. A man my dad's age listening to the same music as me? Very strange.

The cabbie dropped us at a bed and breakfast in Bayswater. The Lion Court Hotel was more of a student hostel than a hotel, with shoes drying on window ledges, bunk beds and cheap towels.

I hadn't brought much: a few changes of clothes and the three records I didn't feel I could leave behind—*White Light/White Heat*, *Raw Power* and *Fun House*. I had a couple hundred dollars to last me for what would turn out to be the rest of my life. I needed to find a job.

We stashed our suitcases and walked up Queensway to the Bayswater Road (not "Bayswater Road," but "the Bayswater Road") and wandered along a parade of outdoor market stalls selling paintings and handbags and crafts. I'd never seen anything like it before. This was real *Alice in Wonderland* stuff for sure. I went from stall to stall and asked anybody I could collar if there was a job going. We ended up with some sleazebag back in the Lion Court Hotel.

The following day, I started my first job, selling handbags in an indoor market called Point on Oxford Street, near Tottenham Court Road. There were about thirty stalls specializing in all sorts: cheese-cloth shirts; "loons" (bell-bottoms); Indian scarves and incense; smoking paraphernalia.

It seemed that cigarette papers weren't the exclusive domain of head shops. A lot of people rolled their own cigarettes (fags, as the locals said). I'd never seen that before. You could buy a pouch of loose tobacco and Rizlas, the paper they all used, which didn't automatically designate "pot smoker." The only time I'd seen that in the States was Bugler tobacco, which came with rolling papers in the package, but only winos smoked that shit (and me in years to come, when I'd get to the States and couldn't find any Golden Virginia or Cutter's Choice—described by Joe Strummer as not a tobacco but a religion).

Another difference was that you could buy ordinary cigarettes in packs of five, like samples, the "trial size" you'd get for free in the States. The cheapest cigs you could buy (that was the other thing, they were a variety of prices, not a standard price) were called Player's No. 6 (the ones I'd discover that English bikers smoked). "Numbies," they called them. They were smaller than an ordinary cigarette but stronger than all the rest put together. Boxes of matches were a nice touch too, with pictures of birds or wildlife on them like collectors' cards.

There was a protocol for everything that I had to learn. For example, you'd never walk into a "newsagent" and say, "Gimme a pack of Rothmans!" That would be considered rude. You'd have to say, "May I have a box of Rothmans, please, and some matches." Writing about it now, it all seems so insignificant, but it was the beginning of my assimilation into English life. After all, immigrants have to learn the language.

My stall in Point was at the back, and I would sit there quietly fascinated all day, watching people mill around. English people: lank-haired guys with seedy complexions wearing short brown leather bomber jackets with lousy collars; girls in flowered dresses and wavy, nondescript haircuts that owed nothing to Vidal Sassoon.

It looked like the sixties had been hijacked by the Amish. I didn't see one Jean Shrimpton lookalike—not a nod to anything that so much as hinted at Terence Stamp.

Still, even the most dowdy English were more glamorous than anyone at the Summit Mall. Everyone was underweight with undernourished, pallid skin tones, greenish in hue. But anything was always going to be better than bulging stomachs spilling over the waistbands of polyester slacks or "shorts," an unfortunate American craze virtually unknown to the English. Best of all were the shoe stalls. Debbie Smith would have gone crazy.

By day three I met some guys who took me to a pub, and I discovered that pubs didn't serve wine. Maybe a bottle of sherry was stashed behind the counter for the publican's wife, but it was mainly beer, which they drank warm. If I'd served warm beer at any establishment I ever worked in I'd have been out on my ear. They didn't seem to mind. Even a Coke came without ice. Nobody was bothered. I asked for a tequila and that too drew a blank. "Okay, then, I'll have a whisky." That was when I noticed old boys in flat caps side by side with teenagers listening to the latest charts: Wizzard, Peters and Lee, Alvin Stardust, David Essex. Weird!

The music itself was surprising. A song called "Tie a Yellow Ribbon Round the Ole Oak Tree" was number one. It wasn't rock and roll. I couldn't have described it—English pop music, I guess.

There were pictures at every newsstand of the hairy-chested Gary Glitter, shirt unbuttoned. He was on the cover of all the teeny-bopper magazines! Why would a teenage girl want to look at that? Where was Mark Bolan? I thought girls wanted effete little things, not big, burly, manly-looking men. It was outrageous!

London was throwing a lot of curveballs I didn't see coming, but I didn't care. The weirder it got, the more I loved it. Yes, I was in love with it.

I got separated from Cindy after getting thrown out of the Lion Court. It turned out you weren't allowed to take bottles and guys there after midnight. I would get used to being thrown out of places. There was a Spanish lesbian called Maite selling leather jackets in the kiosk next to mine, who invited me back to her place in Clapham, south of the river. There was a room going in the house. "I'll take it."

My new life was beginning. The room was £4 ("four quid") a week. Everyone in the house had a padlock on their door and there was one "payphone" in the "corridor" (the alien terminology). We all shared a filthy kitchen and a toilet in its own little cubicle next to the bathroom. To take a bath we were required to put a "shilling," or "5p bit," in a meter for hot water.

You never asked for "the bathroom" in a public place unless you wanted a bath. If you wanted to relieve yourself you asked for "the toilet." You could never say that in the States. It was starting to occur to me that Americans had odd habits too. Seeing them from a new perspective was fun. (Why *would* you ask for a bath when you wanted a toilet?)

I'd never been on an overground or underground train before. At the "top" of my new street, Englewood Road, there was a "Tube station," which was what they called the subway. Crazy language was English in the hands of the English.

I could jump over the turnstiles at Clapham South and go anywhere I wanted on the Northern line for free, as long as I didn't get caught. I didn't get caught—I couldn't afford to get caught. I had to be frugal and careful.

Public transport! (What genius thought that one up? When the word got out in America, they'd all want it!) I could now go wherever I wanted, whenever I wanted. The days of waiting for someone to pick me up in a car were over. For the first time I felt like my own person; I didn't have to answer to anyone. It felt so right, like something I'd been waiting all my life for.

I kept finding that, by not knowing anybody, I got to meet people fast. A guy at a bus stop who I'd only known for twenty minutes would technically be my oldest friend in town. Buses were another shared commodity. They weren't just for down-and-outs or cleaners on their way to work at five in the morning—businessmen in pinstriped suits got the bus too. A guy in uniform patrolled the aisles and sold you your ticket for however far you were going. One stop was 5p, and so on. He'd turn a crank and roll the ticket out of a machine hooked on his belt that made a distinctive noise (which I can only describe if you've ever heard Shane MacGowan laugh).

"Tottenham Court Road."

"That will be twenty pence, please."

(Shane MacGowan laughs.)

Civilization: you could smoke on the top deck of the bus; you could smoke in movie theaters too. They called them cinemas—how quaint. (Everyone coughing their lungs out.) You could drink alcohol in public; the bottle didn't need to be concealed in a brown paper bag.

Every high street had an Indian restaurant; cafés, called "caffs," only sold instant—"powdered"—coffee. That was the one thing I really missed. Oh, and I could have polished off a whole dozen Amy Joy donuts. You could buy a single sachet of shampoo. No jumbo family sizes—a single wash! English guys didn't wash their hair more than once every two weeks, as they were afraid it would make it fall out.

One night, I traipsed along behind some of these new friends of mine to Leicester Square (don't try to pronounce that if you're American), where we ended up in a basement that had been a club in the sixties, Studio 51, and was now used as a dance studio or rehearsal room, or place to score.

I explored the historic cavern, thoroughly entranced. Drumheads lined the orange walls, serving as mounts for black-and-white shots of the early Rolling Stones. Brian! I studied each photo: the checked shirts, Framus and Vox guitars; Bill in his leather waistcoat; Mick wielding maracas, which made him look tiny; Keith when he had teeth; Charlie looking like he'd lost his jazz combo.

The sixties seemed so far away. I'd fallen in love with sixties London, but I'd missed it. I was too late. So to be transported back there so unexpectedly was like waking into an ethereal dream. As I meditated on the photos I heard music coming from the next room, someone playing acoustic guitar and singing in an unimaginably sad voice—a familiar voice. I followed the music and found a handsome but beaten-down-looking American playing his guitar, all alone. It was Tim Hardin.

His song of sorrow and longing drifted quietly as I hid in the shadow of the doorway and watched, like beholding something divine—the last of a species facing extinction. Tim Hardin, a Vietnam vet who had come home a junkie, wouldn't be around much longer.

•

A self-proclaimed DJ came into the market one day. Disc jockeys in England weren't just on the radio; they could play records at parties or events. He was a sixties type—lanky, checked suit, gray teeth, thin colorless hair, vestiges of acne—nothing special but a look I found to my taste. A two-bit hustler, he claimed he could get me a job in a clothing store: "Mates by Irvine Sellar."

"You need to get onto a good scene," he kept telling me.

He wasn't on one himself, as it turned out. He never got me the job, but one afternoon took me by his folks' council flat. (What we Americans would call "the projects," except this was where a variety of working-class people lived, not just those on welfare—socialism!) I waited in the living room with his brother, who was watching a horse race on the TV.

"Do you like horses?" I asked, excited to meet a fellow enthusiast.

"Only when they win," he replied, disdainfully.

Betting on horses was an everyday pursuit for millions of English. Betting shops were on every corner of every high street. Men, old and young alike, spilled out of them and into the nearest pub.

I lost the job selling handbags in the market when I stopped showing up. I didn't even go to collect my wage. I never sold a bag anyway.

One of my housemates in Englewood Road knew someone in a firm of architects, Martineau Jenkins Associates, and told me that they needed an office-boy type, someone to run errands. It paid £17 a week, which would cover my rent and transport, with enough left for food. Well, I could shoplift the rest.

Everything was in black and white, even television. I was walking past an appliance shop with a guy one day who stopped and pointed to the window, saying, "That's what I want, one of those."

I couldn't work out what he was talking about—I presumed he already had a television—but he was pointing to a color one. Good grief—it was a new thing.

I'd get the Northern line to Charing Cross, the District line to Hammersmith and then the bus to Barnes and walk up Castelnau Road to the architect offices, get my assignment and take the bus and train back into town to pick up photos for the firm. I spent many an hour underground. But I never got over the thrill of not having to wait for someone with a car to pick me up. The first time I rode on a train sitting on a seat facing backwards I couldn't stand up as I found it so disorientating. But I liked that feeling.

The streets were made for walking, or horse-drawn carriages. That's what the mews were for, where the horses and grooms used to stay. I wandered for hours, squinting so as not to see the tower blocks and imagining the traps on the streets and the sound of hoofs on cobblestones. I was in England; I'd made it.

I saw St. Paul's Cathedral as I emerged from a station one afternoon and, although I'd never heard of it and so didn't know it was famous, when I saw the office buildings slammed up against it, it made me cry. I had fallen in love with London and couldn't bear to see it fucked with.

I'd wait for someone to enter a "mansion block" (what they called an old apartment building) and dart in behind him before the door closed, take the stairs to the top, find the door to the roof and stand there looking out over the rooftops of London. Beautiful. I was mesmerized by it. If anyone asked what I was doing I'd say, "I've lost my cat."

I heard a sound every morning, eerie, not human. I couldn't imagine what could cause such an unearthly timbre. Then I saw them: pigeons. A city sound.

I learned not to climb into a car with just anyone. A few times I found myself fighting my way out past some salivating creep. Perverts and sadists were universal. I had to stop thinking I didn't care what happened to me, because now I was in London and I wanted to live.

John Martineau had a big house on the river. He lived there with his wife, Deirdre, and son Rupert and a cat called Henry. I'd never met people or cats with names like those before. The offices were at the top of the house. Deirdre would make a big spread of "sarnies" (sandwiches) and quiches and fruit crumble, or we'd all go to the pub on the high street in Barnes for lunch.

Every part of town had a High Street, local shops like a mini-downtown in every neighborhood, all of which had their own names and personalities, all different. Kensington High Street, St. John's Wood High Street (I remembered that name from the Stones song "Play with Fire"), Kilburn High Road, Shoreditch High Street: the list was endless; they were all places in which to hang out and shop and drink and eat and buy flowers.

When I saw the destination Muswell Hill on a bus I jumped on and rode to the end of the line, where I wandered around knowing that Ray and Dave Davies must have walked there too. London—I was a kid in a toy store.

I found every aspect of the city totally fascinating. I woke up every morning, a girl in love—at that stage of love where the object of desire has no faults.

The architects took time out one day to watch Princess Anne get married on television. We could see the pomp and ceremony and the horses all dolled up. I didn't really know who the Royal Family were, but it was easy to see they had the best horses. Princess Anne wore a dress like something Nita would have designed, scooped sleeves trimmed with pearls. Someone said she was a good rider, a show jumper.

There was a picture of Brigitte Bardot on the cover of a men's magazine and posters of her outside every newsagent in town. She was turning forty, so it was an opportunity for the press to celebrate her. In the picture she wore hot pants and tall stonewashed-denim platform boots. Was there a girl alive who didn't want to look like Brigitte Bardot?

I went to Kensington Market and found some cheap-ass knee-high platform boots, cut off a pair of jeans and pranced about like a little sexpot without worrying about being turned over by a fleet of psychos on Harleys.

Kensington Market was, like Point, a bunch of indoor stalls, but much cooler. It was on multiple floors, and the people in there were more rock and roll than the Oxford Street bunch. It turned out that there were rock fans after all, and I was finding them at last.

I had a bootleg reel-to-reel tape-recording of a Velvet Underground performance I'd been guarding since my arrival. (Oh, yeah, that was the other thing I brought with me from Akron.) I got a guy in a shop to make a copy and for his trouble told him he could keep the tape. I also got him to print up an enlargement of a photo I had in my wallet: a picture of Bowie and Lou and Iggy with their arms around each other, Iggy being held up by the other two, a pack of Luckys in his teeth. Now I could listen to "Foggy Notion" on cassette while looking at the picture of my guys up on my wall.

Next door to Kensington Market was a huge emporium, a clothes store called Biba. It was the best place I'd ever seen. You could get blue lipstick and purple nail polish and all sorts of metallic clothes. It was the place that Alex from *A Clockwork Orange* would have hung out, and, for me, something of a concession for missing out on the sixties London that I mourned.

Life was almost perfect and I knew it.

18

THE *NME*

fter a couple blissful months in London, a few home truths were starting to sink in: the radio wasn't as good as in Ohio, and nobody was obsessed with Iggy Pop like I was.

I'd been misled by the backdated *NME* I got at Gray Drug at the Summit Mall. It was a live review and, judging by the enthusiasm of the writer, I'd assumed England was swarming with Iggy Pop fans. I'd stuck the picture of him in his silver hip-huggers humping a mic stand up on my wall, a big inspiration for me leaving Akron.

I was beginning to get inklings that my old, useless, familiar and constantly suppressed depression was creeping back. I nicked a bottle of wine from an off-license (what the English called a liquor store), and got the Tube to Acton in search of an address someone had given me for a party.

I walked in, knowing nobody. It looked like it was a student party in someone's parents' house. Never mind, I didn't plan on staying long. Someone gave me the old "Cheer up—it might never happen" line. I hated it when people said that.

I mumbled, "Yeah, well, it *did* happen. Someone stole my three prized possessions—*White Light/White Heat*, *Raw Power* and *Fun House*," and made my way to the drinks table. Then came a voice from the back of the room: "I know Iggy."

I spent the next hour talking to the first person I'd met who was as much a fan of the Ig as me. He was an emaciated oddball in leather jeans, sporting a tooth earring, Keith Richards style. As I was getting up to leave he asked if I knew of a place where he could crash for the night, so I took him back to Clapham and showed him to an empty room. But first he had a good look at the pictures I had stuck up on the wall of my room: Iggy, Lou, Keith, Dylan.

In the morning he asked if he could leave some things at my place for a few days as he was in the middle of moving house. I said I didn't mind. Two days later, a U-Haul van pulled up, dumping a few hundred coverless records—sticky with yogurt and fingerprints—in the middle of my room; the guy moved in on me!

It was some weeks later that I realized this was the same guy who'd written the article accompanying the photo that had given me the final impetus to go to England. Coincidence? Obviously. Divine intervention or messengers from above couldn't be that twisted. Enter, as they say, Nick Kent.

In a way, you could say I was slowly zeroing in on him—Iggy, I mean, not Kent—but the real question was what was Nick Kent doing at a student party? Dark stuff indeed.

How can we prove that anything is arbitrary? Even what at first sight might appear the most arbitrary encounter can have lasting repercussions, like a car accident. Everything in nature lives according to some order so it seems unlikely that humans live outside this system, even if they try to resist their instincts. That's how we can be sure we're not animals, this refusal to abide by what we know is good for us. If an animal's instinct tells him to avoid something, he has no trouble keeping a wide berth. We, on the other hand, run in the direction of danger if it offers a thrill or satisfies a curiosity.

As far as my meeting Nick Kent goes, in fiction you probably wouldn't include too many coincidences like that because it would seem phony, too unlikely. In real life it happens all the time.

He wore pink nail varnish and black eyeliner to highlight his haunted, staring blue eyes. He smoked St. Moritz menthol cigarettes and subsisted on a mixture of tinned mandarin orange segments and Heinz custard, also tinned (or "canned," as the Americans would say). He often wore a dog collar studded with rhinestones, and a cheap belt with fake doubloons on it, probably from a stall in Kensington Market. He played guitar, not much better than me, and was madly devoted to rock bands; he looked up to Bob Dylan, Keith Richards, Lou Reed, Sid Barrett and Iggy. I suspect Mick Jagger was his guilty pleasure.

Mainly, he was fascinated by anyone in music if they were damaged and weird, or deranged and destructive or addicted. He was happy to meet someone as devoted to the above as himself who he could take along to gigs with his access pass as an *NME* journalist. I was only too happy to tag along. I'd been getting worried that I might not have found the rock mecca I'd been dreaming of after all.

The first show we saw was a band called Kilburn and the High-Roads at the 100 Club on Oxford Street. I thought the singer looked like what Lou Reed should have looked like then. (Lou had gained a few pounds—a no-no for rock stars.) This Kilburn guy was scrawny and, like Reed, a college-professor type, although crippled by childhood polio. It was Ian Dury: a good first gig to get under my belt.

Kent and I spent hours reading back issues of *Creem* magazine (of which he had an Asperger's-worthy collection, Lester Bangs being a big hero of his), while listening to the Flamin' Groovies, *Goats Head Soup*, the New York Dolls—and the Temptations; I would often find him enraptured listening to "Just My Imagination." We all have our soft spots.

One night in a pub I went off on one about some band or other in front of a long-haired intellectual type across the table, a friend of Nick's. The guy leaned forward and said, "You should write for us." Nick introduced me to him, Ian MacDonald, his assistant editor.

The idea of me writing anything at all was ludicrous. My head was disorganized, a tangle of crossed lines. I couldn't conclude a thought on a postcard.

Hi!
It's good here.
Cool stuff.
Saw a band.
Well, it's raining.
Okay, that's all.
Bye.

I wasn't a poet. I wasn't a writer. To begin a paragraph and find my way to a conclusion—Gretel tracking a breadcrumb trail would fare better. I had no understanding of music theory. My only qualification, had I required one, was that I was as frustrated as the rest of them—a frustrated musician (the cliché of music journalism), opinionated, hungover, illegal in the workplace, devoid of ambition and, if I couldn't find a word in my dumb guy vocabulary, I would make one up.

MacDonald, observing this over half a pint said, "Yeah, you should write for us."

These English weren't the same as the wasters I'd been used to. They used words like "quintessential" and the occasional phrase in French. I wasn't sure how I fit into the alien strata, but I wanted to. It hadn't taken me long to sniff out British versions of artistic types, the con artists I gravitated towards who were still too young and fresh-faced to be unmasked as con artists. Only time could reveal that.

I started writing for the *NME*.

The "flourish" came off Hynde (a thinly veiled ruse on my part to throw the Home Office). Nick Kent kept introducing me to people as Chrissie, either because Chris was a guy's name in Limeytown or because he preferred Chrissie, I never asked. Thus I became Chrissie Hynd of the *NME* and no one called me Chris ever again.

My theory, that to make it in this life you didn't need qualifications, was how I'd justified my steady slide as I watched the hard-earned savings my parents had put towards my education disappear down the crapper, so I wasn't going to change my mind all of a sudden and embark on a career. I never called myself a journalist or a writer because I wasn't a journalist or a writer. But, more important, now I wasn't a waitress either.

Ian MacDonald, one of the stars of the *NME*, which at the time was the leader, the most intelligently observed and humorous of the music papers, was a true visionary and humanitarian. But he was wrong this time: I really couldn't write.

He didn't care. He wasn't looking for quality. They were looking for sex. They wanted sex. They wanted a pimple-faced loudmouth to push the male staff around and make them crawl on all fours. Besides, I was fresh from getting the sack from Martineau Jenkins Associates, and this would save me having to find a job. Martineau had offered to train me up as an architect, but I preferred to sit around drawing pictures of the staff and drinking tea. They used my portraits on the end-of-year calendar and then gave me the elbow.

Come to think of it, nobody seemed to care about qualifications at all in England. Me, an architect? I thought you needed an eight-year slog through a university course and stacks of degrees. Nope. Hairdressers too seemed to be set up and raking in the cash *sans* certificate. What a great country it was!

I looked around my room in Clapham, rubbing my hands together as if I'd won the pools. I wouldn't even have to leave the house. I got thirty quid for my first article and figured I could coast on that until I found another job, having not a shred of doubt that I'd be banned from the *NME* offices after the hate mail my first review received.

Pissed-off Neil Diamond fans wanted me dead. The cross-eyed divorcées at Stouffer's who'd laughed at my Bowie scrapbook were Diamond fans and I had an ax to grind. There, that'll teach 'em. It might have been juvenile of me, but this getting your own back was rather good. And it was the English way.

Where American journalists thoughtfully reported the human-interest aspect of a story, the English went straight for the under-belly. Everything was a "riddle," never a straightforward murder but always tinged with sadism. Right up my street.

The more dismissive and poorly written my reviews, the more the *NME* applauded me. They wanted the bad publicity. Hate mail now spilled out of the post room and they liked it. They liked it bad and that was good.

I went with Nick Kent to Ladbroke Grove to meet Brian Eno. I remember the day distinctly because the mild-mannered, feathered bald one invited me to make a pot of tea, and I experienced what was to become an all-too-familiar feeling of cultural humiliation.

I'd never made a pot of tea before, and I had no idea how many loose leaves from the caddy to put in the pot. Twenty? A fistful?

I'd tried all the herbal varieties back in Akron, popular around the same time as incense and pot: Constant Comment was a good one, black tea infused with orange rind and spice; burdock root, another I could get in the one health-food store in Akron, Alexander's on North Main Street. Mu was my favorite, ginseng and an aromatic blend of oriental spices. I thought I was pretty sophisticated in my knowledge of tea, until I got to England.

Faced with a kettle and teapot I felt like a total ignoramus. In fact, the English drank ordinary Tetley tea, but there was a whole method to it, which was kept secret from Americans. The water had to be boiling first, tea bag in before pouring, two schools of thought on whether or not milk went in first or after—but it was never hot. Sounds simple until you get to a hotel in the States and you're jonesing for a cup of English tea. The English had never heard of iced tea, the very notion of which was met with unanimous disapproval.

Eno's loose-leaf tea was another story, requiring a tea strainer—a ton of factors that could go wrong. The only other time I'd felt cultural embarrassment that badly was the first time someone in Limeytown invited me to roll a joint. I was handed the kit: cigarette, box of matches, lump of hash, scissors, rolling papers and a piece of cardboard, but I might as well have been handed a Rubik's Cube and told, "Ready? Begin!"

I figured the scissors must be for cutting off bits of the hash, which I proceeded to do, only to be met with jolly amusement. I worked out that the cigarette was meant to be tipped out and re-rolled with the hash. But what was the cardboard for? It would be a matter of time before I got hip to the method.

The scissors, of course, were for cutting a ticket-sized bit of card to roll into a filter, the matches were for heating the hash up to then

crumble and distribute evenly into the tobacco. Well, if you're reading this you already know how to roll a joint, so you can imagine
what a dunce I felt.

Nick Kent pinched words from my vocabulary, of which there
were about five, and started using them in his articles: turkey, wimp,
twerp . . . okay, three.

They wanted the dumbing down that only a purebred American
could provide. I lucked out!

Little teenagers out in the sticks like Julie Burchill lapped up my
half-baked philosophical drivel and prepared their own versions of
nonsensical tirades for the day when they too could make a "career"
out of it. (I even sold the darling little Julie my typewriter for fifteen
quid when my time was over, like passing on the baton of "how
to fuck off the nation and get paid for it"; she insisted on giving
me £17.)

Good fortune smiled on me, but I knew I was a phony and,
unlike some of my comrades, it bothered me. I learned that the
things you find the most embarrassing about yourself are the very
things the public will love you for.

They kept giving me assignments so how could I refuse? They
bought it. It was like getting paid to shoplift. Steal one and get one
free on top of the one you already got free sort of thing. I couldn't
fathom what I was doing hanging out with guys like Tony Tyler,
who was writing an encyclopedia on the complete works of J.R.R.
Tolkien. I'd had trouble getting through *The Hobbit*.

All I had were opinions, but my employers were intent on turning me into a star attraction of the rat pack of the British music
press. Life was now an endless succession of album launches—early
afternooners, with plates of smoked salmon (no, thanks!), sarnies,

and lots of booze. The *NME* staff would hover over and hog the drinks table, get pissed, then stagger back up Long Acre to write an insulting profile of the artist whose launch it had been.

Record companies were burning money, and there I was, tagging along and scarfing the free lunch with the rest of them. The difference was, of course, that the rest of them were serious writers. Ian MacDonald would one day be writing books on Shostakovich, for Chrissake!

"Chrissie Hynd (who has a thing about black leather)" was a typical byline written by whoever was editing the paper that week. I did not have a thing about black leather; the *NME* staff did.

I guess it was novel to have someone on board who didn't know what the rest of them were talking about. Well, whatever. I was getting paid, and I was part of the team. But it was embarrassing if I got recognized when I went to gigs. Someone was going to call my bluff; it was just a matter of time. I was learning that people didn't care if you were a total quack; if you were more famous than they were, they were impressed. But that didn't feel okay to me, like someone posing with a guitar who can't play it. It's just wrong.

I'd inadvertently started to make a name for myself, while the whole time I'd been wanting to back out. I'd forgotten about getting in a band. I didn't want to be known for something that I knew I wasn't good at.

Then when the editor, Nick Logan, asked me to write a "looking back" piece on the Velvet Underground, I knew it was time to go. I didn't want to look back. But I felt I was letting Logan down; he had been especially good to me, often giving me advances when I was behind in my rent.

Still, I'd spent a year slagging off bands, saying everything was shit, and I was sorry. I wanted to love music again. Part of my constant slagging was a cover-up for my poor writing skills—arrogance over ability. (Hey—I really did have what it takes to be in a band!) It had even occurred to me once or twice that if someone was that critical, they should get out there and try it themselves.

19

CRAFT MUST HAVE CLOTHES
BUT TRUTH LOVES TO GO NAKED

So I wasn't thinking about getting in a band anymore. I'd had designs on it when I first stepped off the boat, and often parked myself in a place on the King's Road to pore over the "singers wanted" ads in the back pages of *Melody Maker* in the only place I could find that had coffee that wasn't instant: an American burger joint. Rank. (The addict will go to any length.)

Mythology would have it that I'd declared, "The next time you see my name, it will be in lights." But that's not how it was. I knew my time had run out. When I left Ohio my only ambition remaining had been to leave.

I met a woman who lived on the King's Road who I occasionally got pot from. Her cat had kittens and I had the notion to take one back to Clapham. I went to her place, above the Barclays Bank, to choose one when I was struck by a glorious sound: "What's that?"

"Oh, that's my son's band."

I went into the adjacent room where four fourteen-year-olds were in full flight. How wonderful, I thought, the crude sounds of raw beginnings. I listened appreciatively to their small repertoire.

Gary Holton, local Keith Richards lookalike singer of the Heavy Metal Kids, lived nearby. "Heavy metal" wasn't a term used to describe loud metal music yet. I think it was still associated with

William Burroughs. (People were always lifting his descriptions for band names. Steely Dan, 10cc, Soft Machine?) Anyway, the young band was struggling to play some of Holton's Heavy Metal Kids songs. I suggested they try some Velvet tunes if they were looking for something basic but tasty. They didn't know who the Velvet Underground was, so I took a guitar and showed them "White Light/ White Heat." They watched and listened quizzically. Who was this friend of Mum's who could play rock guitar and sing cool songs?

It never occurred to me that I still had a shot of getting a band together myself. I was twenty-three, twenty-four now, way past it, but I thought that I could advise this spirited little group, so taken was I with their sound. But with zero business acumen and even less interest in learning about it, nothing came of the encounter except the reminder that I could play guitar and sing. I'd almost forgotten that. I left with a gray-striped kitten I called Mose.

•

Malcolm McLaren and Vivienne Westwood offered me a job as a shop assistant. Yeah! That's more like it. Just being around them was going to be more creative than anything I could do at the *NME*. Nick and I used to go in their shop when it was called Let It Rock and schmooze around en route to Granny Takes a Trip, where all the real get-down boys bought their gear. (Keith got his blue velvet suit with the little flowers embroidered all over there, and naturally Nick had to go there too and buy the same suit.)

"Craft Must Have Clothes but Truth Loves to Go Naked" was what it was now called, written above the door in spray paint. The little shop nestled discreetly in the curve where the King's Road meets the World's End. Malcolm and Vivienne were already the two people I most looked up to.

It felt more progressive to be in the orbit of two genuine English eccentrics than churning out reviews. They saw things differently from everyone I'd ever met. They were "straight," for a start. They didn't take, and never had taken, drugs. They weren't even pot smokers. That made them unique, in my book. They just drank whisky on the odd night out, and they'd never been hippies. It was more like hanging out with Emma Peel and John Steed, or even Laurel and Hardy, than the scruffy roadie types I was used to.

They had fifties stuff on the jukebox in the shop and "Tell It Like It Is" by Aaron Neville. I doubt they'd even heard of Buffalo Springfield, and surely had never bought a Led Zeppelin album. I was intrigued. And they looked great, especially Viv, with her spiky platinum-blonde hair, drainpipe trousers, winkle-picker shoes and fifties rocker shirts. Nobody else looked like her. Walking down the street with her, I knew what Colonel Tom Parker must have felt like walking next to Elvis.

Malcolm, too, had his own look, totally original and subtle—but you noticed: curly ginger hair, pale and sensitive looking, with an inquisitive, almost pervy expression of wonder. You knew this guy didn't play sports. It was all about the clothes; the clothes did the talking. If you saw Malcolm in any police lineup in the world, you would say, "Nope, I'd definitely remember him!"

When the shop was called Let It Rock it catered to Teddy Boys, who wore quiffs (Elvis/James Dean–styled hair) and multiple earrings, and came in to buy drape jackets and brothel creepers—the stuff Rotten and Strummer would be wearing in a few years. I'd never seen anything like it in Akron or Cleveland.

No sooner had the fifties signed out than that look, American in inspiration, was pushed aside and long hair took over in the States.

But even the Beatles wore quiffs to begin with. Brian Epstein was spot-on getting them in mop-top bowl cuts, but you could tell Lennon was born to wear a quiff. He knew it too.

The English kept a tribal thing going indefinitely. I'm sure I stuck out like a sore thumb, being, as I was, a victim of the American mall culture. But I was thrilled to be in on this fifties' reworking into something with sexual innuendo, even though I didn't really know what that meant.

The shop was about to undergo another change. The word SEX, in pink latex letters, would soon appear curiously above the door. Soho comes to the World's End: bondage gear; rubber masks. I think it was meant to be a political statement. I was never quite sure; you couldn't tell with Malcolm.

I didn't think people really used those things—maybe politicians. All that kinky stuff and bondage was for the straight world. My impression was that the whole concept was a send-up and supposed to be ironic—an "up yours" to the establishment.

Nobody I knew thought about fashion. Designer labels didn't exist, not to people like us, anyway. Gucci? That was for someone's sad auntie. But being around Malcolm and Viv, I started to understand the meaning of glamour; that how you present yourself to your fellow man is a way of communicating ideas.

It was still the glory days when, unlike movie stars, what people in bands wore would never make it into the pages of a fashion magazine. They were two separate worlds. Fashion was for shop assistants, a bit of fun on the lower end, and less fun and more about status on the higher end.

Being in a band meant you were exempt from fashion altogether, especially in the seventies which, up until Malcolm and Viv's influence, was nothing short of hideous. The beginning of glam got away with it (the Faces), but by the time of ABBA or pretty much anything you'd see on *Top of the Pops*, it was quite disturbing: bad hair; satin trousers tucked into Frye boots; platform shoes; and sparkly glasses.

In the gay community things were different. The designers had artistic expression, but it was still relatively underground or only for the rich. Yves St. Laurent was making those Mondrian print dresses and men's suits for women—Le Smoking!—but no one on the street was wearing that stuff. We'd loved Mary Quant and Biba and Courrèges, but soon we were to embark on a DIY campaign that would only be considered "fashion" thirty years after the fact.

•

Malcolm and Vivienne were living in her council flat, in a thirties block on Nightingale Lane, not far from my place on Englewood Road, with their young son, Joe. I'd walk home with Malcolm after the shop closed, over Chelsea Bridge and across the Common, and we'd talk about music and how we saw things going. Who was to know that this strange bird, with his seditious take on clothes and culture, and his fierce but beautiful girlfriend were soon to set the whole fashion and music scene on its head with the Sex Pistols?

The three of us went to see the New York Dolls at Biba's Rainbow Room, and I could see the wheels turning in Malcolm's head; you can always tell by the way someone watches a band. That was a pivotal night for all of us, each in our different ways. The Dolls were keeping the flame from going out, our favorite New York band.

That evening was also memorable because Viv launched a bread roll at a waiter over something he'd said and ended up towering above the public on a table, making obscene gestures involving her rear end. Viv could be fearsome and you did not want to get on her bad side—or her backside.

Other than the Dolls, there weren't a lot of new, original bands out there. The mid-seventies sagged. There were some good blues-based pub bands on amphetamines, but you could feel things had to shift. Roots Reggae was the main creative force, but it wasn't storming the charts. The scene was on hold. As always in a transitional period, you couldn't put your finger on it.

A teenage west London delinquent, Steve Jones, hung out around the shop. (I had no idea he had aspirations to play guitar; he had no idea I did, either.) Malcolm and Viv seemed to have taken him under their wing for some reason, to help keep him out of trouble. I guess it was better to let him hang out in the shop than for him to rob the shop. He used to put the grilles up for me at closing.

·

One evening after work, I was just about to light a cigarette at the bar in the Roebuck, the King's Road local, when a feminine hand, long fingernails and silver rings, appeared seemingly out of nowhere, offering a lit match. I looked over to see an androgynous figure, darkly beautiful and possessed of something that would have sat nicely on a biker's petrol tank next to a goblin crossing a sand dune.

As any world traveler will tell you, the French are second to none when it comes to making things appear and disappear. And things were about to appear: this creature was to be my portal into Paris.

It was Flipos who taught me how to walk in backwards through exits when everyone else was leaving (how I got into the Louvre the first time) and how to get into venues for free through skylights. (Don't try it in a cinema. Miscalculating a descent and landing in the projectionist's booth is just embarrassing.) Then after a week or two, like everything he touched, he disappeared.

Malcolm and Viv had by now issued my walking papers, a direct result of the Nick Kent belt incident when he came into the shop, took off his cheap coin-studded belt and started swinging it around, trying to bash me in the face.

He was cross with me for dumping him. Well, perhaps he shouldn't have presented me with, first, scabies, then a virulent strain of something even worse, which had landed me in Hammersmith Hospital for three days.

Malcolm ducked behind the counter just as a local guy who'd been sitting quietly in the corner stood up and knocked Kent out. Good punch! Kent was sprawled out on his back, tooth knocked out, unconscious long enough for me to step over him and run out of the shop. The next day, Viv said they didn't need me anymore. I guess they didn't want some wacko trashing the place because of me.

So I was back in the mode of: "Now what?" In a bizarre twist of events, Star-eyed Stella had come to visit me and married Chris Webster, another tenant at Englewood Road and its resident sculptor. Now she too lived in the house with us, and she got a job in south London working as a schoolteacher. Debbie does Peckham! Now married, she at least was legal. I was on the run.

Webster let me sleep on the desk in his studio as I was underfunded and couldn't pay rent. It was cold, the desk hard, and I was permanently covered in a fine layer of white powder (plaster, not amphetamines). I was dossing.

The payphone in the hall rang. I bounded to get it in a cloud of dust like the Lone Ranger. It was Flipos, inviting me to sing in a band he was putting together.

"What makes you think I can sing?" I asked.

"You look like you can."

I went immediately to three record companies, announcing myself, "Chrissie Hynd, *NME*." I walked out with as many albums "to review" as I could carry, took them straight to Cheapo Cheapo's in Soho, sold the lot and was on the next hovercraft to the City of Love.

20

PARIS

Flipos' band had no name. In fact, Flipos' band had no band. It was the fantasy of a mad urchin and homeless gypsy, a failed magician who could make things appear and disappear but couldn't materialize musicians or guitars or songs. But it was a start. The bee trapped in my bonnet was now a roaring cicada demanding attention.

The dark-eyed *gitano*, whose clanging silver talismans led a trail from up his sleeves, installed me in a tiny house near the Eiffel Tower, home to a Jewish heiress who kept fur throws, Moroccan pillows, Persian carpets and a sofa where I could crash. It was a typically Parisian one up, one down, connected by a spiral staircase, with a tiny kitchen and toilet at arm's reach in a courtyard off Rue Lecourbe. (I was going to have to get used to staying in places whose names I couldn't pronounce for the life of me.)

Her name was Lilian; she had long blonde hair, wore silk scarves and served tea and oranges that came all the way from China. Her Jewishness made me feel like I was back in Debbie Smith's mum's house in Fairlawn, cozy, with a life-affirming full fridge. I came to realize that the Jewish Princess is a universal stereotype regardless of nationality (except in Israel).

Then I met Sasha. Sasha was half-Dutch, half-Chinese and a little older than me, late twenties. I knew she had been a rock singer at some point, because Sabrina, her husband/wife, snuck me a picture showing her all done up like a rockabilly—quiff, short-sleeved checked shirt—and singing real intent down a mic in some basement club somewhere. Amsterdam, probably.

We hid the picture of Sasha in a little drawer in the tiny Indian bureau near the brass tray. Sometimes I would sneak it out and Sabrina and I would laugh, unbeknownst to Sasha. It was one of the things that was understood between us, our only language in common. Sasha no longer looked like she did in the photo. Her blue-black hair fell down her back like a horse's tail and she dressed like a monk now—but not for long.

Sasha was meant to be the other singer in the band, and within a couple of weeks she invited me to stay at the apartment on Avenue Denfert-Rochereau. I bade farewell to Lilian, shifting my worldly goods to *chez* Letronière. Sasha and I had much in common: we both read the Bhagavad Gita, with lifelong devotion, and you can't have more in common than philosophy.

Sabrina was the star of l'Alcazar—a typically Parisian cabaret and one of the last in a great tradition. Sabrina went onstage around midnight in feathers and sequins, dazzling the audience while flying through the air on a swing trailing glitter, and performing French dance-hall classics. She designed all her costumes and was constantly drawing and putting new outfits together.

In civilian life, "Sabo" looked like Lou Reed. "He" wore a motorcycle jacket, jeans, boots, striped mohair sweater and studded leather cap. I loved walking down the street with the Letronières, the only couple I'd met who could rival the reaction that Vivienne and Malcolm elicited.

Sasha did the cooking and whatever administration needed doing, and drove Sabrina about in an old white Mercedes with leopard-print seat covers, steady as a Chinese lieutenant driving a diplomatic car.

Everyone in Paris was an expert at rolling joints—hashish mixed with tobacco and don't forget the filter, usually a spent Metro subway ticket. This common ritual took place hourly as we sat cross-legged on the floor around the brass tray, drinking Imperial Gunpowder or oolong tea.

The brass tray was the centerpiece of the apartment on the fifth floor above an ancient billiards hall with a long view down the Rue Daguerre, which at Christmas was strung with every imaginable beast, from quail to wild boar, hung by their feet, bags tied securely over their heads so as not to splash blood on the cobblestones (a far cry from the frozen food department at the Acme).

I realized that the time I was spending at Denfert-Rochereau was the best of my life so far. I felt like I was starting to figure out who I was.

There was no furniture in the apartment except for a wooden chair and a little table in the kitchen, which overlooked the court-yard. As far as I knew the bathtub had never been used other than to store costumes and we all washed at the bathroom sink. They'd lived on a houseboat in Kashmir before and were used to "basic." The French didn't like to wash much anyway, so it seemed.

Sasha made basic brown rice with tamari sauce and carefully prepared legumes—precisely my cup of tea. She was a good cook. Sabo preferred French delicacies, which included a daily round of fresh Camembert. And I do mean fresh.

Every day, after taking Kalu out (my one duty—walking the dog), I'd climb the five flights of stairs, gasping a smoker's gasp, then open the door to an explosion of Camembert fumes. Gagging, I'd stagger to a window and force it open in a panic.

Sabo loved his Camembert and, as a grateful houseguest, there was nothing I could do about it. Like clockwork every day, he would take the fresh one that Sasha had bought earlier that morning down from the cupboard, give it a good squeeze (squeezing it was necessary for some reason before unwrapping it, maybe to release the fumes) and then sit down at the little table to eat it with whatever you eat Camembert with. Crackers or a baguette, I guess. I never knew exactly, as I cleared off as soon as the Camembert appeared.

One day, while browsing through a joke shop, I found a rubber Camembert that made a loud blurting noise when squeezed. What genius thought that up? I rushed back to the apartment, flew up the five flights breathlessly excited as I replaced the fresh Camembert with the fake one. Then Sasha and I hid in wait for Sabo to unsuspectingly sashay out of his room and attend to his routines, which would inevitably culminate in squeezing the Camembert. We held our breath as he opened the cupboard, took out the dummy and pushed his thumbs into it.

You could hear the screams all the way down the Rue Daguerre.

•

Although Sabo and I couldn't have a conversation, I made it understood that I was fed up with men hissing at me on the street. It really pissed me off, especially because I couldn't tell them to "fuck off!" I seemed to have no aptitude for French while Sasha, being Dutch, spoke four or five languages, including perfect English, so I wasn't required to learn.

It was something of an adjustment for me to be mute, but I got used to it. After the first week around the tray I only managed to understand what *"Tu vois ce que je veux dire?"* meant. Nevertheless, I made my grievance clear, and Sabo proceeded to coach me for an entire night until I could say with near perfect diction, "*L'ideé de vous baiser me fait gerber! Maintenant, foutez-moi la paix!*" with special emphasis on the word *gerber* (vomit). He thought that was the funniest thing ever, making me repeat it over and over as he laughed real tears, especially with my vicious attack on *gerber*! I went on to impress passersby with it whenever someone hissed. The offender, then becoming the offended, would launch into a tirade of abuse to which I would become the dopey American tourist, saying, "I'm sorry, I don't speak French."

There were door hangings made of glass beads with pictures of exotic flowers and birds in all the doorways that made a whooshing sound as you wandered from room to room, which was infinitely more pleasant than the sound of doors opening and closing and made me wonder why everybody didn't have them. There was no phone, or television, and time stood still with nothing to alert you to a schedule of any kind, except for Kalu when he needed to go out.

The stereo was the only modern convenience, and Sasha used to play a lot of Tina Turner and Fats Domino. Smoking the amount of hash we did was a real eye-closer, and not being able to understand a word made it even more of a mind-fuck. I liked it, though.

Every night, Sasha and I would drop Sabrina off and—if we didn't stay to watch the show—go back to pick her up around three in the morning. We smoked into the night until, one by one, we'd go off to our respective magic carpets. I had my own mat in a corner.

Sasha had lacquered the paneling and doorframes of the lounge room red. Moroccan wall hangings lined the walls. They told me that someone had got them from the film set of *Performance*. Sasha's room was pink with gold detail around the coving and light fittings. I guessed that it was what a palace or temple in India must look like. Sabo's room was dark blue, strewn with costumes from days gone by.

Just like a Chinese or Italian restaurant, once inside the apartment there was no way of telling what year it was or what country you were in. I loved that sense of timelessness.

There would often be visitors from the cabaret, including the beautiful Marie France, one of the best singers I'd ever met. I was the resident rock-and-roller, and they all liked rock in the way the French like things, the classic way. Viva la Rock! My natural androgyny, I guess, is what allowed me to fit into the scene. I added a certain amount of yang, more boyish than the rest.

A Templar monk dropped by sometimes in the afternoon, and he loved looking through Sabrina's scrapbooks of costumes. He was very proud to show us his antique gold rings and elaborately embroidered vestments. We didn't smoke in front of him, though; man of the cloth and all.

Most evenings I would walk up to Montparnasse, where there where a bunch of bars and restaurants. La Coupole was an enormous dance hall/brasserie famous for its pillars, each individually painted by artists in the twenties. I didn't have the money to go inside but I could hang around the bar and observe, which was just as good. One night, I picked up a heavy cigarette lighter that someone had left on a table and put it in my pocket. Twenty minutes later, a guy came running in, shouting, *"Mon briquet! Mon briquet!"* He was in a lather, frantic to find it. I handed it to him and he looked like he was going to cry with relief. I thought, "Imagine getting like that over a stupid lighter" (even if it was a solid gold Dupont). Some people.

Sasha bought a little Mobilette scooter that I would race around on, but I had to be careful as people drove in a way that made me think of tadpoles darting through a pond. "That must be why they're called 'Frogs,'" I reasoned.

Paris was so beautiful. I could get lost in a kind of euphoria just tooling around under the *tilleul* blossoms which spilled overhead, filling the streets with their luscious fragrance. The cemeteries were, as in all cities, a haven of tranquility, awash with flowers and the cats who lived there, and I could happily spend a whole afternoon wandering along the cobbled paths, reading inscriptions and meditating on the timeless nature of the departed. Everyone wanted to see where Jim Morrison was. As in life, his poetry followed him to the City of Love.

Despite not understanding French, I was getting the gist of a certain hierarchy which really came to light one day when I was picked up by a policeman on the Metro, in what was, I guess, a routine check. He asked to see my passport and I told him I didn't have it on me, paranoid that he would confiscate it. He hauled me off to the police station as if I'd committed a crime, and he was unnecessarily heavy-handed. I sat there for over an hour waiting for something—I didn't know what. Finally, his superior came in, wondering what I was doing there. When I could see the officer who'd picked me up explaining that I was without papers (surely thinking he was about to score some points for this important coup) I produced my passport and handed it straight to his superior, who in turn waved me away and started shouting at his minion. Ha ha—showed him! Prick.

Everyone under someone else—same as anywhere.

·

I met an Afghani guy, much older than me, about thirty-five, at the Select, another bar/restaurant in Montparnasse. He noticed me in my tight jeans and cowboy boots trying to look hard, and said, "I bet you're a bitch!" to which I replied, "How much do you want to bet?" That must have appealed to him, as he was, I was about to find out, a professional gambler. We started to see each other and he was the closest thing I had to a boyfriend, although I saw him infrequently and would never have taken him back to Denfert-Rochereau. That would have been in poor taste.

He and I had little in common except a love for Jimi Hendrix, but, well, that was all I needed. He stayed out all night, every night, playing poker and drinking vodka. He was, in his own words, "not a good Muslim." He slept by day in a tiny room in a two-star hotel off the Boulevard Raspail after stopping by a bar as the sun was coming up and dunking a lump of sugar into a shot of bourbon for breakfast. I liked his vampiric habitudes and thought he was handsome. With his dark, bloodshot eyes and long face he actually looked like an Afghan hound, the hippie dog of choice back in the day.

He told me that Afghanis were "Oriental, not Arab." (I had a big argument with my dad years later: "Oh, Christy, of course they're Arabs!") He dressed real straight: slightly flared black trousers, thin belt, Italian shirt, black calfskin ankle boots that zipped on the inside, tan sports jacket. He was nothing like the French guys I was hanging out with, who all wore motorcycle jackets, tight jeans and cowboy boots.

One night he told me, "In your country people say, 'Sticks and stones will break my bones, but names can never hurt me.' In my country, if you insult someone, you meet that night in the cemetery and one of you goes home in the morning."

He'd take me to see a film sometimes in the afternoon before going to work—playing poker. He liked crappy American movies but I didn't mind; I never got to see films in those days otherwise.

Once I found him sitting at a bar brooding over something. He was leaning on his elbows, looking down at his vodka and soda and, without looking up, said, "I just want to go back to Afghanistan and get a horse and a rifle."

He had a kind of Wild West thing going. I liked that. I often thought about what he said about insulting people—a good thing to know.

.

Marc Zermati was the French-Algerian entrepreneur who ran the Open Market in Les Halles, a record store that had a definitive selection of vinyl—the Flamin' Groovies, Stooges and all the pre-punk classics. It was as intelligently stocked as any record store in the world. It's no wonder that the word "connoisseur" is French. That's probably the reason so many jazz artists ended up there. The French embraced the best of modern culture, but didn't throw out what was ancient, beautiful and worthy of preservation. (Their appreciation for the offbeat earned them the closing line in Woody Allen's *Hollywood Ending*: "Thank God the French exist!")

Of course, they got it wrong too sometimes. If you looked the part and called yourself a poet, you could go a long way there; it was a poser's paradise.

Under the Open Market there was a series of descending basement caves, maybe three or even four subterranean rooms where Zermati let fledgling bands rehearse. Across the road was an enormous crater that was the site of the as yet unbuilt Centre Georges Pompidou.

I hooked up with a couple of Keith Richards lookalikes (everybody at the Open Market was a Keith Richards lookalike) and we attempted to put something together, but never got as far as finding a drummer. I embarked on a few other misfires too. I was now on a mission.

Sasha had got me a Japanese Les Paul copy, and she and I still talked about being in a band, although she didn't play anything yet herself.

One day, she handed me a big pair of scissors and asked me to cut off her hair. She was fed up with the unwelcome attention of lowlifes on the street. I hated cutting it—it was so long, black and sleek—but she wanted it off. Like the rest of us, she was preparing for something. We could feel it coming. Punk.

Zermati let us all rehearse in rotation in one cave or another. The thing with the French was that they could play, but just not with each other. As soon as one guy started to tune up, another jumped in to "vamp." For some reason it was virtually impossible for four guys to wait until everybody was ready and count in a song. It was permanent chaos.

At first I didn't mind—I like a bit of chaos. But it didn't take long to see that nothing was going to come together in a madhouse. No one spoke English, which was a problem because they all wanted to sound like the Rolling Stones, who were at the height of their "elegantly wasted" period. There was palpable frustration because everyone's favorite bands sang in English, but rock is idiomatic and lyrics have to be written in a first language to nail the nuances.

I could feel their frustration, but feeling my own was worse. Although everybody had an appreciation for the great pre-punk bands of the day, nobody had heard of my favorite: Mitch Ryder and the Detroit Wheels. When you start to get serious, your roots become everything.

Then there was another stumbling block. Paris, where everyone smoked hash, was enjoying a heroin epidemic. Everyone was getting strung out, and heroin, as is its wont, was becoming more important than the music. I woke up one day and, instead of thinking about finding a band, I was thinking about if I was going to score. Alarm bells.

Every day it became more apparent that I wasn't going to find what I was looking for in Paris. What good was paradise to me now? What was the point of the Garden of Eden with no Adam and no apple?

I'd been sneaking around without work papers, no work, and it looked like no prospects. That didn't bother me so much, but I got fixated on Mitch Ryder. I needed to start hanging out with someone who understood my roots.

I loved Paris but it was now standing in the way of destiny. I used my return ticket and went back to Akron, disappearing just as Flipos had done, back to the streets.

21
BACK TO OHIO

Being back in Ohio was a lot crazier than I'd expected. I was less suited to life there than before—a lot less. I knew that staying with my parents was a temporary situation, but it was insane to think I could hold out even for a week.

For a start, after Sasha's place and my mat on the floor, I found I could no longer sleep in a bed. I slept on the floor next to the bed in my room, on the silver polyester shag carpet, in the *Clockwork Orange* house.

I was already back to hiding from my parents. They would have been appalled and furious to find me on the floor. I was already trying not to rile them. What had I been thinking?

My pictures of Iggy were still on the wall, as was the poster of Brigitte Bardot with the cheroot dangling from her lips. How odd it all seemed; it occurred to me that maybe I'd actually gone insane.

I was also to discover that I couldn't sit in a chair for more than a minute before I had to move onto the floor. What the fuck? I couldn't sit on a chair! I'd have to get out of there.

One of my problems was that I did things—everything—too fast. I made my decision and left Paris the second I realized I wasn't going to get a band together there. Now I was back in a self-imposed high-security prison: no money, no job, no setup, no idea and, the most scary part, no hash. I hadn't figured that into the equation when I booked my ticket. What self-respecting drug addict would allow such an omission when making a plan? Did I think I'd just stop smoking and everything would be fine? The expression "climbing the walls" springs to mind.

None of my old pals would have dope, nor would they be interested in finding any. They'd either have jobs or would have moved away. I couldn't even get on the blower and arrange some. I had absolutely no way of scoring.

It was turning into my worst nightmare. I had actually, of my own volition, put myself back in Akron. I knew I had to be calm and find a solution, but a solution to what? That I'd lost my mind? No, I couldn't fixate on negative shit. Think. There's always a solution.

I called Duane. It had been some time since I'd blown off his audition, and I didn't really know him well in the first place. He was someone I'd admired from afar.

"Oh, hey. I'm back in town. What's happening?" I tried not to sound panic-stricken.

Bingo! He was playing a gig at the Brick Cottage in Cleveland, some little cement shithouse bar on Euclid Avenue. I called Debbie Smith and begged her to pick me up and take me to the top of Route 76 at the entrance ramp, where she could drop me off and I could thumb a ride. Only Jeffrey Dahmer could stop me now.

A guy picked me up in a VW. Something was wrong—it was making a terrible racket. He got off at the wrong exit. We were going to some remote place out in the country. As soon as he stopped, I flung the door open, got out, legged it and waved down another car. I was shaking. Welcome back, stupid.

It seemed like years since I'd seen the likes of the Brick Cottage, a windowless bar with a stage surrounded by *Deer Hunter*–type pill heads drinking beer. I didn't care about anything except seeing a band play to steady my jangled nerves, getting a couple of shots of tequila and finding someone with a joint. Surely that wasn't too much to ask.

The band was a sturdy R&B outfit, old school; not a Keith Richards lookalike in sight. And they could play. Duane looked exactly the same, in fact quite exotic, after the French rockers I'd been hanging out with. From one time warp to another.

Oh, how I loved guys in bands. When a band played, time stood still. In between sets Duane introduced me to a couple of his friends who lived in a typical Cleveland apartment building (a dump) just across from the gig. They took me back and let me sleep in the hallway. No problem for me at all; I was fine with the floor. I was like a stray dog let in from the cold. I just wanted to be quiet and not get thrown out. I'd do anything.

Micky "Meadows" and Dot, Duane's friends, didn't mind me being there because I took up no space and they both went out to work during the day. They said I could stay. I loved it when life opened its arms like that and said, "Yes."

I painted the hallway to look like an English pub—glossy red walls with gold trim on the coving sort of thing—and divided the ceiling with a yin-yang symbol. I got a sleeping bag and a candle and some good news: Duane's band, the Mr. Stress Blues Band, was having problems. Their singer, Bill Miller, was in the hospital with throat problems, and they needed a singer to fill in while he was gone. Well, bad news for Miller—but good news for me. I guess I was a glass-half-full person after all.

Duane lent me a bunch of records to study and I was back in action. I would wait until Meadows and Dot, my benefactors, saviors and now best friends, had gone to work, then shut myself in a closet and try to belt out "Precious, Precious," the Jackie Moore classic, and "Sweet Feeling" by the silver-throated Candi Staton.

The conundrum: I knew I wanted to be in a band and sing, but I didn't actually know what I sounded like. I wasn't even sure if I could sing or not. It was a case of "Where there's a will, please, God, let there be a way." So I sang in the closet and hoped for the best.

I went to a rehearsal and tried my voice on a few songs, including those I'd practiced behind closed doors and "Fight the Power" by the Isley Brothers and "Slippery When Wet" by the Commodores. The band seemed nonplussed, but I was just temping so no protests were made. They just wanted to fulfill their commitments and get paid.

Then an astonishing thing happened. Donnie Baker—a guitar hero who I'd seen play in The Case of E. T. Hooley, one of the great Cleveland bands from the late sixties—was back. He'd moved to Florida after Hooley split, but here he was, driving into town in his black-and-white '57 Chevy, just like a guitar hero should. Duane asked him if he wanted to join us and he agreed. It was like a miracle. He named the band Jack Rabbit. I never thought to ask why; anything he wanted was good by me. Jack Rabbit? Why not?

Baker had tousled dark-blond hair and muscular guitar-player forearms like Popeye. For me to share a stage with Duane and Donnie was my idea of heaven. Never mind the beautiful idyll of Montparnasse that I'd left for a place barely a step up from a slum, I was in a band. Glory, hallelujah!

We rehearsed in the basement at Mike Maudlin's, the keyboard player, and got some gigs at the Cellar Door, a subterranean venue in typical subterranean venue mode.

I wore my *SCUM Manifesto* T-shirt and fringed miniskirt that I'd bought from Malcolm's shop. For once in my life I was the best-dressed person in town. We did a couple of reggae songs, "Pressure Drop" and "Johnny Too Bad," which Duane loved, although no one else in Cleveland had even heard of reggae. Who cared? They had now.

I discovered how much I loved to play tambourine while dancing and singing. It was real funfair stuff, more like a Detroit Wheels band than anything I'd tried in Paris, so I guessed I was on the right path.

I thought about Sasha and Sabrina, and our life together, a lot. This was an extreme change that even I, with my lust for change, was finding tough. Not to mention the fact that nobody in Cleveland smoked hash with tobacco like they did in Europe, and I couldn't get used to smoking straight pot anymore. And to think how much I'd hated mixing it with tobacco the first time. Well, people change.

Then one day a package arrived: some photos from Sasha. "Oh, cool," I thought as I unwrapped them. I was a little surprised, though; it was an unusual package to get from her. I put all the photos against the wall in the hall and sat back and looked at them: random photos of street scenes. Hmmm . . .

I looked again at the elaborate way she'd packaged them, so carefully, and precisely, the way she did everything. There was a lot of tape on the wrapping, and then, when I investigated further . . . she had rolled out a huge block of hash, paper thin, wrapped it in foil and hidden it between the cardboard! I was surprised I'd even found it, so cleverly was it concealed.

There was enough to smoke for months. Now that we were all smoking European-style spliffs in Cleveland I had become a bit of a cultural ambassador.

Well, you do your bit.

A letter arrived out of the blue from Malcolm. He was putting a band together. He'd been to New York, met some guys—I think it was Richard Hell or Tom Verlaine, maybe both—and got an idea. He said he would send me a plane ticket if I was interested in coming back to London. I can't remember his exact plan, but I think the idea was to have me just play guitar.

I was still sleeping in Meadow's hallway, happy now that I had something to smoke. But more than that, I was actually learning something, singing in a real band. Granted, it was a covers band in Cleveland, but I was committed to it. We had gigs, and I was an integral part of it. In my heart of hearts I knew this wasn't *the* band, but it's the same with all love stories—you can tell the one you're in isn't going to be there in a year or two, but you have to see it through to its conclusion, so I declined the offer. Malcolm McLaren would have better things to attend to soon anyway.

Cleveland was a city in decline. The steel industry was failing and the downtown was, like Akron's, unloved and unlived in, but, unlike Akron's, very heavy and very dangerous. (If you don't know what Cleveland looked like around that time, watch *The Deer Hunter* again—it was set in Pittsburgh but filmed in Cleveland.)

The national homicide-by-pistol rate saw Cleveland in the top five. Ditto death by fire. So you had an above-the-odds chance of getting shot or burnt to death just by being there. However, it did have soul. Despite the dilapidated inner city, the outskirts were important cultural centers. The Cleveland Orchestra was one of the nation's finest, and there was a hub of universities and medical centers, in sharp contrast to the ghetto within.

As with all American cities, there was a distinct black-and-white divide. Black Cleveland and White Cleveland were like separate cities. There was a criminal undercurrent just below the surface that you couldn't see, but you could reach down and touch it if you were so inclined. The Mafia had big interests in Cleveland, but nobody talked about stuff like that. No one wanted to put themselves in harm's way.

I didn't make any money out of my one-day-a-week residency with Jack Rabbit—I was just hoping to pay for my own mic—but there were no expenses to speak of in our ramshackle Cleveland apartment building. Whoever the landlord was, he wasn't bothered about upkeep. The plumbing was shot and the bathtub out of commission, so I would fill the sink, climb up into it and squat. One morning I was ankle-deep in water when I stood up and banged my back on what turned out to be a live cord dangling from the ceiling. The force of the shock knocked me out of the sink and across the room.

In other words, Micky and Dot's place was a dive, but I couldn't complain. You get what you pay for.

One day, I arrived home after band practice to discover that a freak storm had blown the corner of the building clean off. The winds off Lake Erie could be fierce and we all grew up with tornado warnings where families would regularly go into their basements, listen to the radio and wait till it was over. This wasn't a tornado but something akin to one, and now there was a big hole in the ceiling where we could see straight up into the sky. It would be possible to get by with it like that for the summer, but winter was going to be a problem. Well, we were practically in Canada. Still, that was a few months away—no point overreacting.

I'm not proud to say I was back to drinking MD 20/20, but it was so cheap and easy to get that it was hard to resist.

I knocked on the window of a car stopped at a red light. I could see some Cleveland State University books on the seat, so I thought it was a safe bet to blag a ride from a student. I asked the guy to drop me at the next drugstore, but he came in with me while I bought the bottle of Mad Dog and then invited me to go for a ride along the shore. Having no previous engagements in my social calendar for the afternoon, I agreed. We drove around, passing the bottle, and he asked if I'd tried any of the blue mescaline going around. I said no, and I guess I wasn't paying attention as he slipped a dose in. I didn't notice I was tripping until I saw the black-and-white floor tiles shrinking and expanding in the foyer of the Hotel Sterling, a flophouse in the heart of no man's—or at least no white man's—land in Cleveland's most depressed inner-city neighborhood.

Next I found myself walking around in circles, looking for a door in a room which appeared not to have one. Oh, there it was—behind the wardrobe with which he'd blocked it off. I was naked, my shoes dangling from two fingers, circling the room and now starting to be pretty sure I was tripping my brains out. Something happened in the shower, both of us now naked, followed by something in the bed, all of it about as coherent as the scene in *Point Blank* where the band is playing while someone's getting wasted under the stage. Tripping was disorienting even in the most controlled conditions, when externals were prepared in advance. On this occasion, I felt like I'd been shot out of a cannon. It was grim but, still, it was my own damn fault: what kind of idiot jumps into a car with a stranger in Cleveland? This kind.

He talked about the Watts riots in LA that he'd been in. I asked him if he'd ever been in love (I was tripping, after all) and he said, "She's dead. Dead. *Dead.*"

At that point I really wanted to leave, but he said if I tried to, he'd do something to me with the lamp cord (involving an electric shock and death, if I remember correctly), and throw me into the alley outside the window. I can only guess that he was tripping too. After a blurry length of time he said, "C'mon, I'll give you a ride home." I wasn't overly keen on him knowing where I lived, but I knew, even in my reduced state, that if I went out on the street in that neighborhood on my own there was a 99.9 percent chance I'd meet up with something much worse, so I accepted the ride. Better the devil you know.

He made me go through my pockets and give him whatever money I had. I handed him a five-dollar bill, saying, "Ah, c'mon— that's all I've got in the world," to which he replied, "Well, you can always get more." And you know what? He was right. Just one of the many perks of being white.

Two days later, I was sitting on my own in the apartment, looking at the sky through the ceiling, when I heard someone coming up the stairs. It was the guy. He wanted to give me my five dollars back.

In retrospect, I think he must have been going to college and trying to better himself, but when I got in his car and he dosed us up with mescaline he must have had a "ghetto" relapse. I never wanted to see him again, that's for sure, but I got the impression that the night we spent together freaked him out as much as it did me. Cleveland and I were not hitting it off.

We were just adjusting to the new open-plan arrangement when the building started to burn. I heard our neighbor, David P. Green, calling over from his balcony next door, "Micky—you'd better get out. Your house is on fire."

David P. Green was black, but not in the mode of most black men in Cleveland. For starters, he rode a bicycle to the factory where he worked, something his fellow workers regarded as a very strange thing to do indeed. Jokes like Q: "What do you call a black man on a bicycle?" A: "Stop, thief!" were about as close as you got to a black man on a bicycle in Cleveland circa 1975.

Green also made bread and would bring over a loaf of his famous herb-and-onion once a week. We occasionally walked up to the corner of East 55th and Euclid of a hot summer's night to lean on a wall and watch the pimp cars slowly cruise by. We had a few theories but never quite figured out what the pillows on the back shelves of those low-riding Lincolns and Cadillacs were for.

We were both fascinated by the pimp culture, stylistically more than anything. What they actually did wasn't what interested us, but how they looked—they had an aesthetic unlike anyone else. We'd observe in silence for a while, and finally Green would say, "Why pillows?" Then we'd walk back up Euclid to Mayfair.

Cleveland pimps must have got their suits straight out of the Eleganza catalogue. They all dressed like James Brown. David P. Green wore dungarees. The rest of black America had left those back in the cotton fields.

As for the fire, it looked like a landlord scam, insurance and all that. It would have been nice if we hadn't all been in the building at the time, but now that it was going up in flames, better to leave, not speculate. I ran out and stood in my underpants and shirt on the street as Micky lowered his paintings and worldly possessions down from the balcony with Dot, Green and I shouting at him to get out as smoke billowed up into the purple and orange Cleveland sky, adding a punctuation mark to the already well-established pollution.

Fire trucks arrived and a crowd gathered to watch; I wished I'd grabbed some jeans or a towel, as I was still bare-legged.

When the fire was finally out we went in to collect our things. There was no way we could stay now with a big hole in the roof and the timbers smoldering. I sat on the floor and thumbed through the "for rent" section of the Cleveland *Plain Dealer*. Once a place has been on fire you can never get the smell out.

·

There was an apartment going just up the road. Not being from Cleveland, I didn't realize the implications of moving into Little Italy. It was a mistake but I didn't know it yet, so I walked up the six or seven blocks to have a look. There was a pizza parlor, Presti's, at the top of the street the apartment was on. You could buy a single slice, New York style, out of a big square pie. I tried one—great pizza. I thought that was all I needed to know.

I called Annie, my old co-conspirator. I hadn't seen her since I'd been back, but it was worth a shot to find out if she was still in town. She was, and agreed to move in—fantastic! Annie was one of those rare people I actually wanted to share a place with. She had a "Don't fuck with me, fellas" personality and was fun.

One of the reasons living in Murray Hill was a mistake was that some of Jack Rabbit couldn't come to pick me up for band practice. Our drummer, Bobby Hinton, was black. Not being a Cleveland native and not being Italian-American, I was unaware of how totally racist the I'ties could be; in Murray Hill, being black was a guarantee you'd get shot at.

My own landlord had done time for that very thing, as someone pointed out after we'd settled in. I'd love to tell you his name—David Chase could write a whole episode around it—but I don't mess with those guys anymore. Not after living there.

One day, I had to have my charming landlord come over to fix a light fitting, and once he was up the top of a ladder I blasted him with Parliament's masterpiece "Chocolate City." The song describes the black takeover of America, all the way to the White House. "God bless Chocolate City and its Vanilla suburbs"; it was one of the musical highlights of the seventies.

The guy next door had a tattoo on his arm that said "Cook," but his wife's name was Cookie. I asked him, "Why Cook and not Cookie?" and he told me, "So's in case we split up I can say I was a cook in the navy." Those guys in Murray Hill were a laugh a minute.

I'd walk up 117th Street to Presti's singing "Time Won't Let Me," the Outsiders hit whose singer, Sonny Geraci, was from the neighborhood. I'd always been a fan of Italian guys as, being Catholic and all, not many of them went to my school. They were fine guys to us, with their Italian shoes and clothes and greaser hair, and were good dancers, too, who could do the "dirty dog" better than any guys we knew could.

But living in their exclusive neighborhood was an eye-opener. If you weren't white you stayed out of Murray Hill. There might as well have been police tape cordoning off the whole area, with signs that said, "If you're black, don't hurry back," or, "Dark skin—Don't come in." It made me extra-keen on shoplifting provisions, as all the locals were racist to the hilt so I didn't mind ripping them off. Of course, you didn't want to get caught shoplifting there, either. So I didn't.

The high point of living in Little Italy was that I found a cheap coffee-maker and you could get great coffee in those shops, and having time with Annie, that was great too. But the clock on the wall was talking.

I found it particularly disturbing to witness the unseemly behavior during the celebration of the Holy Assumption in which a plaster cast of the Blessed Virgin was tied down in the back of a pickup truck, her robes fixed with flypaper creating streamers that floated behind her as the truck rolled her along the street. (I personally found that a little on the distasteful side and I'm not even Catholic. Flypaper—really!)

But the weirdest part was watching everyone run out of their houses after the Virgin, sticking ten-dollar bills to the flypaper—or twenties, or even fifties.

So, not only did the sacred icon have to bear the indignation of being tied down in the back of a truck, but she had to be plastered with "the dirty paper with the ugly faces" to boot. Sorry, call me a religious fanatic, but I think that's the sort of thing that would have had Jesus driving them off the streets with a whip. But then, how can I know that for sure?

Anyway, because Bobby was black, the band had to wait in the car at the bottom of the hill under the bridge while someone came to get me. That in itself was an affront, but to make it worse some moron had left a dead dog in a garbage bag under the bridge. You couldn't go near there for weeks without gagging. Just revolting. It was an all-around shitty place to live. The local kids were little bastards and used to moon Annie and me whenever we went out, presumably because we were outsiders and didn't look like Annette Funicello and no doubt their greaser parents had something to say about us. Then, one afternoon, I called their bluff when they started their tiresome jeering by "dropping trou" to my ankles. They wouldn't forget that for a while—and they didn't.

It all went downhill for me and Annie after that. The little pricks took to riding their bikes back and forth relentlessly in front of our place, yelling, "BOX SHOT! BOX SHOT! BOX SHOT! BOX SHOT!" We were like prisoners in our own home.

The whole neighborhood made it crystal clear that we weren't welcome there. I tried to ignore or at least out-glare my inhospitable neighbors, but we were massively outgunned. They wanted us out, and I certainly didn't want the fuckers to start shooting at me too.

Jack Rabbit was falling apart. Stress's singer, Bill Miller, was out of the hospital, Donnie Baker was going back to Florida, and every time I heard the sound of a Harley I'd dive behind garbage cans or bushes, as I didn't want that lot knowing I was in town—I'd never get out again. Cleveland was all played out for me.

The last straw was when I went for a job in the bar of the Hotel Garfield. I thought I was onto a good thing. It said in the paper that I'd get "$100 per week," which sounded right to me. But the first thing they asked when I started was, "Do you know how to use one of these?" I thought they were going to show me a cocktail shaker or something, but instead the guy opened a drawer behind the bar and pulled out a gun: "You pull this back and then you . . ."

Anybody there could have reached over the counter and got his hand in that drawer, so it didn't inspire a feeling of safety in me. Would I really pull a gun on someone? Seemed unlikely.

I got fired after a week anyway, probably for buying some weed off one of the customers. Well, I think that's why—I'll never know. Of all the places I'd worked as a "server," that place was the one I was least likely to succeed in. It was a number-runners' joint, with the regulars starting on bourbon at eight in the morning—a real Don King hangout. A great big fat white guy, a dangerous-looking fucker, hired and fired me. Only a total imbecile wouldn't have got the picture—I shouldn't have been there in the first place. I'd been trying to look like a student, in a fisherman's sweater, but I would have done better to show up wearing crotchless knickers and a tattoo on my ass that said "Pay as You Enter."

I should have seen the writing on the wall in the first week I spent back in Cleveland, when I'd strayed down the wrong way on Euclid on one of my meditation walks. What a dummkopf! I realized I'd wandered into a strictly nonwhite stronghold, so I went to a bus depot and asked around for some spare change, enough to get a bus out. One or two white business-suited types changing buses looked straight ahead and ignored me.

Everyone else looked more fucked-up than me, so I didn't ask them. I went back on the street and asked some old guy which way took me back to Mayfair. He said, "It's that way . . . but if you go that way, you mos' likely end up in the graveyard!"

Annie had a friend and they were going to get a car and drive to Tucson, Arizona. She'd spent some time there and had an ex-boyfriend who might put us up. It was 2,000 miles away. Would I like to share the driving? Hold me back!

I'd made enough at the Cellar Door to pay for my mic, which I left with Duane. The drive was wonderful. Every mile away from Cleveland was a mile cherished. I'm sorry to speak so ill of Cleveland, but c'mon—the place was a fucking disaster zone. And, anyway, I'm from Akron.

22

IS IT GETTING HOT IN HERE
OR AM I JUST GOING CRAZY?

Tucson was hot, unforgiving and it hated me. I'd left the brutality of Cleveland for dust—literally. Annie's ex-boyfriend let me ride along in the cab of his pickup truck as he went about his daily business so I could jump out at bars along the way and ask for work. Me, the cocktail waitress: a good way to ruin anyone's night.

My last such gig at the Last Moving Picture Show in Cleveland (I keep remembering all these loser jobs I've tried to forget) was proof that I didn't have whatever it takes to solicit tips. The only tip I got then was some asshole telling me I should get a different job.

My dreams of getting a band together now seemed laughable as I sat on a barstool in the dark, waiting for the manager of whatever tavern I was in to emerge from a back room while outside the desert sun zapped the living and inanimate without mercy.

I'd gone from being the singer of a cool R&B band to someone resembling a hopeful who'd arrived for the filming of *Charley Varrick* and been turned away: "I'm sorry, Miss Hynde, we already have our quota of hookers for the Beverly Whorehouse scene." I'd fucked up. I'd panicked—too impulsive again.

First thing each morning, I'd go to the yard behind the ex-boyfriend's prefab, where I would sit and meditate in the dirt. It was far too hot for a lawn to grow or anything remotely green, but I had

to get out of the house, away from the rattling, dripping air condi-
tioner which blasted fake cold air to mask the insult of stale tobacco,
incense, pot and the fuming cat tray—the signature of my generation. To make matters worse, the only thing they played in the bars
where I applied for jobs was country music. I wanted to kill myself.

One night, Annie's ex was driving to New Mexico for a wedding
or something, and said I could come and hang out if I didn't mind
riding in the back of the pickup truck. I stretched out on some old
dog blankets, looking up at the stars in their billions, twinkling and
spinning overhead as we bounced at speed along the dirt highway.
I'd never seen stars like it. Of course, the desert is magic. But it
wasn't my magic.

I felt like a real little prize, one that drops out of a machine after
you've sunk the contents of both pockets into it: a troll doll with purple hair, something bass players used to hang from the headstocks
of their guitars. I couldn't do anything about my situation until I
got some money, unless I could hitch a ride somewhere. California?
Denver? The Arctic Circle? Take me!

And then, a miracle. Annie dropped an envelope onto the
kitchen table and said, "This came for you." A telegram:

COME TO PARIS. STOP. SING IN BAND. STOP.
WILL SEND TICKET. STOP. MICHAEL MEMMI. STOP.

Had we even met? He must have seen me thrashing about in
one of my attempts in the Open Market. Oh, Glory on High—I was
saved! I got the next flight to Paris.

•

I knocked on the door at Avenue Denfert-Rochereau with my
tail between my legs. A whipped dog doesn't cry. I was saved. I took

Kalu out for a walk and prayed to God that I'd never do anything so mindlessly stupid again. I was glad to be back.

Michael Memmi was a crazy fucker who rode a BMW like a lunatic but never came off, at least not when I was on the back. He was a rocker down to the ground. He'd been knocked about in the student riots in Paris in '68, and I think he might have been dropped on his head.

His band was due to perform at a festival—the Fête Rouge. I was the last-minute fill-in for another singer who'd come down with something. We worked up a few songs, covers like "You Can't Judge a Book by Looking at the Cover." All of my well-meaning friends from the Open Market took me aside, one by one, before our big debut to pat me on the back and see me right before showtime. It was speedballs all round: the smack dropped my voice an octave and the coke froze my vocal chords.

I got my big lesson in what happens when you get too fucked up before going onstage, and it was a lesson well worth the trip to France in itself. I never did it again. I never went on a stage in that state again. Oh, maybe once or twice I was a little high on weed, but never again did I get loaded before going onstage.

I knew this wasn't the band I'd been holding out for, but it was still devastating to get on a stage and underdeliver so spectacularly. My powers were so diminished that I knew I was heading for a serious depression as soon as I came offstage.

I was so bummed the next morning, I got Sasha to drive the Merc to a hotel where I'd heard some of the British acts were staying. I needed to see someone English. The French agenda of drugs over performance had worn me down. Not to blame the French—it was becoming *my* agenda.

More than anything, I wanted to see Nick Lowe, whose name

I'd seen on the bill for the festival. Nick was one of the guys I knew from Limeytown. He'd been in a band called Brinsley Schwarz, a pub band. He was a stellar bass player, songwriter and singer, and a bit of a riot in the English band tradition—fun and not French. I thought twenty minutes with Nick would restore my strength—but Lowe he was gone.

Sasha and I hung out in the hotel cafeteria for a bit so I could at least take in whatever was left of the Limeys. That's when I first saw them, Chris and Nora.

Chris Spedding was one of England's great, unsung guitar heroes, a die-hard Elvis fan who loyally wore a quiff whatever the stylistic trend *du jour*. The woman he was with looked like one of Sabrina's troupe from the Alcazar; German, blonde, not a kid—probably Sabrina's age, late-thirties—and dressed in a fifties' Hollywood-type glamour outfit that sat nicely next to Spedding in his Teddy Boy gear. To see them, you wouldn't know what decade or country you were in. Nora, in her tulle skirt and stiletto heels, looked like she was about to step onto a yacht in the Med for a drinks party in 1954 or '64 . . . or '74. Obviously, we had to talk to them and invite them back to the apartment in Denfert-Rochereau.

Nora was totally at home in Sabrina's theatrical surroundings—Sabo, in turn, delighted in having someone to show his designs and scrapbooks to. Cabaret was nothing new to Nora. Chris, Sasha and I, die-hard rock fans, talked bands, and Chris stopped by the next time he was in Paris and we forged a friendship.

I'd reached my limit, like Waldo Jeffers; the band I was searching for wasn't to be found in Paris. Once again, London was calling.

23

MICK'S GRAN'S

It was right before it all started to kick off. You could feel it brewing like the ions in the air before a storm; I made it back just in time. Malcolm invited me along to see a band rehearse. They called themselves the Barracudas. That's where I first met Mick Jones, who had "I want to be a guitar hero" written all over him.

Bernie Rhodes, who had been silk-screening shirts for Malcolm, was there. Both Bernie and Malcolm had ideas to manage, nurture or even create a band. My money was on Malcolm, but they would both get there in the end.

The next week, Mick had me come over to his place where he lived with his gran on the eleventh floor of a tower block overlooking the Westway (which, as it so happens, I can see from the window where I'm writing this now). I would get the Tube from Clapham South to Royal Oak, and his gran would make us beans on toast while we put our song ideas together.

It became a regular thing, and I really looked forward to it, especially the beans on toast part, my favorite English dish. It was a joy to get out at Royal Oak and walk over the bridge carrying my guitar, knowing I was doing it, really doing it.

Mick and I would swap ideas but I wasn't really sure who I was in all of it. I had the idea of a band like a motorcycle club: out-law, outside, antiestablishment. The goal was modest, just to be able to play in a little band somewhere, somehow. I wasn't sure what I sounded like as a singer and had little faith in my guitar playing. I used the guitar to write, but would I say I was a guitar player? No. I didn't think I qualified as a musician. But we were on the brink of punk so, you see, I was in the right place.

The funny thing about my unyielding desire to be in a band was that I really had no idea what I was going for. I just knew it had to be hard, not soft. I never liked soft things. Hard for me, every time: tea, strong; coffee, black; ice cream, frozen not melty. Rock? Hard, not soft; aggressive, unapologetic, masculine—that was it.

How I would fit into that scenario, I had no idea. It would have to be something that transcended gender. Rock was masculine but its listeners were feminine. It was never gender-restrictive—men loved to see a woman play guitar; they always had. I'd have to figure it out, as I didn't want to be a waitress again.

I wanted to play rhythm, not so much because I thought it would be easier than lead, but because rhythm turned me on. I'd never once been tempted to play a single note. Chords, for me, three, less is more. All that R&B and James "I don't know K-Rate but I know K-Razy" Brown I'd been gorging myself on was exclusively reliant on rhythm. Someone had to hold the fort. Like sex, if the rhythm changed, even fractionally, the mood was lost.

James Brown was a tyrant, fining his musicians, but I under-stood him. Don't shoot your wad—keep it going. Never change the groove.

Chet Baker singing so softly. Neil Young with his girl's voice. Anita O'Day on the soul train. Janis turning herself inside out.

Sarah Vaughan, so sure-footed. Dionne Warwick gliding, always gliding. Dusty with her angel voice. Those voices. Julie London. Marvin. Otis. Iggy.

It was nothing you could be taught, coming from inside and upstairs: never black or white; never good or bad. Personal, personality—Him up there, that's who we were all talking to. To address another human was one thing, but a singing voice was capable of so much more.

Romance made you weak and love was about suffering. I wanted what the jazz musicians were looking for: the supreme. I wanted my voice to take life by the throat and rattle it until it made sense. "If you go that way, you mos' likely end up in the graveyard." No, I won't. Don't you get it? I can't not be alive.

Singing was direct—heart to brain to ear. I had to sing but had no idea if I could do it. What did I sound like? I couldn't tell down at the Cellar Door. I couldn't tell at the Fête Rouge. I just had the feeling—blind faith, that's all I had.

Those were the thoughts I'd have as the train pounded out its industrial clanging, winding through tunnels, flying overground into sunlight and disappearing down again: cha-chunk, cha-chunk, cha-chunk, cha-chunk . . . I didn't care where I fit in. I'd happily be an outsider. Those women lining up at the tortilla factory, how were they now? And the Canadian with the blue eyes? Don't think sad thoughts. You're almost there.

I'd get to Mick's, have a cup of tea and take out my guitar: a few chords, where to start? But something more pertinent was bothering me: Mick's hair. I was going to have to get rid of it. Mick was having a bad-hair year, and his hair knew it too. I was just waiting for an opportune moment. I had to be patient because I could sense

Posing on the roof
of the *NME* offices
on Long Acre in London

Nick Kent makes himself
at home under my
collage of heroes at
Englewood Road

Sabrina and Sasha with Kalu in Paris

Sabrina, star of the Alcazar

Singer Marie France, Paris

Vivienne Westwood and Malcolm McClaren

Early Sex Pistols gig. That's me in the corner.

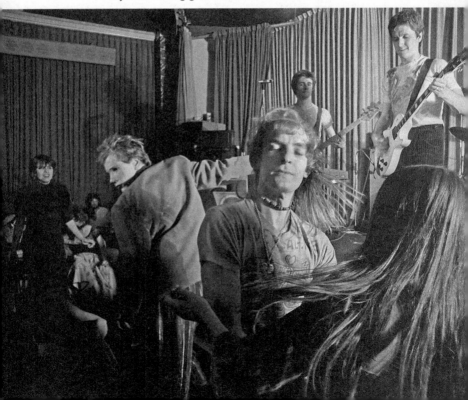

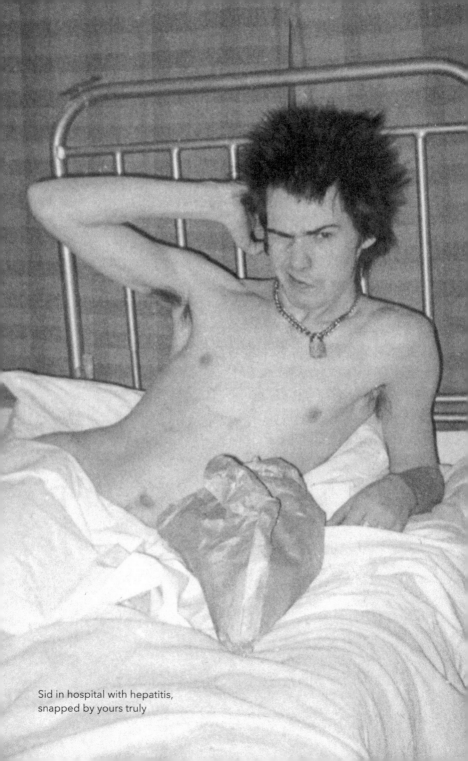

Sid in hospital with hepatitis,
snapped by yours truly

Steve Jones carrying me over the threshold of decency. Paul's seen it all before.

Scabies, Brian James, me on my knees, the Captain, guitar whizz-kid Patrice in the background and Joey Ramone far right

With Marc
Zermati,
Open Market
and Skydog
Records
entrepreneur

Rehearsing
for Steve
Strange's
band the
Moors
Murderers

Lemmy

With Chris Spedding at a Pistols' gig in London, Jordan in background

Don Letts and Andy Czezowski in the doorway of the Roxy

Backstage with the David Johansen band.
On the sofa (*left to right*): Martin Chambers,
Frankie LaRocka, Mick Jones, me and David.

Finally, here we are.
The Pretenders onstage
at Barbarella's.

that Mick was very sensitive about his hair. This was still in the days before I realized all guys were very sensitive about their hair.

I finally lost it, launched into a tirade and he relented. I got him to sit on a chair and went at it with a pair of his gran's kitchen scissors but he kept trying to squirm away to have a look in the mirror and make sure I wasn't taking too much off. Honestly, what a girl!

He remained unconvinced until a week later, when a gig review in the *NME* referred to "a Keith Richards lookalike in the audience." It was Mick in my haircut! *Now* he was pleased, silly sod.

Mick told me about a fight he'd had with his girlfriend. "Ignore her," was my advice. I knew what hurt a woman. When a woman said, "Leave me alone," she meant, "You're not paying enough attention to me"; when a man said, "Leave me alone," he meant, "Leave me alone." I would coach Mick on how to slip the dagger in.

The good thing about working with guys was that they rarely talked about emotional things. I liked that. I was trying to contain my emotions, not inflame them.

The songs were coming along, even if it didn't feel like we were going to make rock history—but, you know, we were trying. Mick had a few good tunes and my specialty was to toughen them up, or so I thought.

Bernie was lurking in the wings, and I knew he wasn't in favor of me at all. At one point he even suggested we call ourselves Big Girl's Blouse. Fuck off, Rhodes!

It all went south one day, when in walked this pretty boy with spiky hair carrying an album sleeve for the Sensational Alex Harvey Band that he'd designed—some kind of art project, or maybe just his own thing. I didn't think he had that student thing about him. It was a painting of a tramp passed out next to a brick wall. Alex

Harvey was worthy of legendary status at that time. Good choice, but never mind that—what was all this about?

I could see straight away where this was going. Mick wanted this kid who couldn't even play to be in the band. I didn't want to be in a band with a bunch of pretty boys. What happened to my motorcycle-club-with-guitars idea?

It was obvious that they were perfect for each other, and I was the odd one out, so I stopped going round to let them get on with their pretty-boy ideas. Within a week they had hooked up with the singer of the 101ers, a pub band who played down the Chippenham Hotel near the Elgin Avenue squat (a kind of headquarters for hopefuls); a guy my age who went by the name of Strummer. Joe Strummer. Shaken. And stirred.

Mick's song "I'm So Bored with You" morphed into "I'm So Bored with the U-S-A!" (referring to the Vietnam War). Nice touch, Joe. Strummer was turning the band into a banner-waving gang of social-conscience freedom fighters. Right on! And there was no denying that pretty-boy Paul Simonon, with his arty aspirations, was proving to be an asset. All that Jackson Pollock stuff *and* he came up with the name: the Clash.

Okay, so I was wrong. Strummer put the aggression in and the songs were better with me out. Good call, Mick.

·

Steve Jones had come up in the world. Malcolm, too. The Sex Pistols were getting gigs and people liked them. Malcolm was acting as their mentor/manager and, with Viv, he now had a band to dress and feed ideas to. Johnny Rotten (named after the state of his teeth) didn't need much in the way of ideas; he had plenty himself.

They looked like Alex's gang of droogs times ten. Steve was

playing guitar and it was thrilling to see him finding himself—still a thieving delinquent at heart, but now with a creative outlet.

The Pistols got a studio and headquarters which doubled as Jonesy's pad behind a shop on Denmark Street, home to most of London's music publishers and music stores. I was round there one day, Jonesy and I having tea and a sarnie in the local sandwich bar, Batista's, when I spied a flamboyant-looking character, Philippe Sallon his name, and on a hunch asked if he knew where I might find work. "Try St. Martin's—the art college next door." I did, and it got me through the next year or so.

I modeled regularly at St. Martin's for the fashion department, in my modified street clothes, standing still for twenty-minute slots while looking longingly at my guitar stashed in the corner. Frustrating, but I could collect my £7 at the end of the day, enough to get a bus and have something to eat. (Those fashion students couldn't even draw.)

My other job was cleaning houses, which was the first time I met someone from the "upper" classes.

"What should I call you?"

"Well, my name's Christine."

"Oh, that won't do. My daughter's name is Christine. Have you got a middle name?"

"Ellen."

"Ellen! Oh, dear. I don't like that. Elaine. I'll call you Elaine. Elaine, you can start upstairs."

*

There was already dissent within the Pistols. John tried to undermine Glen Matlock's performance every show. Glen was a good bass player and helped write the songs, but Rotten was ferocious and intent on caving Glen's head in with a mic stand. It was only a matter of time.

Steve was also wary of John's malice, but Paul Cook, the best drummer ever to come out of Shepherd's Bush, helped keep things in place. John had a few sidekicks but Sid was his protégé, and more of a doer than John—a doer of violence. Sid was always game for a spot of thuggery, the perfect entertainment for Rotten. Hence the title "Vicious." It would take only a nudge and Sid would have a length of chain out, clearing a dance floor, a pinwheeling threat to anyone who was in the way (including Nick Kent). The formerly well-respected denizens of English rock were getting pushed aside by a bunch of punks. All that was missing was a score by Ludwig Van to complete the Burgess-prophesized scene.

Johnny Rotten was a strange brew. He looked like Steptoe crossed with Joni Mitchell, was a fan of Van der Graaf Generator, and his singing voice, if you could call it that, sounded always on the brink of tears—tears of mirth, pain, outrage and frustration. A mesmerizing presence onstage.

*

I moved into a squat on Caversham Street. Pride of place was given to the Japanese Les Paul copy Sasha gave me and a practice amp Spedding had lent me. I got a little padlock at the hardware store on Chelsea Green near Halsey Street, where I cleaned for another woman and her RAF husband. That cleaning agency would hire anybody: I even got Rotten a few jobs with them. Imagine seeing him come through the door to clean your house.

The little lock with the "R" on it offered no security to speak of—if you had a screwdriver you could pop it off like a bottle cap—

but at least I'd know if someone had been in sniffing around my guitar and Spedding's amp. Sid put the lock on a chain around his neck and I don't think it ever came off again; not for sentimental reasons—he just didn't take the key. He also never wore socks under his heavy engineer boots, and no shirt in the winter. Comfort didn't seem to be his thing.

I got Sid to come along to St. Martin's to model a few times, and the other pretty one, Alan Alan aka Alan Drake, was another face you'd see. We called him the Barbie Doll Kid because he was so pretty. Those fashion students got the cream. It would show up thirty years later when the influence of punk was revisited on the catwalk.

·

I invited Spedding to come with me to see the Pistols one night. He wanted to get in on the scene but was way too accomplished a musician to be able to downgrade to punk. His solo albums had come out at exactly the wrong time, just before punk kicked everything that came before in the teeth. The pop-rock sound of his records got flattened in the crush, although I was grateful for the chance to sing backing vocals on them. (I wasn't a backing singer, but then I wasn't a journalist, either. I'd blag whatever I could.)

The Pistols were playing the 100 Club and they did not disappoint. The whole show was chaos. John collapsed to his knees in tears while singing "No Fun," then crawled off the stage, legged it up the stairs and ran out onto Oxford Street. Jonesy was so pissed off that yet another show had ended in one of John's tantrums that he yanked all the strings off his guitar. When Rotten, after sneaking back in, realized that Steve was rendered unable to play, he jumped back onstage, grabbed the mic and announced the next song, fixing Steve with his inimitable evil stare. Now Steve was the one in tears. Rotten could be a real little bastard when he wanted to be. The show was over.

Spedding had watched in stunned silence as the audience merrily spat, or "gobbed," as was the parlance of the time, at the band. It was nothing like a Roxy Music show, one of the bands he'd been playing in.

After the debacle John was desperate to get out before Malcolm got to him, so I told him I was with a guy who had a car and he, along with some other stragglers—Rat Scabies among them (that's where the gobbing started: Scabies gobbing at Jonesy, Jonesy gobbing back and everyone joining in; the one thing I hated about punk)—all piled into Spedding's Chevrolet Camaro.

Off we sped to the Last Resort all-night restaurant in Fulham. En route, we passed some poor sod bleeding on the pavement. There were always fights on the streets of London outside the boozers, like a sport—the old ultra-violence.

"Pull over!" I yelled, and Chris screeched to a halt. I bounded over and cradled the guy's cracked head in my lap until an ambulance arrived, and then got back in the car and on we went to the restaurant, where everybody ordered tons of food and drink and left Chris with the bill. All in all, it was a good introduction to punk.

Eventually, Spedding ended up recording the Pistols' demos. Chris Thomas, who I met while singing on two of Spedding's albums, went on to produce *Never Mind the Bollocks* (and later the Pretenders). Rotten eventually went on to marry Nora Forster (the only lasting love story to come out of punk that I can think of), and Ariane, Nora's daughter, went on to be the singer of the Slits.

So you see, that gig in Paris, the disastrous Fête Rouge, had legs after all. Funny how seemingly insignificant things sometimes turn out to be links you can't see at the time.

.

I was starting to need more than links: my visa situation was now a constant source of high anxiety. But I couldn't leave London, not now. What, and go back—to where? Paris was too rife with drugs and, anyway, I'd need to get a visa to stay there too. Akron? Oh, dear God, no. Cleveland? Just kill me now.

I was illegal, scrounging, suffering from severe band-deficiency and having real problems staying in the country. I knew they were no longer going to give me a "leave to enter" visitor's stamp in my passport. The next time I went to leave, I might not get back in.

I'd been going to Paris on the hovercraft (a fiver if you were under twenty-six), borrowing some cash and returning a week later, getting a fresh "leave to enter" stamp. But the last time I'd tried it, after borrowing a couple hundred quid off Sasha, the customs official at Calais clocked me, saying, "Didn't you come through here a week ago with £7 and a guitar?"

Imagine remembering me among all those travelers? I guess that's what those guys are trained to do. I had to hitch all the way back to Montparnasse.

My situation meant I couldn't get a job, so I was doing dumb shit to get by. Some girl I met in Paris had a plan to do a traveler's check scam, so we hitchhiked to Amsterdam, went straight to the famous Paradiso club, met some guys who got us smoking smack with them, got real fucked up, stayed in the club all night, then thumbed back to Paris, where she reported the checks stolen. I thought it was all too much hassle and dropped out of the scheme. I didn't want to be questioned and have to lie, or get turfed out of France once and for all because of some flaky girl. I also "lost" my passport and got another one, hoping to start over with no multiple-entry stamps to incriminate me.

Life was becoming one big hassle. Rotten offered to go to a registry office with me and do the unmentionable so I could stay in the country, but as the agreed date approached the Pistols had stirred it up something "rotten" on the nationally televised *Today* show, presented by Bill Grundy when they appeared as guests along with Siouxsie Sioux and other assorted punk rockers. Overnight, they were a household name and all over the tabloids. Jonesy had called Grundy a "dirty fucker"—among other things—when the hapless presenter had asked Siouxsie what she was doing later on that night. I say "hapless," but Grundy was goading them, and they took the bait. It was a field day for the British press—everything they live for. Headlines said things like "Filthy Lucre"; I loved that—so British!

John was catapulted into the limelight as the band's front man. He had expressed foreboding about the way things were heading, and now his premonitions had become reality: he was famous.

Fame was not the name of the game. I don't think anyone particularly thought about it, let alone sought it. The idea was to make some noise and, hopefully, a bit of dosh, but fame was not the objective. Nobody was prepared for it.

So when I saw Rotten in the Roebuck on the King's Road and asked if he was still up for our plan, he buried his head in his hands and groaned, "Oh, Gaaaaawwd."

He was preoccupied with his new status as public-enemy number one. Sid, who hadn't been party to the scheme, darted out of his seat and blurted: "What—what's going on? You want to marry him 'cause now he's a rock star you can have his baby and get his money!"

Everyone was shocked by this weird bit of conjecture. Sid sat back down slowly, surprised himself by his bizarre outburst. In an attempt to redeem himself, I guess, he offered to stand in: "I'll do it! But there has to be something in it for me."

I said I'd give him two quid and it was on. We had to go to Sid's mum's council flat in a high-rise in Hackney, east London, to get his birth certificate, as he was underage. I needed to have him stay at mine so I could make sure he'd get to the registry office in the morning.

There were three of us on my mattress that night, as he was intent on some girl he'd picked up somewhere along the line. All night, I kept getting jabbed by bony knees and elbows. It was like trying to sleep in a sack of ferrets, but I just had to hold out until the morning. I had to get a permanent leave of entry—it was a matter of life or death now.

(The thing about that house was that everyone who lived there was too cheap to leave a toilet roll in the bathroom—real student stuff; you'd have to take your own roll when you went. Chris, the sculptor, tacked an artful poster up in the bog. I couldn't stop smiling later that week when I saw that Sid had torn off the corner to wipe his ass. Sidney!)

Morning came, and we arrived first thing to find the registry office closed for an extended holiday. Bollocks! The next day wouldn't work, as Sid had to go to court for putting someone's eye out with a glass.

A thousand people since have asked about my marriage to Vicious—it never happened.

Malcolm had another idea. He said he'd met a great kid, a drummer, at a party—although he'd never seen him play. The thing about Malcolm was that he really could tell just by looking at someone.

The idea was that I would be standing in the background, seen as a boy, not singing, just playing guitar, with two singers up in front, a blond one and a dark one. Sure. I'd do anything by then. The band was to be called the Masters of the Backside—probably not my first choice of name, but at least I was going to get to play guitar.

Malcolm and I set off to meet the singers. Even going on the train with him was something of an adventure, as he always saw things in an unexpected way. He told me about the singer we were going to meet, a kid he'd found working in a clothing store in the East End: David White, the blond one.

We got the Tube and walked to the council flat he shared with his parents and brothers. He looked the part, but the problem was that he didn't want to sing or be in a band. That didn't seem to bother Malcolm at all. Then we went to Euston and got the overground to Hemel Hempstead to meet the other singer: David Zero, the dark one. This one was more game, the opposite of the other David; he was dead keen on fronting a band.

Some rehearsals were scheduled in a church hall that Malcolm had found on Bell Street, off Lisson Grove. The drummer kid brought along a friend to play bass, who looked totally out of place with long, wavy hippie hair, but he could play. The blond David was a no-show but the other one turned up eager to get cracking. We worked up some songs, including a version of "You Can't Judge a Book by Looking at the Cover," on which I could display my Bo Diddley rhythm technique—my only technique.

Malcolm, Viv, Little Helen and a few other SEX-shop regulars showed up for our "showcase" to see what, if anything, we had to offer. Vivienne was impressed.

"Chrissie, you really can squeeze some chords out of that guitar," she remarked in her ever-surprising Derbyshire accent.

In fact, the Masters of the Backside's debut was probably just as well forgotten, and I never heard from the others again. But the next week, there was a new band in town. Chris Miller, the drummer kid, had changed his name to Rat Scabies. Ray Burns on bass had cut his frankly obnoxious hair (offensive even to the hippie in me) and was now wearing a nurse's uniform and going by the name Captain Sensible.

David Zero manifested something you could describe as a Gothic-Elvis-meets-Nosferatu look—and changed his name from Zero to Vanian—and I'd been replaced by a good-looking guy who could play a damn sight better than me called Brian James. In fact, without me, they were probably the most musically accomplished punk outfit in town. Ladies and gentlemen, I give you the Damned.

Sid had only been playing bass for three days and was in a band with Keith Levene—the Flowers of Romance. One night, uncharacteristically deep in thought, he announced, "I've got really bad news. John asked me to join the Pistols."

He couldn't just walk out on Keith, could he? I mulled over the news for a minute and said, "But it's like you already *are* in the Pistols."

We looked at each other and didn't talk about it anymore. He walked out on Keith the next day, because he already *was* in the Pistols.

24

DAYS OF PUNK AND POSES

The squat on Caversham Street in Chelsea was just a stone's throw from Margaret Thatcher's house on Flood Street. Mick and Keith both lived a few streets over, near the river on Cheyne Walk. Location, location, location.

Coming from the USA, I had never heard of a squat and was incredulous when someone tried to explain what it was to me.

"What, you mean you can actually break in and live there?"

"Yeah."

"You can break the lock and move in and you won't get arrested?"

"Yeah."

"But what about the guy who owns it?"

"If it's unoccupied, you can break in and set up the electricity and gas and live there legally, just paying the bills, and put your own lock on it."

I was finding out that England had almost nothing in common with the USA. Unemployed yet able-bodied student types could claim welfare, called "the dole," and anyone could break into an empty property, set up house and stay there protected by the law. You could also get medical assistance, including dentistry, for free on the National Health Service.

I was constantly imagining a couple of comic or sci-fi writers at the end of the fifties, stoned on weed and speed, trying to outdo each other with outrageous scenarios of the Beat world of the future. It was called England.

I would hear people complain about the trains running late—people who had never bothered to learn to drive and never needed to buy a car to get to work to pay for the car—or complain about waiting to get an appointment on the free health-care system. To an American, it was just unfathomable that these services even existed.

My dad's voice, always a ghostly presence: "Christy—you don't get something for nothing. That's breaking and entering; don't you know that?"

But to me, living in a squat was like winning the lottery. Anyway, it was a given that, whatever I was doing, my folks would disapprove—I only mention it to illustrate how vast the English–American cultural divide was.

A friend of a friend knew a low-key junkie who didn't want any trouble. He let me in and showed me the empty room at the top of the house. I guess I passed inspection because no one asked me to leave.

There was a cool, very bohemian couple who seemed to be somewhat in charge: Billy and Rae. She was over six feet tall, a beautiful Australian, and he was even taller, a handsome American intellectual. They had a baby and went out every day to a free concert or exhibition, making the most of living in London with a copy of *Time Out* at the ready, opened to the free-events listings.

One day, there was a dispute in the house about something and the junkie was told to "Clear out!" by Billy. "You can't tell me to leave—I have as much right here as you do!" cried the junkie, to which the tall American said, "Oh, yes I can, because I'm bigger than you." And with that, the dispute was settled, law-of-the-jungle style. Normally, I would side with the scrawny underdog, but this time I liked the common sense of the quiet American.

I painted my room and found some junk in skips to use as furniture; I taped a brown bag from a fruit-and-veg stall around the overhead lightbulb for ambience, stood back and saw that it was good.

There was only the one toilet, out back through the courtyard. All those London townhouses were like that, built for workers a hundred years earlier, which was absolutely fine with me. Bathroom? How passé. Being on the top floor meant taking out a bucket and emptying it into the street every morning. No problem at all— the price was right.

There was a public baths on Chelsea Manor Street, nearby. For 40p you could have your own cubical, big bathtub and all the hot water you wanted for an hour.

Rotten stayed over once or twice while wrestling with his impending fame. We'd walk and talk, a little like me and Nita back in Akron. He was shy but funny—troubled, though. A troubled youth.

Another friend I met in Malcolm's shop when I was working there. She'd walked in, all arsey in a tailcoat, wearing a top hat. I was in conversation with Malcolm and could see her behind him as she took a T-shirt off a hanger, tipped her hat, popped the shirt in, replaced the hanger and then replaced the hat, all in a split second while keeping her eyes fixed on mine.

We left together and became big pals immediately. I didn't really like her ripping off Malcolm, but what finesse! She was the worst of all the drug fiends I'd ever met, often covered in scabs like something you'd expect from radioactive poisoning, but a laugh—a one-off. She was born to be a rock star but far too fucked up to pull anything like that off. She and I often stayed up for two nights under the green lightbulb installed at Caversham Street. Pill heads.

I had some French rockers stay for a few weeks—a rare talent named Patrice Llaberia, who I'd met in Paris, and some of his marginal friends. Patrice was a hot-shot player, the type of which you only encounter every ten years or so. These types are amiable enough about the mundane, but they aren't paying attention to ordinary stuff—politics, religion or society—they don't bother with opinions as those things don't concern them. Playing guitar concerns them. Life for them begins and ends with the guitar. That's the kind of guy you want in your band.

I found a rehearsal room on Lots Road. It was £3 an hour, and I could just about scrape that together as I was willing to do anything quickly and discreetly if it meant an hour's rehearsal. But Patrice *et ses amis* were eventually forced out of London by the appalling food and general frustration of not speaking English. He did make an impact on the London scene in the short time he spent in it, though, and I know that for a fact because, after the Damned saw Patrice catch fire in our rehearsals, wilder and with more panache than any of the London boys, the Captain visibly upped his game.

25

MOPED MANIA AND WHITE RIOT

The Roxy on Neal Street in Covent Garden was the place where we gathered every night to watch bands who, even if they couldn't actually play, put on memorable shows. Don Letts was the resident DJ.

I first met Don when he was working in John Krevine's shop Acme Attractions in the basement of Antiquarius on the King's Road. I wandered in one afternoon to find a wonderland of old stock: button-down collared sixties shirts, fifties wire sculptures, African masks, vinyl American car seats, Jamaican flags and zebra rugs.

Don was a professional Black Man, in much the same way the English were professional Englishmen when they went to the States in the late sixties, getting jobs at radio stations or clothing stores on the back of an English accent. Don's accent was dreadlocks, leopard-skin waistcoat and dark sunglasses, which never came off. He really looked the dog's bollocks: Rasta Four Eyes!

I asked him if he played anything and he told me he played bass, the cornerstone of reggae. I took his number, and first thing the next morning I called him, hoping to set something up. Jeannette Lee, his girlfriend, who looked like a perfectly formed miniature porcelain doll, answered the phone. She sounded surprised when I asked for "Don the bass player" because he'd been lying out of his ass to impress me.

Judy Nylon and I designed T-shirts, one of our many small-time money-making schemes. She'd write the text and I'd draw the corresponding portrait with a Magic Marker, then we'd sell them to Don for the shop. Nylon and I looned around the King's Road, pooling our resources; if we had enough, we'd buy a box of Dunhill—never No. 6. We weren't trying to save money—we had class.

Most of our T-shirt designs were inspired by *Evening News* or *Evening Standard* posters, which I unclipped and liberated nightly from newsagents. The corridors in Englewood Road were lined in them, Caversham Street too; all my places were.

Judy, the brains—me, the brawn; that was us. A typical design would boast a picture on the front—such as Keith Relf, the Yardbirds singer—with the day's news headline on the back—"Pop Star Found Dead." Relf had been electrocuted while playing an ungrounded guitar. One design I was particularly fond of featured a portrait of Nick Kent on the front, and a recipe card for how to cook a turkey on the back.

Nylon was an exotic giant of a beauty from Boston, or maybe Florida. She had platinum-blonde hair cropped to an inch of its life, and wore tiny striped T-shirts and trousers held up with suspenders. She was an intellectual who favored medical texts. She had a high-cheekboned, model-type face, but when she smiled she turned into Howdy Doody, in much the same way Iggy went from brooding street-walking cheetah to Alfred E. Neuman.

Nylon was my introduction to Patti Palladin, another American. Patti was from Brooklyn, had a smoky laugh, a dark wit, was devoted to the Rolling Stones and drove a Morris Minor done out like a Puerto Rican ride. I felt like white trash around those two big-city players.

One day, I took Nylon to Caversham Street and said, "Check this out."

I plugged my guitar into Spedding's amp and proceeded to thrash out the chords to "The Phone Call," the song I was working on. The look on Nylon's face! I could read her mind—she was thinking, "If this hilljack can do that . . ." Before you could say, "Key of E," Patti and Judy were doing gigs as Snatch, recording albums on an eight-track and startling everyone with their super high-end glossy artwork—all done in-house.

I, meanwhile, continued to peer out from under bus shelters in the rain, guitar by my side, looking for a band like a hunter having his prey chased away by animal rights saboteurs.

While I was busying myself going nowhere, Sasha had taken up the drums and was in a crazy little outfit with a couple of French girls, PoPo and ToTo, calling themselves the Lous. They came to London and were knocking around the scene, with the city now the main breeding ground for bands.

Every rag-trade merchant wanted a band to manage and every record company had a subsidiary label to sign the punk hopefuls to. The Lous and a bunch of other loose ends parked themselves with Sebastian Conran at his dad Terence's elegant Nash house on Albany Street, Regent's Park, where the newly formed Clash hung out.

Sebastian had a café racer, and with me riding pillion we'd zoom through Regent's Park, past conker trees with their candelabra-like blossoms, and weeping willows, their sad branches dipping into the ponds where the Queen's swans competed for space with lily pads.

The English liked speed of any description and didn't have the roads to accommodate the big hogs American bikers rode. Sebastian's little brother Jasper would be sewing all day down in the kitchen and I happily joined him. Everybody was making their own clothes, but Jasper Conran had loftier ambitions than ripped-up cast-offs.

Another player on the scene, Barry Jones, had me round to his basement flat in Maida Vale one day and we swapped song ideas, knocking out R&B chords, but when he flatly stated that he didn't like the sound of the female voice singing rock, I could only agree with him. I think Barry got in a band with another hopeful, Steve Walsh, but it's hard to remember because everybody was at it.

.

I moved into Don's house in Forest Hill, which he shared with Jeannette and a bunch of mates of similar Jamaican background—Leo, J.R. and T. Jeannette's friend Janice had committed suicide there, and I got her room.

The guys had dragged their mattresses into Don's room because they were too scared after Janice's death to sleep on their own. I was reminded of something Duane had told me back in Cleveland in case I ever got mugged by a black man: "Pretend you're either crazy or seeing something, because black guys spook easy and they'll run off." I couldn't resist looking over Leo's shoulder, pretending to see something, just to test Duane's theory.

"Oh, Chrissie, mon, don't!"

I did it at least once a day.

Don was a regular "wide boy," the term the English used for an all-around hustler. He had all the cool state-of-the-art gear: stereos, Ford Zodiac, hundreds of albums and every new gadget going.

His album collection was as definitive as a WMMS playlist, but when he took his New York punk albums to play down at the

Roxy, the punters told him to put them away because everyone only wanted to hear reggae. The Roxy, apart from the live acts, was a reggae club—whose patrons were predominantly working-class kids in modified clothes and haircuts, which got weirder and weirder. The music you liked defined your identity more than race or class; England was tribal like that.

The guys, second-generation Jamaicans all, worked behind the Roxy bar. They sold spliffs under the counter, while Don was in the DJ box next to the stage and I'd be right in front, where I could see the bands up close. We were always stoned, watching the bands, none of whom had any fear or shame about not being able to play and got on with it defiantly.

I'd look over to see if Don was watching what I was watching, and sure enough he'd be as amazed as me and we'd crease up, crying real tears of painful laughter.

One night, as a band left the stage I asked one of them if they were using their own tuning. He looked at me as if it was perfectly normal and said, "No, we just don't know how to tune our guitars." I loved that.

Don had schmoozed a woman who then bought him a camera, and he ended up shooting the definitive Roxy film. I was never featured in it myself, as most of the time I was shoulder to shoulder with him holding up the heavy light (you're welcome!). You see Shane MacGowan before he went Irish, a London punk in a Union Jack shirt, pogoing—priceless!

Every night after closing, we'd pile into the Zodiac and I'd say, "You guys ought to get in a band." It would go all quiet and I realized that, like everyone else, it was exactly what they were dying to do. Eventually, J.R.—the genius of the house—taught Don and Leo how to play. T could already play drums and they would become the Basement 5, a reggae band in the spirit of punk.

It was in Janice's room that I wrote "Private Life," which Grace Jones eventually recorded with our heroes Sly Dunbar and Robbie Shakespeare. (I remember the first time I heard it in a club in Germany on tour with the Pretenders—a stand-out moment.) My room was a sanctuary, as no one would come anywhere near it. Joe Strummer took it over after I left.

•

I was back in a guitar shop on Denmark Street, a regular hangout of mine, where I'd go to imagine owning one of the guitars during my breaks from modeling at St. Martin's. I'd loiter for a while and then buy a plectrum. I was always losing them, and I swore that one day I'd have them stuffed in every pocket. (That's why I use orange ones—you can always find them.)

I saw a card on the noticeboard: "Bass player seeks groupie."

I went to a call box and gave it a shot: "Do you mean groupie or group?"

"Well, both," said the voice at the other end.

I got the train to Thornton Heath and met Fred Mills, a talented bass player and pianist. He had a mate, Dave Bachelor, who played drums. We worked up some of my Mose Allison rip-offs, and it was the closest thing I'd got to having a band.

I named us the Unusuals, although we never got a gig so we never got to use the name. I referred to them as the Berk Brothers after Fred pointed to a photo of Charlie Watts on an old single of the Stones and said, "He looks a right berk."

It turned out that Captain Sensible lived nearby—they were

all mates. I referred to the lot of them, collectively, as the Croydon Express, which Fred, for some reason, loved.

I'd regularly get the train to Thornton Heath with my guitar. We practiced in Fred's parents' front room, in a terraced house which, if I remember correctly, had copies of the *Daily Express* lying around. Some nights I'd stay over on the sofa, and we'd often go to the Captain's and have a feedback free-for-all in his parents' front room.

They were all in awe of the local Croydon legend, the already mythical Johnny Moped. They'd each played in bands with Moped, but he would habitually disappear for weeks and months at the behest of his girlfriend, Brenda, which everyone thought bizarre—not because he would disappear so much, but because Brenda was forty.

They gave me a tape of his "I Hate Students" and "London to Brighton Moped Race" and then I too was smitten, but I never got to meet the elusive Moped himself. He was always on the missing-persons' list.

The only time I actually got onstage at the Roxy was with the Berk Brothers when we did a version of "Baby It's You" changed to "Johnny It's You," me wearing a cardboard pirate hat I got off Fred's little brother. I used the name "Sissy Bar," although I doubt any of them got the reference to the passenger's backrest on a motorcycle. They probably didn't understand what I was doing there at all. And I admit, I was—as usual—the odd one out. I was getting used to that. But every band needs songs to play and a shitty original is still better than a good cover—and I had some shitty originals.

We went a few times to Andy Czezowski's rehearsal place, where he stored old jukeboxes under one of the railway arches in Rotherhithe, but the Unusuals' fate was to be another in a persistent line of misfires.

One day, while browsing through *Sniffin' Glue*, the punk fanzine

we all read, I saw an ad for a band: "Guitar player wanted for Croydon based . . ." Hang on a minute! I called the number and Fred
answered. They had failed to tell me that I'd been sacked. Fred said
I was the only person to answer the ad.

The Unusuals' story went on to have a happy ending when they
found guitarist Slimey Toad and somehow corralled Moped himself.
The result was the Johnny Moped *Starting a Moped* album featuring hits like "Groovy Ruby" and the classic "Darling, Let's Have
Another Baby," a pop delight that Fred wrote. A couple of years
later, Fred threw himself under a train. I blame the booze. The Captain would one day name his son after him.

●

While hanging out with Steve "Jonesy" in Batista's, we saw
Mick Jones walk by, grabbed him and went over to Denmark Street.
We had our guitars and the three of us set about making a racket.
Mick's girlfriend, a pretty schoolgirl type, sat quietly on the floor in
the corner watching. So this was Viv—the one I used to coach him
on how to torture.

I met Viv again on the street somewhere and we started hanging
out. It was like a club, everybody wanted to get in a band. As far as
I knew, Viv didn't play guitar, but she wasted no time learning. One
summer evening, we were walking down the Fulham Road. Viv was
in a contemplative mood and said, "Chrissie, the Slits have asked
me to be their guitar player." The Slits were one of the most exciting bands in town, with the fearless Ariane—who Strummer called
"Ari Up," as in "Hurry Up"—as their singer; a cool-looking Spanish
girl, Strummer's then girlfriend Palmolive, on drums; and a sultry
English-rose type, Tessa, on bass. Viv was undecided: "I don't know
if I want to be in an all-girl band."

Viv Albertine obviously was the missing link. To add her to the line-up, a buxom blonde schoolgirl type wearing a crotch-revealing miniskirt would turn the Slits into the kind of band that Russ Meyer would have wanked himself stupid over. Rock and roll is all about gimmicks, after all. Who cares if you're girls or garden gnomes, as long as you've got a sound and the world's attention.

The Slits went on to make one of the stand-out albums of the day, the first truly punky reggae album, with a famously unforget-table cover—bare-breasted, slathered in mud, wearing grass skirts.

Everyone I'd ever met in my whole life was now in a band. I now had absolutely no hope that it would happen for me, but I was so used to failure that, like a cart horse en route to the glue factory, I just kept going.

I bumped into Paul Simonon at Dingwalls in Camden and started hanging around with him. (I guess I didn't mind a pretty boy, after all.) The Clash were about to embark on their first tour, White Riot, and Paul invited me to come along.

It was a blast to travel with my old buds on their bus, steal-ing pillows out of hotels, getting wasted and just lapping up being on the road for the first time with a great band. The audiences, mostly blokes in Mecca ballrooms and university halls, went ballistic nightly as the paint-splattered foursome hammered out their aggres-sive brand of political punk rock. Britain was caught up in pogo mania, and to stand in the audience watching my mates tear the place up was exhilarating. Except for the gobbing part; Joe looked like a statue covered in pigeon shit after every show.

Joe Strummer was a ringleader, always the one to commandeer

the troops. He and I crawled out of a student union in single file on hands and knees one afternoon, we were so drunk. It was paramount to him that everyone was having a good time at all times, but he was quietly thoughtful and truly concerned about social injustice. He had the most activist mentality of anyone on the scene, but thrived on gang participation.

The Clash was a band of and for rogues, and I loved to see them getting the whole nation behind them. I'd always found watching a band inspiring, leaving a venue fired up with resolve to get in a band myself. The Slits were actually to join the tour as the support act. I still had no band. I left the White Riot tour tail between my legs feeling like a dog not allowed in the house.

.

I'd found a rehearsal room in the basement of Eddie Ryan's drum shop on Langley Street in Covent Garden through Chris Brown, a drummer I tried to get something going with, but I couldn't even find the £17 a month to pay for it, and I was soon in arrears. I knew I was going to lose it if I didn't find some readies soon.

I had a mate, a drug fiend who used to shoot up using the water out of public toilets, and I don't mean the sink—I mean the toilet.

"Oi, Chris—come in and hold the door shut for me."

She'd dump the contents of a Seconal or some bullshit she'd copped straight into a dirty syringe—no cotton, spoon or lighter for her, waste of time—and plunge the needle into the back of her hand while I tried not to barf. Nothing could satisfy her insatiable need, which cost money, but she was in no shape to get a job—too fucked up even to stand in line and claim the dole. She told me she went to an Arab for money. I didn't ask what she had to do—she got the money. Not my first choice, but my options were getting thin on the ground.

I owed two months' rent to Eddie Ryan. St. Martin's only paid £7 a day, cleaning jobs no better. Think, think, think . . . I heard the payphone ring and flew down the stairs to answer it.

"Is that Chrissie?" the voice at the other end said. "My name's Tony. A few people have told me about you and I thought you might like to come to my office and we could meet."

Game on.

Tony Secunda was an entrepreneur and creative mastermind of the UK music scene. He had been involved with the Move, Marc Bolan, Steeleye Span and a bunch of others, and always lent a madcap bent to proceedings, guaranteeing publicity and raised eyebrows.

So when punk bludgeoned its way onto the sagging seventies music scene, I can only imagine how much it put his considerable nose out of joint not to be part of it. All the irreverent "up yours" mannerisms and ploys of punk had at one time been Secunda's personal domain. But now he was on the outside looking in.

Well, that's what happened when punk came along. Everything that went before got thrown onto the rubbish heap with no respect or apologies. So when someone told Tony about an American girl with a guitar and an attitude who'd been skulking about on the scene for some time to no avail, he must have thought it might be his way back in.

My problem—part of a long list—was that I did not want to be solo, a singer-songwriter on my own, in any shape or form, or do anything at all other than play guitar in a band, write songs and sing as part of a band setup. Being the sole focal point was not the plan.

I'd been about as far down in the food chain as you could go for long enough to see no reason at all to compromise my ambitions. As Dylan said, "When you ain't got nothing, you got nothing to lose." Compromise was not a word that fit into my worldview.

Jake Riviera, the debonair smoothy and brains behind Stiff Records—"If it ain't stiff it ain't worth a fuck"—had even called me to say that Nick Lowe had played him an early demo I'd recorded of "Precious" and wanted to know if I'd like to join the Stiff roster.

"I'll let you know when I get a band together." I would have loved to have been part of Stiff—you bet I would—but on my own, under my name? No chance.

Tony Secunda had only heard me thrash out the chords to "The Phone Call" in his office on the little Spedding amp while staring him down with a defiant glare. He had not heard me sing, or seen anything that he could use to big me up to a record-company exec. To his credit, Tony humored me—he paid off the £40 I owed Eddie Ryan and took me around town in his little Fiat as his new protégée. Tony truly was as mad as a March hare, and would bypass traffic by mounting the pavement in his tiny car and to hell with any pedestrians who might be in the way. I liked his daredevil attitude and he liked to display it to someone who appreciated it.

Tony had plans to put me on the map. He pointed out a billboard that overlooked Shepherd's Bush roundabout and told me my face would be on that soon. He loved grandiose, attention-grabbing, in-your-face stuff.

I was furious! I wanted to be *in* a band, not singled out. How many times did I have to say it? But the truth was something more than that. With his ambitions it seriously dawned on me for the first time that if I continued my quest, fame could follow in some form.

It's one thing to admire rock stars and imagine how great it must be to live like them, but to really get inside the possibility of total exposure was daunting. I went back to my room, sat on the foot of my bed and cried. I saw my freedom slipping away.

But being in Tony's orbit was fun and he knew some of the coolest London movers and shakers. Keith Morris, the photographer, was one of his mates I especially liked, with his blue Lancia, his flat in St. Mary's on Paddington Green and his general knowledge of all things interesting pre-punk. He was the guy who'd taken all those photos of Bolan in Anello & Davide pumps with the little strap (that Debbie Smith had tracked down and sent away for). I liked being with people older than me who didn't live and breathe only punk—people from the sixties!

But despite Tony's cool friends and all the larking about, there was something missing, and that something was coming from my end. I was all talk and no action; Tony had taken me under his wing and I could tell he believed in my potential, but so far I had offered potential only—where were the goods? He kept broaching the subject of a demo. How could I make a demo without a band? It would mean a session band, and that would be more solo than I was willing to bend to. Tony put it like this: how could he get interest from a record company if nobody—including him—had ever heard anything? Even I wasn't sure what I sounded like. I had to concede to his logic.

I agreed to go into a small studio and record a few of my songs, and found a bass player and drummer to go in with me, with an engineer. One of Secunda's pals, John Cale, former member of the now-defunct Velvet Underground, was in town and they were hanging out. I didn't want anyone in the studio so I told Tony to stay away and let me get on with it. But I needed to record the "pips," the sound you used to get on a public phone before you put your coin in: the sound you hear on the first demo and subsequent album version of "The Phone Call."

I arranged for Tony to call me from a pub and, as if by magic, the pips fit perfectly in the intro of the song. Because Cale was with Tony when he placed the call, he told everyone that John had produced it—typical Secunda! Name-dropping publicity monger! It certainly sounded better to say "a John Cale production."

So now I had a demo with "The Phone Call" and "Hymn No. 4" (a song inspired by Rotten's dark moods and the Mighty Hannibal). Then I met Steve Strange.

He wasn't called Strange yet, though. He was just some kid from Wales who accosted me one night in the Vortex—the club on Wardour Street that had taken over after the Roxy's demise. He came over to where I was leaning on the bar with a bunch of song lyrics written out and paper-clipped together, and started singing his songs a cappella. I liked his shameless determination, singing like that with such unself-conscious belief. And the songs were good too; all about underworld gangsters, Al Capone, the Krays—famous English villains, mostly—and a stand-out little tune called "Free Hindley."

The Moors Murders had happened before my time, my time starting in 1973 when I arrived in the UK, so I didn't really appreciate the impact a song about Myra Hindley and Ian Brady, the serial child-killing couple, would have, with a chorus imploring the public to "Free Hindley."

In nineteen hundred and sixty-four
Myra Hindley was nothing more
than a woman who fell for a man.
So why can't she be free?
Free Hindley!
Brady was her lover
He told her what to do
A psychopathic killer
Nothing new
So why can't she be free?
Free Hindley!

When Steve asked if I would help him out—play guitar on a few tunes for a showcase he was planning for some record-company guy—I was happy to get on board, mainly because he promised that, as we'd all be wearing bin liners over our heads, no one would know who we were. So I saw no reason to think that this little jaunt would in any way have an impact on my own plans—and I would get to play! Great!

We cooked up some songs in a shitty little rehearsal room under the Waterloo Bridge arches. My mate Jane Suck, who had taken over my room in Clapham and was writing for the *NME*, came along for a laugh. Jane had changed her name from Suck to Solanas in tribute to Valerie Solanas, who was the author of the *SCUM Manifesto* (Society for Cutting Up Men) and, more famously, the woman who shot Andy Warhol. The most memorable part of the rehearsal was that it was the only time I'd ever punched someone in the face. (Jane—after she threw lager all over my guitar.)

The showcase went all right, I guess. Steve introduced us, bin liners obscuring our faces, using alias names. Mine, unfortunately, was Christine Hyndley. The next week, we were on the cover of *Sounds*: The Moors Murderers—Chrissie Hynd, former *NME* journalist, and her band.

I was mortified. I don't think Steve was happy, either. He was all set to garner the notoriety for himself. Then it got all over the tabloids. Steve was overshadowed completely by me, as I was already a known entity after my *NME* days. I was devastated—totally fucked off to have my cover blown after all the effort to keep a lid on my thing until it was ready. And it wasn't even *my* band!

Tony, the master of outrage, was appalled when he saw me in the tabloids. Plus, as my manager, I could see how it looked like I went over his head on this one. I really had no inkling that I'd be implicated or even detected. I just wanted to play my guitar and have a laugh. But, for all intents and purposes in the eyes of the British public, well, I might as well have gone to New York City and started a band called Adolf Hitler and His Girl Commandos, featuring Christina Braun singing "*Mein Führer*—Don't Let Him Be Misunderstood."

Tony was so exasperated after an agitated conversation, during which I launched into some lame defense, that he put the phone down on me. And me being the badass with an attitude that I was, I wouldn't speak to him again. "No one hangs up on me!" I thought. (Although a hundred boyfriends have over the years, and I call 'em straight back. Crying.)

Now I had no manager and was back to square one, though I was now armed with Tony's demo, "produced by John Cale." Ha ha.

"Ace Doran" was a name that Randall Lee Rose had seen written on the side of a truck in Ohio, and ever since wished he could use for something. So when I hooked up with him after a chance meeting on the King's Road (he being the only other Kent, Ohio, escapee in London I knew) and he offered to manage my musical venture, what with Tony out of the picture, I agreed.

It was clear to me that I'd never get involved with the business side of anything—just not my bag at all. Take a tape to a record company and try to sell myself? That was never going to happen. I needed a manager to do that—and all the other dirty jobs besides.

Ace Doran worked in the rag trade so I started selling flannel shirts—old American lumberjack-type gear—at Portobello Road Market on weekends for him. Now I had a job *and* a manager; all I needed was a band.

Ace had been one of Kent's get-down boys. In fact, he was one of the most stylish and well-turned-out guys I'd ever met, anywhere, so I was surprised to see him trying to flog that pre-grunge American stuff. But he was onto something—people bought it, just not from me. Whatever it takes to be a salesperson, I didn't have it.

Ace had good ideas but wasn't really coming from a music-business background. However, working in the rag trade meant that he met a lot of like-minded would-be managers, like Dave Hill.

Hill was working as an A&R man for Anchor Records, a small label whose offices were on Wardour Street, near the Marquee Club. He was always out and about on the market stalls, his interest being mainly Second World War flying jackets; he was fascinated with American things—from flannel shirts to Elvis to, well, soon me.

Ace played him my demo and Dave was interested. He'd started his own small label, Real Records, and had one band on it, Strangeways, some kids from Wakefield in Yorkshire. He was about to take on Johnny Thunders too, who had just left the Heartbreakers.

Hill was so impressed with the demo that he offered to manage me. Nothing else was shaking but the leaves on the trees—but something was about to.

26

LEMMY

I was still kicking around with my guitar, doing menial jobs and trying to write songs in between three-day marathons on speed in and out of some bikers' clubhouse in Eltham, in southeast London.

I'd seen a girl in various toilets and clubs who always seemed to be wearing the same haircut and clothes as me. Her name was Jenny Money and she knew the Heavy Bikers and lived near their Eltham Clubhouse. We were so twin-like we fell in with each other naturally. We modified clothes from local Oxfam stores, writing free-association words with Magic Markers on tightly pegged white jeans and generally hanging out.

Other times we froze in a country house in Whitstable on the coast with a drug-ravaged countess and her makeshift crew of tooth-less ex-cons and aristocrats. They ran an amphetamine/sulphate lab and languished all day in soiled bedding among stray needles, when not organizing scavenger runs to rubbish dumps for discarded ward-robes and chairs to chop up and cast onto the fire, while the genera-tor in the barn provided enough electricity to keep the lab going.

The sergeant-at-arms of the London chapter of the Heavy Bik-ers (I guess you could say he was my boyfriend) asked if he could store something in my room. Don't ask me how I hooked up with them after all my troubles with the club in Cleveland. Unlucky I guess. Drugs.

I ended up with a stolen Trident motorcycle engine in the corner of my room with a blanket thrown over it for two months. (The Home Office would have loved that.) He used to take me for rides on his chopper (whenever it was uncharacteristically on the road), which had no passenger seat so he tied a sponge to the back fender for me. The things I'll do for a handsome man!

I felt like public loser number one. The one good thing about hanging out in the gutter was that there was always someone worse off, so I was staying in the middle, or at least low down in the middle. It's all relative, after all.

.

Lemmy was built like a brick shithouse. He was big, hard and looked like he could only belong to one of the world's more savage motorcycle clubs—except he didn't. He played bass in a band. Pretty much everything a girl like me was looking for.

"Lemme a quid."

The first time I clapped eyes on him was in a shop on the King's Road. We exchanged no words at all. He eyed me up and down, moved in close, dipped the silver tube he wore on a chain around his neck into a plastic bag of white powder, shoved it up my snout, then turned around and walked out. I was up for three days.

Motörhead was the name, and bleeding ears was the game. On-your-feet-or-on-your-knees loud! You'd better believe it. It was no surprise that he too hung out with—a mascot if you will—the Heavy Bikers' Windsor chapter.

I'd lost no time in rooting out anyone who wouldn't be out of place on an S. Clay Wilson greeting card in Limeytown. Why did I do that? By accident, really; I didn't go out of my way to look for it. I must have had some heavy karmic debt and was still making payments. There I was again, making myself as available and useful as an oily rag. It was as if I had come across them instinctively. Or maybe I should say they came across me.

Lemmy and I liked bikes, music and drugs. In this case, the bikes were more often than not off the road; the music was omnipresent, and the drugs were too—and then some. Drugs now permeated everything—it was just a fact of life. A life without drugs was unfathomable: tranqs, speed, downers, smoke, smack too. Cocaine was so expensive that we assumed it must be good—the oldest con in the book.

Lemmy was hip to the trip and didn't touch anything except amphetamines, smoke and Jack Daniel's. Clean living. We liked the same things—we were mongrels with an appreciation for the finer things in life. He was a Beatles fan at a time when the Beatles were like a throwback to a distant, almost forgotten past. He was far more musically knowledgeable than anyone who ever saw Hawkwind or Motörhead would have suspected. He kept it well hidden.

We started, for no reason that I can remember, a game of seeing how long we could reel off dog names until one of us faltered; a momentary lapse meant defeat:

"Champ!"

"Charger!"

"Silky!"

"Window!"

"Bootsie!"

"Fugsley!"

"Alfie!"

"Pronto!"

"King!"

"Princess!"

"Smokey!"

"Shadow!"

"Molly!"

"Mazie!"

"Bruno!"

"Brutus!"

"Lassie!"

"Luna!"

"Sport!"

"Scout!"

"Carl!"

"Hang on, you can't call a dog Carl."

Game to Lemmy.

Lemmy and his band of pirate lookalikes, sexy Latvian shop assistants and Ladbroke Grove goons of all shapes and persuasions snorted lorry-loads of powder and stayed in bed until well into the afternoon, watching cartoons. Lemmy, being the intellectual of the lot and having an interest in the Second World War, would read *Mein Kampf* while cartoons ran with the sound down.

True to the ethos of rock, Lemmy was forever unchanging. It's one of those inexplicable phenomena inherent to rock stars, the opposite of reinvention. Give him a line, put him in front of a one-armed bandit, stand a pretty girl next to him and time stands immovably in the exact place it was two hours or twenty years ago. Wherever he may be, he remains in a pub off St. Luke's Road, the actual location totally irrelevant. Not so much time travel, as untravel.

When punk came along and its followers unconditionally dismissed the bands that had come before, no matter how grand, Lemmy could still hold court and command the admiration of all and sundry. Lemmy was bigger than punk, so if anyone was to be trusted to give sound advice about the construction of a band, he was your man. He might have an idea—he knew all the local bands.

He had recently got out of Hawkwind and into Motörhead. The whole Ladbroke Grove crowd were a sort of bridge between hippie and punk: Tyrannosaurus Rex when Bolan went glam; Powis Square, the centerpiece of *Performance*, was just a hop, skip and a jump from Lemmy's. It was hippies gone into overdrive on class-A drugs all round. Lemmy's turf, and the Pink Fairies.

The punks said they hated hippies, but that was all part of the pose. What they hated was complacency, and drugs only make you complacent if you can get them.

Ladbroke Grove was the domain of antique dealers, drug dealers, hippies, bikers and Rastafarians. When punk arrived, those in mohair jumpers, spiked hair, bondage trousers or rubber gear made a colorful addition to the streets of Portobello and its surrounds. Anyone who called himself a punk listened to reggae, and if you listened to reggae you smoked spliff, without exception. And if you smoked spliff, you went to Ladbroke Grove to score.

There were no other occupants of Ladbroke Grove, other than the odd aristocrat who had found the only way out of the shackles of the class system in which they—and all the English—had been born. Rich or poor—and many aristos were on their uppers despite the prestige of their titles—the only way to drop out was to become a heroin addict. It was the one thing that would ensure certain expulsion from the club of which one was otherwise a lifelong member.

No doubt there were a few scruffy writers slumming it there too like Richard Tull, the protagonist in Martin Amis's *The Information*.

(Amis must have been living there himself at one time, obvious if you read his stories.)

It was certainly the best place to be in London, as far as I could see. I thought it was the best place I'd ever been. I was in love with London, in love with England, and in love with the thoroughly seedy but titillating streets of Ladbroke Grove, the place where hippie met aristo met Rasta met punk, out of reach of establishment trends like fashion and wise investments. I crashed on many a sofa in Ladbroke Grove.

So I walked up the cobbled mews to Lemmy's flat off All Saints Road and knocked on the door.

Oh, boo hoo, I whimpered, hoping he would feel sorry for me and give me something to cheer me up. But he didn't. He was annoyed more than anything. "No one said it was going to be easy!" he smiled.

I was like the student in a Zen fable that the master cracks across the back of the skull with a length of bamboo. Ouch! For once, I had nothing to say. It was true. He was right. Then, to ward off any self-pity sneaking up on me, he put his arm around my shoulder, peered down my shirt and said, "You wanna check this drummer out, calls himself Gas Wild." He went on to describe a Jeff Beck lookalike who could be found somewhere among the dregs in Ladbroke Grove.

Ready, steady . . .

Chris Brown was a drummer I'd met when I had it in my head that a drummer was the first step in finding my sound—drums being the backbone of the sound and all—as I had some weird time signatures going on and wanted something you could dance to that would still be hard-ass. This is how I got the rehearsal room at Eddie Ryan's. Brown knew Eddie, who had a setup making drums, Eddie Ryan Custom Drums, and he let us rent a room in his basement to rehearse. In urban environments, a rehearsal room can't be taken for granted—not like setting up in a basement or garage out in the sticks. Finding a rehearsal place was the number-one stumbling block for most bands.

Chris and I bashed through a few of my tunes, which sounded pretty good with just the two of us but nothing that was going to set the world on fire. We didn't last long, but I kept the rehearsal room.

Sometimes, during a no-fixed-abode period, I would stay the night in Eddie's basement and sleep on a vinyl car seat, although it was cold and scary as hell in those underground caves, which extended way farther than I cared to explore on my own.

I had a Gannex raincoat like the one Harold Wilson famously wore—that I'd got at Laurence Corner on Drummond Street, where everybody got all the good military gear, next to a bunch of vegetarian Indian restaurants. I loved that street.

If I wanted to keep the two-bar heater on, I had to put up with the fluorescent overhead strip light, as they were both on the same plug, so I kept the coat over my head as a black-out blind. I was way too scared to turn the light off anyway. There was a supernatural aura down there that kept me awake.

Covent Garden was largely empty: the markets had closed down, the huge glass atrium stood empty and the place was like a ghost town, apart from the opera house and some council dwellings. I was petrified in the caverns underground there on my own, *Phantom of the Opera* and all that.

One night, I got that supernatural frozen-in-terror thing, so I threw off the Gannex coat and bolted. I ran up Long Acre to Leicester Square and got the night bus to Ladbroke Grove. Vivien Goldman lived above the Coral bookmakers next to the bridge.

Viv was a writer I knew from *Sounds* when I was at the *NME*. She was an actual journalist, though, not a phony posing at it like I'd been. I stepped off the bus to find scaffolding all up the front of her building so, as her flat had no bell, I hoisted myself up to the second floor and banged on the window. She flung back the curtains, stark naked, her Page Three breasts pressed up against the window—an eyeful of a Robert Crumb moment for the two officers down below who were stepping out of their squad car. They watched in silence as I went in through the window. She didn't even wake up.

For the next few weeks Viv let me crash at the bottom of her bed. My party trick was washing windows. I was something of an expert with a bucket of water, washing-up liquid and stack of newspapers, which ensured I was a welcomed houseguest.

It was a Saturday—the day Portobello Road came to life with all the antique stalls and hippies and punks and Rastas swanning around for the afternoon like extras in a Robert Altman film. I was polishing Viv's windows, when . . . bingo! I spied Gas Wild on the Street, just like Lemmy had described him.

I struggled with the sash window and forced it up. *"Are you Gas?"* I shouted over the din of the street.

A skinny rocker in tight jeans, studded belt, biker jacket and white scarf spun around, turning his hollow cheeks up in my direction and yelled, "Yeah!"

"Wanna get in a band?"

"Yeah, but I haven't got a drum kit."

"I'll get you one."

I threw a set of keys down and he let himself in. And that, essentially, was the beginning of the Pretenders.

27

CLOSING IN ON DESTINY

took Gas Wild to Dave Hill's office on Wardour Street. Dave looked taken aback to see me with a Jeff Beck lookalike who was all affectation and swagger and peppered his conversation with the word "baby."

He was a very straight guy, Dave, not like other managers who would stay up till five in the morning in hotel rooms gossiping and getting loaded with other managers. He kept to himself. I never once saw him at the bar having a pint, even. But I suppose after being in Johnny Thunders' world, Wild's slurring and stumbling must have seemed like child's play.

Gas was from Hereford, a town in the West Country near the border of Wales and home of the famous SAS—the Special Air Service, part of the British Army and internationally recognized as the number-one badasses without rival. Hereford is also famous for the magnificent Hereford bull, one of which makes a cameo appearance in my cowboy film of preference, *Appaloosa*.

Gas told me he knew a bass player from home who had just got back from Australia, where he'd been touring with an Aussie band called the Bushwackers. Enter Pete Farndon.

Farndon came along to a rehearsal, if you could call it that with just a drummer and my primitive skills. I won him over with a funky but punky version of "Groove Me," the King Floyd song built around a tasty bass line which he had to pull up to work it out. He was visibly impressed with the crazy time signatures of my originals.

My time signatures, I was to discover, would be considered "clever," although the reason they were unusual—not 4/4, 7/8 or 3/4—was because I couldn't count anything. I was used to guys trying to work them out and saying, "But that's wrong," or, "How do you count that?" to which I would answer: "Just memorize it."

Farndon was a fan of the current punk scene, but he didn't look it. He had a classic quiff and wore a biker jacket. Gas Wild also was right out of step with punk, looking like he did, a throwback to the Keith Richards school of rock, admittedly never completely out of fashion. So the three of us looked convincingly like the motorcycle club with guitars, not bikes that I had long-envisioned—and three makes a band, even if we were a band short of a guitar hero.

We started going down to Eddie Ryan's and it was beginning to feel like something might happen. Pete and I spent a couple days in Eddie's basement attempting to soundproof it. Apparently if you stuck egg cartons all up the walls and ceiling they acted as insulation.

I'd been having serious doubts that this band idea was ever going to happen, but now I had a rhythm section, a rehearsal room, a manager and some songs. (And I wasn't wearing a polyester dress and hairnet and asking some trucker if he'd like sour cream or butter on his baked potato.) My expenses were negligible as I was still crashing where I could and didn't have to come up with rent. I was a low-maintenance number.

Typically, just as we started we began to fall apart. Gas was getting too fucked up. We all were, of course, but when the drummer falls off his drum stool mid-song, it's red-card time. And then we were two.

*

I was still hanging out in Ladbroke Grove, and now crashing at Mick Farren's ex Joy's place. Mick was a writer for various leftist publications I'd met at the *NME*. He was white but had a big afro, which I once trimmed like a bush into more of a Gene Vincent, which he was quite pleased with. He had an album out called *Vampires Stole My Lunch Money*, which I think I sang on. Joy's place on Ledbury Road was just around the corner from the squalid digs of Philthy Animal Taylor, Motörhead's drummer. I wanted Taylor for myself, but that was something I would never have said out loud. Taylor was of the Keith Moon school—a wild man and a showman—but he was the property of Lemmy.

I would never dream of poaching anyone from another band even if I could, but word on the street was that the Heartbreakers had their sights on Taylor. There were always rumors that Motörhead might be splitting up.

If the Heartbreakers had designs on Taylor, well, I couldn't let that happen. (I don't remember what was happening with Jerry Nolan, the Heartbreakers' superb drummer at the time—I just remember the rumor.) I had to think of a way to let Philthy hear what Farndon and I were doing, then in the event of a Motörhead fracture he would at least have had a taste of what we sounded like before the Heartbreakers pounced.

I came up with a plan. We'd tell Phil we needed a drummer in order to hold auditions for guitar players. That way he would only be stepping in to help out, and inadvertently getting a lug-hole of our repertoire. It was a good plan. You have to go by the book once in a while. Now all we needed to do was find some guitar players to act out the charade.

Pete said he knew a guy in Hereford, a local guitar-hero type, who would probably be up for the crack. I asked for a full description and it turned out that the guy was married and had a kid. My face screwed up when he told me that part. Then he added that there was another guy—the little brother of a girl he'd gone out with briefly. He could find out from her if the little bro was around still.

He was dialing the local guitar hero when I reached over and put the receiver back in the cradle. I figured that if we were going to bother with the audition, even if it was just a setup with ulterior motives, then why use a guy who's married with kids when there's one who's unattached? We could kill two birds with one stone.

Enter James Honeyman-Scott.

Jimmy Scott was lanky, pasty, blotchy and blond. He worked in a music store in Hereford. His mother was Welsh, his father Scottish. He had a girlfriend. He liked the Beach Boys, ABBA, Neil Young, Dave Edmunds, Nick Lowe and John Lennon. He particularly disliked punk music, which he didn't find in the slightest bit interesting as it was devoid of musicality and melody. He didn't give a toss about attitude.

I had forgotten about any melody I might have had within; Jimmy Scott was about to reawaken it.

We didn't particularly like each other at first. He probably thought I was just some loudmouth, and I thought he was too smooth a player and was slightly offended by his total dismissal of punk. But making music together would change all that. Jimmy would transform my songs in a way I could only have hoped for in my wildest imaginings, and my songs gave him a platform to be the guitar hero God intended. Still, at this juncture I didn't recognize any of that.

We didn't go through with the deception to poach Philthy as it turned out that Motörhead was definitely not splitting. Jimmy Scott went back to Hereford, without me realizing who he was.

Dave reckoned we'd need some demos so he'd be able to play something to record companies, and we asked Jimmy back for a day to record some of my songs with us. We found a good enough drummer, an Irish guy, Gerry McIlduff, who we'd had down to Eddie's basement once or twice. Dave booked us into Regent Sounds Studio.

I still didn't see it. It was clear that Jimmy could play, but I was too blinded by punk to remember how great a great guitar player was. I had temporarily forgotten the magic of Jim McCarty, Buzzy Feiten, Jeff Beck, Jimmy Page—the transcendental feeling when seeing Mick Ronson blow the roof off the Music Hall that night with Bowie in Cleveland.

We spent a day recording six songs, including a spoof country song I'd written about the drive out to Tucson with Annie called "Tequila and Precious," my ode to Cleveland, a sweet little Kinks cover, "Stop your Sobbing," a revamped, punky version of the Troggs' "I Can't Control Myself," and another one I'd written, inspired by Pete hanging around in pinball arcades, called "The Wait."

I casually waved goodbye as Jimmy got on the train back to Hereford, without thinking about when or even whether we'd meet up again. Then I sat down to listen to the demos. I was stunned. I listened again; the songs had taken on another life. These weren't my songs anymore—they were ours. James Honeyman-Scott was the one I'd been searching for. It was him.

28

IT'S ALWAYS SOMETHING

Now I was faced with my next dilemma: how could I convince Jimmy to leave his home, his job and his girlfriend? Think, think, think . . .

Nick Lowe was everything that punk was not. Jimmy didn't acknowledge punk and neither did Nick, who had no time for "angry." Jimmy adored Nick's music and all the bands that he'd produced, especially Rockpile, Jimmy's favorite group. And Nick was a friend of mine!

All I had to do now was convince him to produce our first single and Jimmy would be incapable of resisting. It was obvious that Jimmy was one of those guitar players who put the music above everything. I wanted him badly.

I hadn't been long enough out of the birthing pool to think logistics yet, but, yes, Nick was perfect for us. I'd been on hold for so long that I was slow off the mark, but this plan was as watertight as a duck's ass and I knew it.

Pete and I took a cassette of the demos over to Nick's, pushed it through the letterbox, gave him just enough time to listen to it and then called him from a payphone in Oxford Street Station.

"Oh, hi! [Nick's "endearment."] I just finished listening to your tape and I definitely want to get in on this Sandie Shaw song," he said.

Glory on High! He obviously meant our version of "Stop Your Sobbing." Good Lord, I thought, he's going to do it.

"Stop Your Sobbing" was on the first Kinks album, and I'd pulled it out of the air when we were in rehearsals at Eddie's, surprised that no one had heard it before. Never mind that it was the one song I hadn't written—of course Ray Davies was a million times better songwriter than me—Nick was in, which meant we'd get Jimmy.

I tried to contain my excitement as I dialed the Hereford exchange. Jimmy answered but didn't give me a chance to speak: "Before you say anything, I've been listening to the demos and I want to be in your band."

·

The next week, we went into Nick's studio, Eden in Chiswick, and recorded "Stop Your Sobbing" backed with "The Wait." Under pressure from Pete, I gave half the songwriting credit of the latter to him, even though he'd had no part in the writing—he'd just suggested a key change during the solo. Jimmy took me aside and said, "Don't *ever* give your songs away!" He was pissed off about it and thought Pete was bullying me, using the fact that we'd slipped into a romantic liaison to get around me.

It seems like a trivial thing to mention at this stage, but songwriting credits are the number-one reason bands break up. Well, that and girlfriends.

Our first single, A- and B-side, was recorded in a day, but we forgot to add the backing vocals, which Jimmy had sung on the demo, as we were in such a hurry. Nick sang them himself after we'd gone—what an excellent touch, having the man himself on our record! Elvis Costello, who Nick was also producing at the time, was hanging about with Nick after we left and suggested repeating the "Stop it" on the chorus.

Jimmy's virtuosity and range was becoming increasingly apparent. He claimed not to be a fan of solos but, if egged on, could knock one out of rare magnitude. He used a chorus pedal and was the master of rhythmic arpeggios—nobody else had a sound like his. Even his humor came through in his playing. That was the other thing about Jimmy—I was getting to understand that he was the funniest man I'd ever met. He could have me crying by just pulling a face and popping his false tooth out.

He oozed melody and I was remembering how important that was to me. On the odd timing of the ragged "Tattooed Love Boys" he later admitted that he'd just been hanging in there. Because he couldn't count it, he just followed the chords, adding chiming notes and hoping it would sound like he was on top of it. The results were magic and he let rip with a stand-out solo. Anything he came into contact with was imbued with melody, including me. He just had the magic. He played all the right stuff and never more or less. When he played he became fully alive in the mode of a true guitar hero. How this rare diamond appeared out of the rolling hills of Hereford is anybody's guess. How I managed to locate him is mine.

It transpired, as coincidence would have it, that two years earlier while I was staying at the house on Englewood Road in Clapham, Jimmy had been staying with a Welsh guy in the house next door. I remembered hearing someone playing some sweet guitar and wondering who it was. I could hear his unique sound floating over the gardens and into my room; he had been near me all along.

His mum and dad came from the same places as the Hynde and Roberts families respectively: Dunfermline and Caerphilly. He would one day get married on my parents' wedding anniversary. I don't usually place too much meaning in little coincidental things, but they seem to point to everything being in the right place. I know I'd been searching for him for a long time.

James Honeyman-Scott is the reason you're even reading this because, without him, I'm sure I would have made only the smallest splash with my talents—probably nothing very memorable.

The four of us, Jimmy, Pete, Gerry and I, worked up a set but still had no name. Dave got us a tour—some gigs in France, including a show at the Gibus Club in Paris. We had to put a name on the billing, so we called ourselves Dinosaurs Eating Cars—a description Nick Lowe had used of a sound we got in the studio.

We were traveling around France doing shows, feeling like the Beatles touring Germany. Jimmy, Pete and I were a little gang and the music was coming alive, but there was one thing that didn't sit right. Gerry was a competent drummer, but he was working in another band on the side to pay alimony. He was a couple of years older than us and had other responsibilities, and I wasn't at all happy if anyone had an agenda that took precedence over the band. But that wasn't the main thing; he got the job done, but musically something just didn't fit.

We were all, apart from Gerry, living in Tufnell Park in north London. Jimmy moved in with Pete, who had found the house because fellow Herefordian Andy Watt, a cameraman, was living there: Hereford House.

I was round at theirs most of the time because of the no-men-allowed rule at my place on Carleton Road, which was run by a strict Irish Catholic couple. Plus, it was bloody cold at mine, up in the attic where I had to keep the two-bar heater on at all times and sleep in my clothes, including boots—and still froze my ass off. The Brits were famous for keeping the heat off.

I did write some good tunes in those rooms, though, like "Tattooed Love Boys" and "The Wait." It's well known that adversity is a great friend to the artist as, by the same token, domesticity is the enemy.

Seymour Stein, the legend and visionary who signed a ton of bands to his label, Sire Records, wanted to sign us. Dave realized that being our manager was going to be a full-time job so he forfeited having his own label to look after us exclusively. We would keep the name Real Records, but be on the bigger label Sire, which went out through Warner Bros. Seymour was encyclopedic in his knowledge of music, and he wasn't shy to sing in public. One night, while driving through Manhattan, I watched the cabbie's eyes in the rearview mirror as Seymour produced the most tuneless a cappella version of James Brown's "Prisoner of Love" ever heard. I thought the guy was going to drive up a lamppost.

So we were signed. I'd read about bands popping champagne corks when they finally scribbled their X on the dotted line, but it never happened like that with me. I just wanted to get on with it, bypassing any fuss. I was as happy as the next person to get a deal, but I accepted it in silence and left it at that.

•

We could all see that Gerry was the odd man out. The other two often talked about a drummer they knew back in Hereford who they reckoned would be perfect, but they'd lost touch with him and had no idea where to find him.

Martin Chambers had been working as a driving instructor

and hadn't had a proper job since playing with his band Cheeks in Hereford. It turned out that he was not only living in London, but right up the road in Kentish Town. What were the chances of that? Sometimes things work. Good for Martin, bad for Gerry. I guess you don't get a winner without a loser.

We met up in the Black Horse pub in Tufnell Park. I think Mart thought I was a bit of a dick (he told me he did later, as a matter of fact) because I sat at the bar reading a book, ignoring the three of them while they got on with the obligatory "catch up." I was paying attention, though. We invited Martin to come along to our studio that night. Gerry had a gig with his other band so it was behind his back but—hey! Never mind . . .

We launched in. As soon as I heard Martin thumping away on "Precious," I started laughing so hard I had to turn my face to the wall. When I recovered my composure I turned to face the band I'd been searching for.

．

We had to dump Gerry now. Why is it that there's always something? Why can't it ever just be easy? It was shitty but it had to be done. There's never a nice way to give someone the elbow.

It was the day we were going to the photographer Dennis Morris to have the photo taken for the single sleeve. Gerry was expecting us. When we arrived at his flat in Camden, he was still shaving and getting ready, excited and happy like the rest of us. Jimmy and I waited in the cab while Pete ran up to tell him: "Sorry, mate. It's not happening—we got someone else."

Cold-blooded, but that, I'm afraid, is show business. He got paid for the session but ultimately he wasn't the man for the job. There are no rules in rock, but there is a rule: loyalty. And the loyalty is to the music. We went and picked up Martin, who appeared on the single sleeve. Martin Chambers was born to be in the band. Who could stop destiny?

There was only one detail outstanding. We had the single, we had a manager, we had each other and we had the photo. But we still had no name. The payphone rang in the hall of my Carleton Road lodgings, and I belted down the three flights of stairs to answer it. "We're about to print the sleeve. We need a name!"

Think, think, think. I remembered a story I'd told two nights earlier to Vermillion, one of the chicks who hung out with the Heavy Bikers in London. It made us both laugh.

The story went: I'd been with the sergeant-at-arms, the one I'd been seeing, in the clubhouse in Eltham. He took me into his room and bolted the door. He didn't want any of his brothers to hear. Then he put his arms around me as if to dance and whispered, "Sweetheart, I want you to hear my favorite song."

No wonder he didn't want the others to hear. This wasn't the Stones at Altamont—it was Sam Cooke singing "The Great Pretender."

29

SID, SID!
LOOK WHAT HE DID!

Someone tossed a copy of the *Sun* onto the bed where I was still asleep in the house on Dalmeny Road. "Huh? What's this?"

It seemed that Sidney had stuck Nancy in the stomach with a knife and killed her. Oh dear. Jimmy was undisturbed. He had no time for junkie business, or for anything to do with punk. If it wasn't musical it didn't concern him.

Pete, on the other hand, was duly stunned. He had already embraced his own version of the "Chinese Rocks" lifestyle and was languishing in its thrall.

Me, I was sad to see Sid in the pickle he was in. The only thing good about the story was that it was over. Well, the Sid and Nancy part was.

Normally, in a situation like that (happens all the time), there would be an emotive response from family and friends alike: "Sid? He would *never* do anything like that—not to the woman he loved!"

However, the nonchalant shrugging of shoulders like a Mexican wave making its way across London's punkerage was palpable. No one who knew them was particularly surprised to hear that Sid had inserted a blade into exhibit "N." We were only surprised that he'd stuck it out as long as he had, being half of Sid and Nancy.

Who could forget that shriek, a sound not unlike that of an untrained cockatoo? "Sid—SID! WHEN ARE YOU GOING TO MAKE ME MY FAMOUS CREAM-CHEESE BAGEL? SIIIIIIIIIIIIIIIIIIIIIIID!" or, "Sid—SIIIIID! MY HAIR—MY HAIR! AAWWOOHH! SIIIIIIID!"

Another colleague of mine, a bass player visiting from Paris who I'd brought over to Sid's Pindock Mews hovel to meet/score from the now-famous Sex Pistol, had slammed the door, inadvertently trapping a few of the klafte's peroxided curls in it.

These junkies can't walk through a room without pictures crashing off walls, bottles smashing, ashtrays flying. It's all part of the chaos—smack's poltergeist. But it was an easy mistake to make, what with the harridan hovering at such close-range at all times, making sure that nobody came between her and her pride of one.

With speed and bad intent Sid came flying out of an airless room, thrusting an eight-inch stiletto at the Frenchman's throat. Although only a tiny drop of black blood appeared—the attack poorly aimed—the message was clear: Don't fuck with my woman!

Hey! That's not how we think in the Land of Punk. Sid—what script are you reading from? (I remembered his weird comment about me marrying Rotten for the money.)

Sid looked at me, nonplussed, fartoost. He'd surprised even himself this time. Not because of the knife wielding or the obnoxiousness of his actions, but because of what he had become: pussy whipped, cowed. It shouldn't happen to a dog!

In those last days he was usually far too gone to notice how fucked up he'd become, but that night his expression conveyed a sheepish, "Oops!" An exclamation mark seemed to float permanently over him, conceding to the universal dismay of recent months. He must have been as fazed by his reaction to Nancy's relentless demands as the rest of us were, as he rushed hither and thither to accommodate her every whim.

It had just all happened too fast for Sid. The fame, the drugs and Nancy had merged into one. His face had become a smeared, distorted version of itself, his features twisted by sickness and a lifetime's worth of hen-pecking packed into a few unenviable months.

My French friend stood temporarily arrested by the greeting by knife, blood now trickling down his neck, but by the same token he was impressed by someone even more off the scale than himself. I resumed normal protocol and made the introductions.

The pair of bass-player junkies were more evenly matched than Sid and his American honeypot, but then few men could match that kind of abuse. To show the solidarity of newly forged friendship, both of the boys cut their arms in some kind of weirdo ritual, becoming "blood brothers." Any excuse to get the blade out, the flesh open.

Hanging around the Vicious household with the two lovebirds was not for the fainthearted, and we left young Sidney, his spiked hair grotesquely thick with Vicks VapoRub, to Nancy, who seemed greedily relieved to have her sex slave back so they could resume the all-consuming pastime of perching on the can, constipated or retching, smack's flowers of romance.

As we trundled down the cobbled mews I could almost hear Nick Kent's voice, though now little more than a distant echo, still making a succinct point as only he could, with an exasperated "WHO NEEDS IT!"

The first time I met Nancy she appeared on the doorstep in need of a place to crash. A mutual "friend" had put her onto me. Cheers! I made her a bowl of popcorn, let her have the mattress and moved over to the corner with my sleeping bag.

Nancy Spungen had stowed away with the Heartbreakers and was seeking a husband so she could get a "leave to remain" stamp in her visa. The Heartbreakers, the breakaway faction of the magnificent New York Dolls, minus leader David Johansen, had blown into town and shook up the Roxy audience with an unprecedented move—they could actually play.

Yet, even more than through their musical excellence, they impressed everyone because they were more fucked up than all the Roxy patrons by a long shot. But no one was to be excluded. They were about to break up the dance by switching the drug of choice from speed to smack, and everybody was invited to the after-party. London punk was about to die a death. The Heartbreakers introduced three new elements into the mix which would bring the house down:

1. MUSICALITY

Up to now, punk had not been beholden to musicianship. In fact, it was frowned upon if you played too well—that was getting into prog-rock territory. But even the London punks were impressed with the flair and musicianship of these New Yorkers. It just validated what everybody already knew, which was that, although you weren't meant to say it, everybody had musical heroes and always had done.

Now, for the first time on the Roxy stage was a band that musically—and only musically—had their shit together. Overnight, everyone wanted to get better on the guitar, as is the usual habitude of a musician. But punk was about attitude; musical aspiration would not bode well for it.

Malcolm was prudent in trying to shield his band from learning too much and trying to keep its poet under wraps.

2. ANARCHY, ANYONE?
Here's the heroin!

3. NANCY SPUNGEN
I wouldn't go so far as to say that Nancy was a drug mule, but she could fit a length of rubber tubing, spoon, zippo lighter and box of handy wipes up her flue and still have room for a can of Elnett and a box of Milk Duds.

The Elgin Avenue squat where Sid had learned to play bass—shooting speed and staying up for excruciating forty-eight-hour Ramones-fueled marathons—became just another junkie shooting gallery.

The squat wasn't a crash pad for me, more of a place to hang out and eventually watch the others shoot speed. I didn't share a fascination for needles, and regarded them as one addiction I could do without. There was nothing you couldn't ingest by smoking or swallowing—shooting up was just the cheaper way of doing things. I wasn't that desperate—or at least I didn't think I was. The moment smack arrived it took approximately three weeks for the whole scene to stall and grind to a halt.

Johnny Thunders showed up with his guitar and his habit. He was already idolized—nobody at the squat had known virtuosity before—and, to their ears, the American catalogue was untapped.

"Johnny, c'mon—you must remember 'Pipeline'!" I would

prompt him to dig into his bag of tricks (being the same age and having grown up listening to all the same radio) and he held the room enthralled as he reeled off the AM charts like a card shark dealing hands. He had the look in spades too, the erstwhile angel with bloodstained sleeves, the cowboy saddlebags slung over his delicate shoulders and dark doleful eyes that said, "Feed me."

He'd been all set to play professional baseball but got waylaid by rock and roll, and yet, metaphorically speaking, was still spending most of his time in the dugout. However, apart from the usual junkie characteristics of lying, stealing, cheating and going missing for days, he had a sweet nature that even the drug could not fully compromise. He was looked up to, and with admiration came the inevitable aspirations to emulate him. (That would bode particularly badly for Pete Farndon.)

·

When was the last time I saw Sid? I think it was the Music Machine—Siouxsie & the Banshees. I clocked the noxious duo, who stood out in the crowd as if they had that wavy outline around them that you got in cheap porn flicks.

My first impulse was to go over and say "Hi," but there seemed no point after noting the catatonic, disconnected look that had taken over the spotty face of our old pal, so I kept walking and made my way to the bar.

Five minutes later, after Nancy bade him fetch her some bar snacks, he was standing next to me smiling and animated, just like the Sid of yore, excited as a child on an errand outside the watchful view of Mommy. Then he slunk back to Nancy's side and resumed his pretty vacant demeanor.

Everyone was fed up with this downshift in personality, and

whispered plans were afoot to grab Nancy off the street, bundle her into a van and speed off to Heathrow, dumping her on the pavement with a one-way ticket and a resounding chorus of "NOW FUCK OFF AND DON'T COME BACK!"

But the more his mates implored him to ditch her, the less likely it was to happen. Of course, Malcolm was beside himself with frustration at her Yoko-like omnipresence, which gave Sid even more reason to refuse to budge—all he had left of his self-esteem was his obstinacy.

Now that I had my own band to think about, Sid and the rest of the Sex Pistols had been consigned in my story to "See you later." However, in Sid's case that was not to be.

The Pretenders' first London gig, on West End Lane in the Moonlight club at the Railway Tavern, was a huge deal for us. I mingled before the show with a bunch of mates who'd shown up to cheer us on. It's all the more nerve-racking, hometown gigs, when you have to deliver to people you actually know.

I thought I'd do a Mose Allison, go straight from the audience to the stage, no fuss. It was 8:45. Time to get my skates on—here goes. But, just as I faced to approach the stage, I heard a voice say, "Oh, man, what about Sid?"

I turned. "What about Sid?"

By mutual agreement no one was going to tell me of Sid's death that day, until after the show. Too late now—never mind. I climbed up, plugged in and we were off.

We dedicated a raggedy version of "I Can't Control Myself" to him.

30

MAKING ROCK HISTORY

The Pretenders' first public appearance in England had been at the famous Barbarella's in Birmingham, supporting David Johansen. We were thrilled to share the same stage as the princely Johansen, who we idolized.

It's a strange feeling when you go from listening to, following and looking up to someone, to sharing a bill with him. I felt like I should have been standing in the audience.

Johansen's band was made up of a gang of New York Italians who looked like what the Murray Hill gang back in Cleveland wished they did: suave, stylish and cool, as opposed to thuggish, out of shape and menacing. They all had perfectly sculpted quiffs, and there was a lot of hairdryer action backstage. Pete especially was enamored with them. He wanted to take his place in it but you got the impression that he didn't quite believe it himself, like it was a blag on his part. I didn't notice it much at the time, though. I was too busy feeling out of my depth myself. I never really thought I could pull it off—I just did what I had to do. All I knew for sure was that I was in love with the process. Not in love with the stage like an actor, but like a vagrant who finds a nook at the side to hide in and crash out for the night.

Anything that made me self-conscious horrified me: publicity, press, cameras—even fans, eventually. I figured out that confidence was a bluff. In fact, everything was a bluff expect the actual music. As long as everyone else thinks you know what you're doing, you're practically home free. As far as self-esteem and all the New Age psychobabble stuff, I didn't worry about that. I read the Bhagavad Gita and knew that all that ego and self-esteem stuff was a load of hooey anyway.

I liked that I could buy some cool clothes, new boots and a good guitar. I loved taking my songs to the band and having them transformed. I knew I loved singing, but it took me a long time to feel like I owned it. But I knew it owned me and always had.

The feeling of being at home overrode the rest, and that feeling came with a guitar slung over my shoulder while standing in front of a microphone. Home at last.

The onset of being recognized in public was as squirm-making as I'd expected. I wanted it all, but I didn't know what to do with it. You take the bitter with the sweet, but it's still hard to swallow; like sucking the sugar coating off a pill but not being able to spit it out, and having to keep sucking indefinitely.

I knew to stay in the middle, keep my head down, not let anything get too big—the middle way. You can see it with a guitar tuner when the needle's not bouncing into the red: stay in the middle. I even asked someone once how to remember which side of the road to drive on, and he said, "Just make sure you're always in the middle."

One day, a guy on the Underground platform kept staring at me. I rounded on him in my usual manner and said, "You see something you like?" But instead of backing off and walking on down the platform, he said, "Ooooh. Superstar!" He recognized me and I hadn't seen it coming. What was I supposed to do? Smile and wink? Sign his train ticket? I turned and walked off, feeling like a twat.

I couldn't be aggressive before someone else got aggressive any-more. I never saw that coming. For the rest of my life I would never see it coming.

We did gigs around the UK, but I didn't look forward to shows at first—if anything I hoped something might prevent them, like a meteorite dropping on the venue. I was just scared, stage fright, the same stuff everyone suffers from.

They say that if you're not a bundle of nerves the show won't be good, but I hated the nerves. The feeling inevitably, however, was a bit of a turn-on. Any personal insecurities were compensated for when I saw my magnificent band take off around me: "Look, everybody—look what I found!"

The shows happened and people liked us. The band was magic one night, but inconsistent and shit the next. I never knew what to expect. But that's what's good about a show—the unpredictability. It's sex, after all.

It was all new to us, being in a band and traveling around—what each of us had always dreamed of. All I had to do was sing. Talk about a scam! Nothing to learn. I was part of the crew; I belonged there. I was part of the happening, just like the girl in the second row—the girl that I always was.

We played a lot of student places, university dates. My love of the Johnny Moped "I Hate Students" tape stayed in my head, and every time we did one of those venues I would berate students just for the hell of it. I could see people walking out in disgust, but I couldn't help myself. It's funny how you say things onstage even after you promise yourself you won't. The more I'd tell myself not to say something, the worse it got. The band didn't like it either, but I couldn't stop. I was eventually telling entire audiences to "Go fuck yourselves!" whenever I'd smell a burger van.

The hotels were basic, often with no phones in the rooms, but we didn't care about stuff like that. In England the meaning of "basic" was a law unto itself. Jimmy went down to the front desk in Wales one night and asked if he could get a Coke. The woman at the desk acted like she'd never heard anything so preposterous in all her life: "At this hour? A Coca-Cola? You can't do that!"

"You can't do that!" in a singsong Welsh accent became a band catchphrase. Every band had catchphrases.

Pete told me about a cool reggae band playing down the Rock Garden in Covent Garden. It was a small club and looked even smaller because the band had eight people onstage. Pete was right—they were great. I made my way backstage to see if they'd be interested in touring with us. The sax player seemed to be the most approachable in this tight unit that had a family vibe about it, very exclusive.

I introduced myself and asked in an apologetic sort of way if they'd be interested in supporting my band. They weren't signed so it was a long shot, but worth pursuing. I couldn't understand a word any of them said in their insane Birmingham accents, but they agreed, and the band who called themselves UB40, a reference to the British welfare system, came along on our first major tour and became like brothers.

A favorite story of Pete, Martin and Jimmy's, which I heard repeated often, was the Bobby Moore story. The iconic footballer Moore—Captain of England—tore his shorts during a game and someone ran onto the pitch with another pair while the team gathered around so he could change into them. From the stands as the hushed crowd waited for him to emerge, one Hereford voice rose up over the pitch with a mighty "BARE-ASSED BOBBY IN YA?"

Onstage in London, early 1979

Flight case with every band's dream: our own stencil

James Honeyman-Scott plays guitar

Pete on the tour bus

Dave Hill, Pete and Mart while filming the video for "Kid" at a fairground

Jimmy Scott proudly displays his guitars

Me and Hoover, Scotty in the middle. Here comes trouble.

Jimmy and Mart, Primrose Hill

Me and Ray. Always laughing.

1984

"Bare-assed Bobby In-ya?" I heard that phrase every day for a year and it never failed to induce juvenile sniggering and hilarity in the others.

We got to one hotel, where every room had a speaker on the wall playing muzak, which was impossible to turn off. There was a knock on my door as I battled to find the nonexistent volume control.

"Here to fix the speaker!" said a gruff workman's voice. It was Jimmy. He marched in, wrestled with the offending speaker and finally yanked it off the wall, leaving a tangle of wires dangling, then walked out and on to the next room to "fix the speaker"; he went on down the hall like that until it all went quiet.

When Jimmy started hyperventilating with laughter, he made a high-pitched sound like that of a young girl weeping. He had absolutely no control of himself unless he had a guitar in his hands. If I were to clear my throat or so much as hint that it might be the wrong time or place to let rip with a blaring fart, it would only make it worse. I was excluded from a lot of the schoolboy humor, and was thankful for that.

One of the more embarrassing nights was in a tiny restaurant in Paris. The chef had worked for Jacques Brel on his boat, and was very proud of it. Jimmy farted so loudly it stunned everyone, just as a Jacques Brel song came on and the chef was serving us. We were all of us mortified, especially producer Chris Thomas who was present, and a friend of the chef, who was very sensitive about his beloved and recently deceased Brel. It was obvious that we were all appalled by Jimmy's behavior, which only inspired him. He was so drunk and encouraged by our attempts to ignore him that he rounded the evening off by wearing an ice-cream cone on his head as the rest of us slunk out ashamed, leaving him to his farting and snerking.

You especially didn't want to share a flight with Jimmy. After a few drinks he couldn't keep his hands off a stewardess. "Gee's a go on yer mams, love!" he'd say, as I hid behind the in-flight entertainment guide.

Passing a guy on crutches while driving was another thing you'd hope to avoid. Jimmy couldn't drive but would roll down the window of the car I was driving and shout at the top of his lungs like a Herefordian farmer, "Get out the road, ya bloody git!" sending the poor guy flying.

He was like the obnoxious little brother you were loath to take anywhere. Good at math though.

One night, after sharing the bill on a show with them, we had a dinner with Dave Hill's other band, Strangeways, from Wakefield. (Wakefield produced another medieval-sounding northern accent.) I overheard someone inquire if anyone had "picked up dry cleaning? Any brass in pocket?"

I thought that was a good line.

·

"Stop Your Sobbing" got some airplay and we did *Top of the Pops*, the biggest music show in Britain. Everyone—mums, dads, granddads, dogs, kids and budgerigars—watched it every week, gathered round the TV: a national tradition.

You got all sorts on *Top of the Pops*—the occasional jewel, but more often than not some pretty dodgy stuff. (Now, that was a time you'd wish there were stylists.)

In the UK, everybody listened to the same music as there were only a few radio stations. I was still amazed every time I went into a pub and saw blue-haired old dears inadvertently listening to the

Stones on the jukebox. It was an "all for one, one for all" mentality. When Marianne Faithfull got busted naked, wrapped in a fur blanket with—allegedly—a Mars Bar up her flue, it was front-page news in all the tabloids.

You wouldn't see that in the *Akron Beacon Journal*.

Getting on *Top of the Pops* was the sign that you'd "made it"—well, you'd made it onto *Top of the Pops*. I don't think it counted for anything else, a few more sales the next week, but did it a career make? Who knows, but it was the only chart show there was.

And we did a few kids' shows, including *Tiswas*, where bands regularly got a cream pie in the face. The presenter, Chris Tarrant, pushed one in my face, and it was a stinging surprise to find out they used shaving foam, not whipped cream. It was all in my eyes, burning, and live on television, so I couldn't react.

Another big show in the UK was *The Kenny Everett Video Show*. Kenny was a camp DJ who specialized in being outrageous. We all got dressed up in kooky gear for that, I don't know why, but we went along with it. I held my guitar back to front and had my hair up in some dumb bun, and was dressed in sci-fi gear. Jimmy wore a gay-boy leather cap with a harness of chains and no shirt, exposing his pasty and, frankly, flabby stomach and hairy blond chest. As he walked past the camera crew someone called out, "That reminds me, I must remember to pick up some lard on the way home."

That become another band catchphrase of sorts: "I must remember to pick up some lard on the way home." Yeah, I heard that a lot.

The idea of trying to be sexy was repellent to me, something I'd never deliberately do. Certainly not after one time in Biba's Rainbow Room a few years before, at an Ann Peebles show. That night, I was wearing a rubber skirt from SEX with a pair of fishnets and suspenders under it. I liked that prostitute look, real in-your-face punk, like the New York Dolls, a bit glam. One of Mott the Hoople was at the bar and kept buying me drinks—probably because of the rubber gear. I'd never turn down a drink.

After about five or six shots of Southern Comfort I passed out in a cubicle in the ladies. I was so sick I couldn't pull my leg into my own cubicle, so anyone going into the next stall had to step around it and sit on the can with my leg in between their feet, but for the life of me, I just couldn't move it. I already knew about those goddamn rubber skirts from my time as a cocktail waitress at the Last Moving Picture Show in Cleveland, but I wore it anyway. The hotter you get, the tighter it gets, which is just what you don't want when you have to throw up. I finally managed to drag myself up the toilet bowl and, with a great effort, got the rubber tubing down around my ankles so I could pass out again in relative comfort.

After the venue closed, a big, fat cleaning woman found me and hoisted me up to a standing position. It took ages for her to get the skirt up over my sweaty thighs and stomach. How embarrassing—painful, too. Why anyone would wear bondage gear for pleasure, I never could fathom. I guess that's why they call them perverts.

I never tried to dress sexy after that. Fuck that. Over-the-knee boots was the limit. You know, if Iggy would wear it, I would. (Although if anyone could pull off a rubber skirt, it would be him. But I digress . . .)

The romance between Pete and me had turned bad, as indeed involvement within the ranks always does—something to be avoided in a band like a bad haircut. Our thing had got underway early on and was a total violation of every code in the book. But how do you stop it? Who can? Nobody I've ever met.

You see a girl in a band out there? Any money she's having a secret affair with the sound mixer. There's always something going on, and with the girls so outnumbered . . . well, do the math.

We were dismantling it and dealing with it—a nightmare to do while having to work together, especially with me as the boss. And I was the boss, no messing. That was the one thing I really was good at. I always knew what was right for the music. I never doubted it. That was my main, possibly my only strong point—natural instinct. But laying down the law to the guy you're breaking up with is not something that guy is going to like. Too bad, buddy boy.

I was my own worst enemy, but we were all getting wrecked— it's practically in the job description. If you were still standing and could play your instrument, that was all that mattered.

I wouldn't allow any photos to be taken of me on my own, even though as the singer, which implies "sex symbol," it was expected. But I held my ground. The Pretenders were the four of us, and I was pathologically insistent that we be perceived as such. I hadn't spent all that time resisting walking the plank on my own to botch it up now.

One magazine did get me alone on its cover by cropping the rest of the band out of the picture. I saw it on the newsstand, a big picture of my face on *Time Out*, and went into a black mood that lasted the whole week the magazine was out. No one could talk to me.

There was already friction. When "Stop Your Sobbing" came out, the B-side, "The Wait," got a lot of notice, which was good because we were more of a rock band than "Sobbing" suggested. Plus, it was a good example of my songwriting, along with Jimmy's superlative guitar playing and our sloppy-but-tight rhythm section. But, as could have been predicted, when people saw Pete's name on the credit next to mine they assumed that he wrote the music and I wrote the words. I felt publicly humiliated—it really stung.

It had taken me a long time to figure out how to write a song, long hours alone in a room with a guitar. Pete had never written a song in his life. I was bummed. Jimmy was right about giving away song credits, but the damage was done. My songs weren't well crafted; I knew that. They didn't have traditional choruses or whatever they were meant to have, but I had something unique. Now people assumed I was just the singer/lyricist and that one of the guys was the musical director.

I felt more degraded than when I'd been bounced around a room and roughed up by a bunch of speed-crazed bikers. Much more. Pete had been adamant, and I felt like I'd been emotionally blackmailed, wanting to please him rather than have him reject me. Well, it was too late to do anything about it, and Pete was only too happy to bask in his new status.

He was already showing certain weaknesses of character, exasperated by the imbalance of power, which was inherently in my favor. He had started out by being the life and soul of the party, always up for anything, always a good laugh. Everyone loved him, especially me. He'd accept any challenge.

One day, I dared him to put Tiger Balm under his foreskin and he did it! Who else would try that? (He never did it again, though.)

All the things we saw happening to other bands were now happening to us. It took us by surprise. The "overnight" success; having to explain ourselves to the press, where we were open to be judged, even laughed at—same as we'd so often laughed at others. And the in-band resentments: only a few months in and we were already living the clichés of the trade.

There was a lot to take on board once we got on the radio and people started to know us. You see a guitar hero or front man—a giant of authority onstage, but put him on television, ask a question and he becomes an inarticulate, bumbling know-nothing trying to hide at the back of the class. *Les idiots savants.*

But for the most part we were riding the crest of the wave, and we all felt good. The negative aspects were relatively small. The irony, as is commonly the case with bands, was that we were raging drug abusers but perceived as "wholesome" because of our poptastic, melodic records.

We spent a lot of time kicking table legs, choking on beans on toast, bent double with laughter at motorway stops. I liked being on the inside with these Herefordians, with their stories and shared history. We were having more fun than any of us had ever had before.

You could never get bigheaded about success, not in England. In general, unlike in the States, people were very up front about their dislike of anyone getting successful. One lovely spring morning, when I was walking through Soho, feeling enlivened by the joys of the season, I passed a dustman who shouted loud enough for the whole street to hear, "*The Pretenders are crap!*"

·

Nick Lowe wasn't up for doing our album; he was just too busy. We never had an A&R man. I don't know why, we just didn't. Usually there was someone from the record company to advise and steer a band. Maybe someone at the top thought we were managing okay without it—I was okay without it.

I called Chris Thomas, who'd produced the Spedding stuff I sang on. He agreed to produce us. I never thought to listen to a person's work to decide if they were right for the job. If I knew them personally and liked the vibe, I'd go with it. It had worked so far.

Not that Thomas didn't have immaculate credentials and then some. I just knew I could hang out with him.

Chart positions and reviews were things I avoided. Good or bad, I tried to keep an even temperament and not react either way, and the easiest way not to react was to never look or inquire. I found a good friend in Moira Bellas, who handled the publicity at Warners. She would explain what I was to expect as I went to what, to me, felt like "slaughter," then give me the gist of any press that came out so I wouldn't have to read it myself. I needed someone diplomatic so I wouldn't sink into a depression, knowing I was in the papers; Moira saved me over and over.

Liz Rosenberg, her American counterpart, had the pleasure of watching me have many a meltdown. She'd meet me in the morning if I was in New York City and we'd go to Central Park to walk her dogs.

·

After writing a song, there's first a feeling of elation followed by the sinking feeling that it will never happen again, and you go back to thinking that you can't do it. It creates an ongoing feeling of inadequacy.

I didn't know how to write in a team; I'd been doing it in solitude for so long. There was the occasional collaboration by accident, such as "Brass in Pocket." I heard Jimmy playing a riff I liked, and I put it on a cassette and wrote the song around it. That was a true collaboration. But I didn't know how to sit in a room with someone and say, "Okay, what are we doing?" I would learn that much later.

Mick and Keith, the Glimmer Twins, had churned out stunners year in, year out. I struggled on my own, but it was all I knew.

I moved into a house on Endell Street in Covent Garden, just the next street over from Neal Street, where the Roxy had been. My new housemates were Steve Mann, who typeset *Private Eye*, the satirical political weekly, and Kevin Sparrow, who did artwork for bands—record sleeves such as the famous Stranglers covers and the one for Eddie and the Hot Rods featuring Aleister Crowley wearing Mickey Mouse ears.

Kevin and Steve were perfect housemates, interesting and smart. Steve was a bit of an intellectual, and Kevin had a Keith Richards thing going on, the tooth earring, the get-down haircut. And now they had a little recording artist at the top, in the room next to Kevin's.

Like all my rooms, I had a mattress in the corner and my guitar within reach. Simple. I'd really moved up in the world; I had a single out and an actual paid-for room in Covent Garden. I felt good.

An incessant squeaking noise kept me awake one night. What the hell was it—something in the pipes? I couldn't work it out but hoped to get to the source in the morning. But by then it was too late. When I pulled my mattress out to make my bed I found a mouse, flat as a pancake. It had got trapped under my mattress and I'd killed it! I was horrified as I picked the poor thing up by the tail and took it down to the street to bury it.

The next week, we got a ginger tomcat, the only solution we could think of, and we were all pretty pleased to have this addition to our domestic arrangement. We named him Basher after Nick Lowe, which was what those working with Nick called him: "Bash it down."

It was Christmas Day, 1979. "Brass in Pocket" was riding high in the charts. Randall Lee Rose, aka Ace Doran, invited me to spend the holiday with him and his wife, Laura, in their little mews flat on Rabbit Row in Kensington. We were finishing dinner and listening to records when the phone rang. Randall passed it to me. Who would call me here at this time? I wondered.

It was Steve Mann: Kevin was dead. He'd died on someone's kitchen floor after a combination of whisky and heroin had got the better of him.

I went back to the house on Endell Street and sat there with Steve. We'd been given an eviction notice the previous week, so we had to pack up and get out soon. I noticed that one of the jigsaw puzzles Steve had spent weeks on was broken up and ready for the rubbish. I'd admired that picture of symmetrically placed blue-and-yellow pills, about sixty of them in rows. I'd thought it was quite an achievement to put that together and now it was back in pieces again, which bummed me out, the symbolism of it. Then I saw his jigsaw of the Lone Ranger rearing up on Silver, also in pieces. It was too much to bear.

I went up to Kevin's room. All he'd owned were the few tin toys he collected and a small pile of dirty laundry. I couldn't have anyone finding his laundry like that, so I put it in a bag and went across the street to the launderette. I watched his clothes go round in the machine knowing that he'd never wear them again.

I returned the little pile and shut his door behind me, then walked into my room and looked around. The Sony radio-cassette player that Dave Hill had given me was facedown in the corner. It had seemed so shiny and big, the most expensive thing I owned, at first; now it looked small and insignificant surrounded by all my new boots and jackets. I went back down to sit with Steve.

There was nothing to say. We were surrounded by packing boxes and he'd taken everything off the walls. Our cat hadn't come home for the night. That wasn't like him.

Suddenly, we heard an enormous howl. It was Basher. He'd come in through the cat flap and was running like a dog, tearing from room to room, meowing like mad. He'd never done anything like that before. Steve and I looked at each other, our eyes like saucers. It was as if the cat was frantically looking for Kevin, and we got the impression that Kevin hadn't completely left yet. Basher finished his search mission and belted back out the cat flap. Then silence. We couldn't speak.

We both slept in the front room that night.

Two weeks later, "Brass in Pocket" went to number one. I knew then that victories were always just the other side of tragedy.

.

When "Brass" was released I'd felt a modicum of regret, having said, "It goes out over my dead body," at the first playback. But I had been unanimously overruled, so when it raced up to the top of the chart I could only remark, "See, I told you I was wrong!" Walking down Oxford Street and hearing it blasting out of shops increased my unease. I didn't like that feeling. I wanted to be heard but I could see that containing the outcome and not letting it get bigger than life would be where to put the smart money. Stay in the middle—the *Tao.*

Nothing was going to compromise my freedom to walk the

streets whenever, wherever and with whomever I wanted. I saw fame as being akin to living in a high-security prison, and I didn't want to go there.

How can you win just enough and then leave the table? Go to a Gamblers Anonymous meeting and you'll see it's easier said than done. I'd have to be very careful not to let things get out of control.

I resolutely avoided looking at charts, bank balances, reviews, radio or television appearances, and carried on like nothing out of the ordinary had happened. The last time I ever looked at a bank statement was when I saved the $500 to go to England.

31

FOR THE RECORD

Chris Thomas had taken us into the studio and shown us who we were. The process was obvious after a while, but not at first. We were all over the place. That's what a producer does: one mind on it. If everybody's trying to get their ideas in, nothing gets done. Democracy is just a word used to placate everyone.

The producer spends a lot of time playing psychologist. Late night phone calls from me, panicking, unable to finish a lyric or pleading to change something that had taken seven hours to get down on tape. The band disagreeing about everything. Hungover late arrivals, defensive ill tempers. The list of the producer's peace-keeping duties is endless.

Martin was always a calming presence and arbitrator from within. Chris Thomas himself, who we soon referred to as the fifth Pretender, was highly strung and cantankerous, often more like one of the artists. I was scared of him, terrified of pissing him off—we all were. The tension kept us wound up tight. Chris used it to his advantage to control the sessions like a captain getting a ship through all manner of weather, and it worked.

Basically, the recording process for the album went like this:

The band got in a room together, the amps miked in separate booths. The band played a song and everybody's part was recorded on a different track. The best drum track was chosen or edited using a combination of different takes—the best fill here, the most consistent feel there. This would take some time as the tape op would have to splice the tape with a razor blade in the exact spot, then tape it back together.

Then the bass would be replaced to the edited drums. That's what an overdub is: a guy alone in the booth or the control room wearing headphones and playing along. Then the guitar overdubs. If the drummer played to a click track (a metronome he's got in his headphones), it's easier to edit because the tempo is consistent. Using a click track was not a popular thing to do because it fucked with the ebb and flow of the feeling, but it was necessary sometimes to get the best backing track if edits were required.

Then, everybody was asked to leave while I, silently having a nervous breakdown while frantically finishing lyrics in my notebook, added the part that turned the whole thing into a song. No pressure.

It might be another hour before I'd get a headphone balance I was happy with, but more likely it was a ploy to stall for time. Then I'd sing it five or six times, and Chris and I would comp the best lines together, or get it in one take if it satisfied us—but more likely make a comp.

The songs had been run in and played live, so the whole process could be done relatively quickly. The engineer was a crucial factor: Bill Price was Chris Thomas's right hand.

For the album cover photo I wore the boots I'd had made at Costa's, a little Greek shoemaker in Kentish Town. There had been a bootmaker in Toronto who some of the get-down boys had come back from, wearing block-heeled Faces-type things, and I'd always wanted to do that, design and have my own boots made, so it was the first thing I'd done when I got the band together. That and buying an eight-ounce bottle of Fracas from the shop on Shaftesbury Avenue that had wigs and a big Durex sign in the window.

Oh, and my red Lewis Leathers jacket. I had recently discovered *Enter the Dragon* and fallen in love with Bruce Lee. When I heard that he was dead I went into mourning and painted a black armband on my jacket and couldn't quite get the dye off for the photo.

We walked in off the street wearing what we wore every day. I tried to smarten the guys up a bit. Pete was mindful of how he looked, especially after the gig supporting Johansen's band at Barbarella's. I'd stitched the Triumph badge onto the sleeve of his biker jacket. He liked that.

To be fair, Mart, Pete and Jimmy all had their own looks, just not very good ones. Neither did I. Martin especially planned out his wardrobe to the letter: three-piece suits, the country gent (farmer), or his American football gear for live shows. I couldn't criticize, as I'd had a bunch of jockey silks made up and would go onstage with a riding crop. A football player, a jockey, a biker and a cowboy onstage: we looked like the Village People.

We stood there in a studio in Covent Garden, sulking in front of the camera as Chalkie Davies snapped away. We were always uncomfortable posing in front of cameras. No one rose to it or liked it; we saw it as a necessary evil and nothing more. Besides, the guys were wasted after eating a shitload of marijuana brownies. We'd been in Joe Allen's in Covent Garden for lunch before the shoot, where they were already incapable of getting through a simple bowl of black bean soup without collapsing into insane, pot-induced laughter. And it continued into the photographer's studio.

"C'mon, shuddup, we're trying to do this thing!"

Jimmy farted. "Smell that focker!"

That was the cover.

32

PRETENDERS

The album, *Pretenders*, went in at number one in the UK. Some people said it was hyped into the charts—maybe it was. If so, thank you, John Fruin, head of Warners. The music business? Everyone knew it was corrupt—payola everywhere. Record companies sending in office-worker types to buy up their artists' releases in the designated chart shops. *Top of the Pops* even had a little scam going. You were supposed to (union rules) re-record the song in the BBC studio and mime to that version for the show, but most of the time your plugger, in our case Clive Banks, who held our hands throughout, would show up with the tape in a can and then switch it for the single version just before going on. Everybody knew it and everybody did it.

But with or without the hype, people liked our album and they liked us. *Pretenders* was also a huge success in the States. American audiences revered guitar-based rock, so we were home free with Jimmy, and my being a Yank helped too; Americans like American things.

Dave Hill explained that I should meet some industry people in New York. I balked at the idea but I had to do what I had to do. We wanted a US tour and I had to learn to meet and greet—or kneel and suck, depending how you looked at it.

So I went with Dave, without the band. We got to New York and, to my total amazement, who did I see leaning up against the wall of the Iroquois Hotel on Forty-fourth Street as our cab pulled up? Iggy Pop.

I went to my room and sat on the edge of the bed, dazed to have seen him again. I'd just finished taking off my make-up when Dave knocked on the door. "Iggy is in the bar," he said. I drew my eyes back on and, as nonchalantly as I could manage, slipped down to the bar.

"Hey! This is great," he said, looking like Alfred E. Neuman and shaking my hand. He seemed as happy to meet me as I was him, as he introduced me to his girlfriend, Esther.

In accordance with everybody else who'd met him, I found out that you either got Jim Osterberg, the straight-A Midwestern bookworm, or Iggy Pop, the drug-crazed, platinum-blond lunatic. The guy in the bar that night was Jim Osterberg.

So now I'd actually spoken to him. I took that as auspicious, a good beginning to my introduction back into America. I had, after all, gone straight from Akron to London, so I now felt almost like any English kid in a band coming to New York City for the first time.

I was going to have to go into the offices of Premier Talent the next day and spend a couple of hours listening to Frank Barsalona describe how he'd been responsible for bringing all the big acts to the world and inventing touring. That was going to take superhuman strength, but now that I'd been touched by divinity I was more than equipped.

Barbara Skydel, "the Yiddle," took over and did all our bookings out of Premier; she became not only a best friend, but my Yiddish teacher—me, the shiksa.

"Good evening my shayna maidels! Not you in the third row, you meeskite!"

Barbara Skydel and Liz Rosenberg were the soul of New York City as far as I was concerned. I didn't hang out with the band much on downtime. They wanted to go to bars or record stores. Give me Zitomer with Barbara or Liz any day. We could spend all day at the perfume counter then go to Three Guys for a grilled cheese or blintzes—or both.

Dave Hill hired Marianne Campana in the States to oversee all of our affairs down to the most minute detail. She essentially was our American manager. I could get a proper cup of tea and her home-made Italian stuffed artichoke whenever I was in Venice Beach. She more or less ran the Pretenders single-handedly in the US.

.

The only way to do it right and get a loyal audience was to tour your ass off, and we went for it, especially in the States, which was the essential market to claim if you were serious about staying in the game for life. Like elephants, the Yanks never forgot. A guitar-based rock band could tour there indefinitely.

Weeks on end on a tour bus is something that all guys love. Well, why wouldn't they? After the show, after getting loaded in the dressing room with their guests, the band would climb onto the bus and stay up till three or four a.m., listening to music at a silly volume and getting hammered on the remains of the rider and on the buds that fans had thrown onto the stage, then stagger off one by one into soiled bunks, leaving it to the driver to do his best to clean the bus sometime later in the week. Guys don't mind sleeping in brown polyester sheets for six weeks at a stretch and sharing a toilet with a driver, band and tour manager. I didn't mind it, either.

We all loved it. Anyone in any band loves the bus, no matter how rank it is.

I could never sleep on the bus, and I spent many hours up front in the cab with the driver. Whenever we'd pass a cattle truck in the night I'd get that old wave of horror and indignation—then I really couldn't sleep.

Sleeping in the bunk is an art in itself, a discipline I couldn't crack. The roaring, churning, changing gears beneath and jostling, jerking motion is not everyone's cup of Jägermeister. Passing out certainly helps, rather than trying to read by the little overhead light in the coffin-like bunk with the curtain shut to get you off to sleep. The curtain can't block out the sound of the party going on three feet from your head. Passing out really was the only way.

Sleeping on the bus was an ongoing dilemma and the source of not only insomnia, but the fear that keeps all singers up at night: losing your voice. Rock singers aren't schooled to take care of their voices. There is no training involved in singing rock and roll. If anything, voice lessons or a voice coach would probably work against you, as would anything that might make you sound like someone else.

Distinctive voices in rock are trained through years of many things: frustration, fear, loneliness, anger, insecurity, arrogance, narcissism, or just sheer perseverance—anything but a teacher.

·

The things that really could mess up my voice were lack of sleep, smoking and air-conditioning. The rest was psychological. Opera singers warm up, rock singers light up.

When we finally arrived at our destination, the band would de-bus and go to our hotel rooms after skulking through the lobby, hoping that no fans would be lurking in wait to take a picture. If there were fans, we'd fumble around through our jacket pockets looking for sunglasses while dragging suitcases behind, trying to look cool—belt undone, shirt on back to front, still drunk.

Now was our downtime—time to make phone calls and the last chance to get some sleep. Trying to go to sleep knowing that I only had three hours before soundcheck, probably with drilling going on somewhere close to my room, was tough, and knowing that if I didn't go under I might have no voice by showtime would keep me awake.

Then we'd be off to the soundcheck and dressing rooms, and the little stack of clean underwear that came out of a bag labeled "Band" that the runner (if we were lucky) would distribute fresh from the local laundromat, where he'd spent his morning.

Jimmy would check his pedal board. I would check my mic, "one, two, one two . . ." and Pete his with a rhyme:

Won One was a race horse.
Won Two was one too.
Won One won one race.
Won Two won one too.

The guys, after soundcheck and catering (most likely lasagna if you stipulated "vegetarian" on the rider), would go off to a record store to trawl through the bins for the next two hours. (Lasagna got struck off the rider after three weeks.)

I would rarely leave the building after the soundcheck, preferring to sit in a chair in my dressing room, inert. Every dressing room's the same from gig to gig—as long as it's dark and there's a candle, I'm happy. I don't like to see anyone before a show, so I can have what I call "tour sleep," which is a wakeful state of remaining still with eyes shut and, although not being actual sleep, could fool a fly on the wall. Even though I wouldn't do any kind of preparation, my meditation time—meditating on nothing—was essential and a way of dealing with stage fright.

Half an hour before the show, and everybody would get into their stage gear: the same thing or a version of what they had on the day before. I myself tried a variety of looks, all of which I later regretted.

"*Five minutes!*" was the warning, called out by Stan Tippins, our tour manager. Stan was instrumental in putting the right set list together, and all sorts of other essentials that the public takes for granted, but which can kill the vibe if not meticulously attended to.

The inevitability of it—that's what I liked; the birth and death of it. Then the final knock on the dressing-room door would come before we'd meet up, gig-ready, which meant looking marginally less like one of the crew, but twice as scared.

I'd look around me. Yeah, they were nervous too: Martin like a prizefighter in his robe, punching the air. He had the SAS motto "Who Dares Wins" stenciled onto his drumsticks. Ha ha. Born to it. The other two—Pete fixing his collar, Jimmy just waiting—like dogs at the gate. Who's the hare in this scenario. Me? Naw, they were chasing something, though. We all were.

Then the intro tape, Wagner's "Ride of the Valkyries" from *Apocalypse Now*, sounding like the helicopters were right over head, just to make sure that if we weren't already shitting ourselves, we were now. Coming to the moment, the lights going all the way down. Okay, Mart first, Pete, me next, Jimmy behind me . . .

I'd walk up to the mic ("Hello, Cleveland!") and then . . . hang on, oh yes, there—at the top of the set list: Cincinnati. Of course.

We'd sling on our guitars and I'd be thinking, "This is perfect." The call of destiny; we were home now, standing next to each other. Home. And they wanted us! Then I'd see them. "Oh no, you gotta be kidding—they're up the front again. How many shows has it been—seven? Good Lord!" Well, if not for them . . .

I couldn't help it, I'd already be laughing. Let's do this thing. I'd take the mic and deliberately wouldn't look at them, but they'd know who I was talking to. Here we go: "Are you ready, girls?"

If we didn't have a good show, we'd all be desperate for a drink and thinking of nothing else by the third song to the end of the set. During the final bow it really would be ALL anyone could think of while smiling weakly, or just glaring at the audience for infringing on our drinking time.

There would be a number of factors that could ruin the show for us, starting with sound problems. The monitor man is as important as a dealer to a junkie—our life in his hands. Confusingly, what the audience was hearing out in the hall would bear no relation whatsoever to what we'd be hearing onstage.

For example, I'd have problems hearing myself because all I could hear was the bass. I knew my singing was way off and pitching probably a semitone out, or more, and I'd abandoned singing altogether and was shouting instead. By the middle of the set I'd be so distracted by the strain of trying to concentrate against the wall of noise I'd start to forget lyrics, especially if we'd done the same song for more than fifteen nights running and I wasn't sure which verse we were on.

My guitar playing at that point would be a total load of bollocks. I'd look into the faces up the front and read the cartoon bubbles over their heads, which said, "My nine-year-old brother can play better than that."

After the show we'd meet a guy from the record company, excitedly informing us that "the sound was amazing—I could hear every note." I'd need a drink more than ever then, knowing that the whole audience just heard me crystal clear, singing and playing at my very worst.

Or sometimes the sound onstage would be perfect—we could hear everything and really settle into what felt like a great performance. We'd come offstage with a rare sense of elation, only to find that nobody could look us in the eye because the slapback in the venue made it impossible for anyone to hear anything from where they were standing, and it sounded like I was singing in the wrong key altogether.

There were infinite combinations of the above and we explored all of them. We would know if someone who came back after the show hadn't enjoyed it, because instead of commenting on it they would say one of the following:

"So, where you heading next?"

"Lights were great!"

Or "Who wants a line?"

Another surefire factor in fucking up the night was pissed-off looking fans, especially the ones who'd been at the front of the stage for the last eight consecutive nights. Even if they weren't pissed off, they soon would be when, having traveled a few hundred miles and waited out in the freezing rain, they were greeted by my telling them, "Fuck off!"

I'd be glad they'd come (again), but it would make me self-conscious, telling the same gag from the previous night's show—and the night's before—knowing they'd already heard it. In fact, the only thing that made doing the same songs night after night make any sense was playing them to a new audience.

(By now, the die-hards would be driving back to Ohio, never wanting to see me again.)

I can still remember when Dennis Wilson threw his sticks and fled the stage at the Akron Civic Theatre in 1970. Fuck-ups and things going wrong always make for a memorable show. Obviously, those shows are better for the audience than the band, but that's what great bands are made of. You don't want too many of them, though.

.

On a subsequent visit to New York I again met Iggy Pop, same hotel, the Iroquois, which, back then, he described as: "a dump, but dirt cheap." He seemed to live there.

We ended up at the Empire State Building, two Midwesterners sightseeing. At one point in a stairwell, I leaned out a window and it seemed that, for a split second, he had in mind to take me from behind but then thought better of it.

We wandered the streets, not hand in hand, but it felt like it to me. It was early morning and he hadn't been to bed, so it made sense to buy a bottle. We had to huddle together in a phone booth to drink it out of the bag, as you could not drink on the street like you could in the UK: a stand-out moment in my life.

.

Who would have thought that rock and roll could be even slightly complicated? We are, after all, talking about three lousy chords played by high school dropouts. But the complications are life threatening.

Alcohol poisoning: every band has gone onstage shaking after barely being able to stand up to do the soundcheck. You can see pictures of the gods of rock reduced to mere mortals, passed out on flight cases daily.

There is nothing quite like the looks of desperation and fear exchanged at the side of the stage before the lights go down, with the whole band undergoing the shared experience of total alcohol meltdown. "Can we do this?"

To see grown men, ashen-faced, with the look of the condemned about to face a firing squad is truly pitiful. It's just, after all, a rock show for a few hundred excited girls who work in shops wanting a bit of fun.

The intense feeling of wanting to call the whole thing off, stagger back to the bus and crawl into a soggy bunk and cry would be dashed by the terrifying strains of the intro tape, the smell of adrenaline, and the faint sound of weeping. Wearing looks of resignation, one by one, the band would take their places onstage, the front row gasping when confronted with something resembling a reenactment of *Night of the Living Dead*.

Throughout the show the entire band would be thinking, "Never, never, never again," then leave the stage totally drained, thanking God to have got through it. Some die-hards up ahead would inevitably be waiting, and we'd hardly be able to look them in the eye, mortified that anyone had to witness the messy pile-up we'd just delivered. Yup, they're waiting to say something—probably that they want their money back.

But no, it's a look of pure joy on their faces as they step forward, trying to touch a band member's sleeve and gravely announcing, "That was the best show of the tour!"

Back to the dressing room, sitting in a huddle. "They said it was the best show of the tour and I've seen them at the front every night for the last month."

"I thought they were going to try to beat us up."

The reason it was so good was that everyone had to dig deeper than they ever had before just to remain standing for an hour. And those party to the debacle loved it all the more, having witnessed the sweating, struggling and suffering, thrilled by the validation of seeing someone more fucked up than they'd ever been.

"Thanks for keeping it real" is the highest compliment that can be paid to a rock musician. So, instead of swearing off as you'd promised yourself during every song, the band triumphantly toasts the first drink of the night . . .

There is a code, unspoken, but adhered to by everybody: "What happens on the bus, stays on the bus." Nobody violates the code or goes home tittle-tattling. Being a girl, I never got on the receiving end of the groupie phenomenon, but every single male member of any band has. It really would be rude not to. There is no denying that this is the very thing that motivates most guys to learn to play guitar. A guy on his own facing his sexual future is one thing, but a guy wielding a guitar is a different animal altogether. This doesn't mean that everybody's only in it for the sex—you can get endorsement deals and free strings too.

·

"Get yer hand on my cock!"

I was in a hotel room—I knew that much because I could see the fire-escape route on the back of the door. I was wearing my T-shirt and underpants. Okay, that was a good sign. Nothing had happened, not in this bed, anyway.

But who was Mr. Naked next to me? Hang on a minute—I recognized that voice!

I rolled over and saw the dark blond hair spilling over the pillow. A manly scent rose up from under the sheet. I directed my eyes into his, a sea of green with a bloodshot sun rising.

It was Iggy Pop.

Never had I been so pleasantly surprised in this unseemly, though not entirely unusual happenstance. Are you kidding me? I'd won the Big Daddy Jackpot! I'd been in love with this Class A piece of tail for my entire band life and before. I was categorically in bed with Iggy Pop.

The cock being referred to has been so well documented that I see no point in expanding on it. If you're reading this, you've probably already indulged in multiple viewings of *The White Room*: the see-through plastic strides; maybe you've seen it in person—thousands have. Every rock fan in the world knows as much about it as I do. He's had it out onstage more times than Jim Morrison could say, "I'll get to you next, honey."

The Pretenders were playing the Agora in Cleveland, and I saw on the bill that Iggy Pop was to play the next night. The next day being a day off, I didn't take the bus with the rest of the band overnight to Columbus. I'd catch them up.

He was happy for the company. We'd been drinking Yukon Jack, "the black sheep of Canadian liquors" (as stated on the label), all afternoon in a darkened bar in Cleveland—and no bar can get darker than that. To have him sitting across from me in real life and real time, the glass of liquor, the smoke, the baritone tones of the Swedish-colored lord of sex and rock-and-roll, contributed to it being one of my better days.

He let me come back to his hotel room before the show but made it perfectly clear that if I wanted to hang around from there on in, I would have to keep my mouth shut. This was, after all, his show, not mine. "Don't say one word around *my* band."

I was spellbound watching the most captivating performer of all time. I'd shimmied up to the rafters for a bird's-eye view, never one to shy away from seizing the best vantage point at a gig. (Many times had I crawled on hands and knees to the front of stages through forests of legs so stealthily that I'd be through before anyone had a chance to say, "Hey, fuckhead—I've been standing here all day. Fuck off!")

But I almost fell from my perch and back into the audience when I saw him come out for the encore wearing the red Lewis Leathers jacket I'd left on the floor of the dressing room.

We went on to a local radio station to play some records. (See, that's what I'm talking about: Cleveland radio having Iggy Pop on at midnight to spin records—the best.) They asked me if I'd like to feature a Pretenders song, and I had them play "Tattooed Love Boys" so I could watch his reaction to Jimmy's superlative solo.

"Hey—ha, ha—that's real good!"

We went on to some little club, raging drunk by now, practically incoherent as we climbed onstage, ousting the local band and—me on guitar and him on drums—performed an unintelligible version of "Louie Louie."

Oh, yeah, it was all coming back.

My old helluva-driver friend Hoover was still in northeast Ohio but remained true to form and would drive up to see us play even if we were a hundred miles away from Akron, where she was now managing an Italian restaurant. I called her one day from the West

Coast. Things did not seem to be going her way: a boyfriend wanted by the FBI was only one of her grievances.

"Why don't you come and hang out with us for a few days?" I asked.

"Oh, Chris, I can't. I have too much to do here."

I didn't like the tone of her voice. She sounded depressed, something I'd never known her to be before. I told Stan to get her on a plane and not take "no" for an answer. So he didn't ask her if she was coming or not; he just told her the flight details.

She arrived two days later. I got her on the tour permanently, where she became our first wardrobe girl. Luxury for us—no more washing underwear in hotel sinks—and luxury for her—she got to travel with the crew and not live in Akron. That story had a happy ending. Hoover went on to become one of the most sought-after wardrobe girls in the business, and moved to San Francisco.

We did all the hip television shows in the States, such as *Saturday Night Live*, with Andy Kaufman, and David Letterman's show so often that I used to present him with contraband Cuban cigars I brought in from England.

                                  •

A couple of weeks later we were doing a soundcheck in Orlando, Florida, when a runner brought me a bit of folded paper. Every venue has a runner who is there to run errands for you if you're in the band. Where else in life is the service that good?

I opened it: "Hi. Remember me? I'm in the parking lot. Scotty."

How could I forget? It's another part of getting success; the people left standing on the other side of the velvet rope of fame always think that you won't remember them. People you sat next to in school for eight years will greet you by saying, "You probably don't remember me . . ."

I went to the parking lot and there he was, sitting on the hood of a 1967 Corvette Stingray—a sight for sore eyes. He ended up joining the tour, ostensibly to "help out," but anyone could see it was going to end in tears. It always does. It totally broke the rules of the road, but I did it anyway. I cannot emphasize enough how terribly unwelcome this "tipping of the balance" is to the organization and the cracks became more pronounced by the day.

We had a great time in New Orleans, fulfilling the regulation bar-hopping like a honeymoon for the mentally challenged. The signs were there. It was just a matter of time.

One afternoon, after rolling off the bus in an unbecoming state, we entered the bar of one of the nicer hotels we were lucky enough to stay in, but were turned away as there was a dress code. No problem—we could always find a bar in town. My charming escort, however, decided to involve himself beyond the call of duty. I watched, captivated with wonder, as the thin white fluke sought out the hotel manager standing in the lobby, grabbed him by both wrists and rotated them downward while locking eyes like a defiant seven-year-old. The drinks the manager was holding now saturated his shoes, and within seconds the entire band and crew were ejected from the hotel.

A disgruntled Stan scrambled about for the rest of the afternoon to find us alternative accommodation. It was obviously time for me to make other arrangements for my guest. But I held my ground. Pete, by now, was shooting up on the bus behind my back, no doubt pushed to doing so by the presence of my bad-boy companion.

A night off in Memphis saw another telling incident. The band

and crew were getting loaded in the bar of the sophisticated and popular haunt Friday's, where I decided not to wait in line for the ladies' room, opting instead for the men's. Scotty took exception: "You don't go in the men's room when you're with me!"

"Who are you, my dad?"

We were sitting on our own at the back of the restaurant as staff put chairs up on the tables. Someone told us we had to move. I was in full-on argument mode and took exception to the fact that the guy didn't say "please."

The band and crew, unaware of my distress, were having a merry time when a second fight broke out, this one involving two bouncers, culminating in them standing on me as they waited for the police to arrive.

Handcuffed in the back of the squad car, I forced my hands out of the cuffs, rolled down the window as the officers were taking down details from the security, and said, "Excuse me, officer, I believe these are yours."

The Memphis Police, not known for their ribald sense of humor, dragged me out of the car, recuffed me with my hands behind my back, and put my ankles in shackles too. It was all a bit of a frenzied blur after that, but I guess I freaked out and kicked the windows out of the back of their cruiser.

The night in jail ended with Stan bailing me out in the morning, with Scotty in tow. Dave Hill came to my room, where I was feeling remorseful, my wrists swollen and bruised very badly.

"We're not going to mention this ever again," he said. That sounded fine to me. I wanted to forget about it myself.

I did the show that night, tail between my legs, and, thankfully, nobody mentioned it—or looked at me, for that matter. I think the whole band thought it was bang out of order, as it would have been the first show we would have ever canceled. (I say "would have"—I never cancel.)

But the next week, the incident was reported in *Rolling Stone* magazine for the whole world to see, and I found out that, in the crazy world of rock and roll, embarrassing incidents like that actually bump up your rock credibility and add mythical status to a reputation.

(The most embarrassing part was going back to Memphis for the court case. They dropped the "drunk and disorderly" charge, leaving me only with "destruction of public property." Now, I ask you, why would I have done that if I wasn't drunk? It gave the wrong impression altogether.)

The good thing to come out of that night in Memphis was someone putting "Brass in Pocket" (never my choice) on the jukebox, despite all the mayhem in the bar; I realized that, once again, Chris Thomas was right—this time about keeping the vocal up in the mix, something we'd argued bitterly about. It really did cut through and you could hear it over all the bar noise.

Scotty didn't last much longer. I watched him a few nights later through the back window of the bus, getting smaller and smaller, waving frantically through the falling snow in the dark where we left him on the side of the road at the Canadian border.

33

THE LAST SHOW

We went back into the studio with Chris Thomas, a little less the fresh-faced bunch than before. We'd taken a battering in all the obvious ways—a bit ravaged from all the touring—but it was still early days and we still wanted it. We recorded some songs in Paris, among them "Message of Love" and "Talk of the Town." I felt at home in Paris.

Dave Hill was panicking, desperate to get a second record out, but I didn't have the songs written yet. I hadn't had the time. I thought writing on the road would have happened, but it never does. Every songwriter thinks touring is the place to write and will often set up the back lounge on the bus for it. Never happens.

I rarely ran ideas by the band at soundchecks because I was too neurotic about strangers listening—I'd even had policemen thrown out of the venue before. Unless we were faced with the actual audience, I hated having an audience in or out of the studio.

The management was so desperate to get a record out that they jumped the gun by releasing an EP of the stuff we were working on for the second album. Americans had never heard of EPs (a record with about five songs on it), which were common in the UK. We released it in the US and called it *Extended Play* to let the Yanks know that it wasn't an album, but it was a mistake: they thought we'd gone soft in the head by releasing our much-anticipated second album, *Extended Play*, with only a handful of songs on it.

The band had befriended tennis-player John McEnroe, who was taking Wimbledon by storm. I never joined them, not being a sports fan, so I hadn't met him myself, but knew he was a rock fan and always up for hanging out with musicians—especially the Pretenders, who really were a riot.

One morning, in a cab on my way to Wessex Sound Studios in Highbury, I heard an English news presenter report one of John's outbursts on the radio. He'd shouted at the umpires, saying, "You guys are the absolute pits of the world!" I thought it was funny hearing the very American rant spoken in a proper English accent, and walked straight into the vocal booth and started the song "Pack It Up" with it. John thanked me for it later. Apparently, it cheered him up after getting fined $1,500.

The second album cover caused a ruckus between me and Dave after someone at the record company airbrushed the cover photo. I hated how it looked so glossy and fake. But all the airbrushing in the world couldn't conceal the green pallor of smack that had claimed the face of our soon-to-be-defeated bass player.

After we'd released "Stop Your Sobbing," a publisher sent me a cassette of "I Go to Sleep," the original demo, just Ray Davies singing and playing the piano. None of us had heard the song before. We were enthralled to hear the nineteen-year-old Davies singing this early offering. We recorded it, adding the sultry French horn.

Lisa Robinson and her husband, Richard, were American journalists for *Hit Parader*, and they knew everyone. When we were having "our fifteen minutes" in New York, Lisa called me in my hotel room and asked if there was anyone I wanted to meet while I was there. Earlier the same afternoon, I'd spoken to Dianne on the phone. She'd moved to New York around the time I'd taken off to the UK. She'd been sitting at a table next to the window in a pizza joint enjoying a slice, when who should walk by? Ray Davies. Well, why not? Lisa was delighted to assist. She arranged a rendezvous in a place called Tracks. Later that night, he and I met in the noisy club. He asked if I wanted to go to a newsagent with him, as he wanted to know Arsenal football club's results. I saw him every day after that, whenever we were in the same town, but we were not suited to each other.

We'd always laugh after the fact about the absurdity of our fights, but there was nothing funny about them. We went in New York to Peppermint Lounge one night to see Junior Walker & the All Stars and walked out after a bout of jaw-dropping proportions.

We went to see Elizabeth Taylor and Richard Burton onstage doing *Private Lives*. Compared to the two of us, Liz and Dick's onstage outbursts seemed like the picture of compatibility.

I kept going back into the ring, so to speak. After all, he was handsome, funny as hell, smart and interesting—he was Ray Davies!

One day, in a rage, I threw some new shirts I'd just bought him, still in their wrappings, out the window. We both leaned out the window and watched as they descended the five floors and hit the ground, bouncing across the pavement below, beautiful pin-striped shirts with white collars—the kind he looked so good in. I suppose one of us would have traipsed down the stairs to retrieve them, but before we got the chance an old tramp appeared, stopped in front of the scattered, unopened packages, stooped over and popped them under his tatty old mac and kept walking, now with a little bounce in his stride.

Ray often likened himself to a tramp, so it was particularly apt to watch this comic drama from on high. I tried my hardest to remain angry but the tears of laughter came. Ours was a battle of wills.

·

If the band were playing near Akron the band and I would stop by my parents' house, and my dad and Martin would go for a walk out in the woods to look for hawks. Martin was an authority on any kind of wildlife and my dad was happy to have someone to take out in a field with a pair of binoculars.

My mom would make a carrot cake and everybody had a good time. Although I knew the Herefordian accent was barely decipherable to them, my folks beamed at this validation of my success. But I was always in a nervous state when I went home, knowing how much my folks hated it if they read any press with me swearing in it. Their disapproval was now mixed with pride. It was all too weird. Doing shows anywhere near Akron was nothing short of traumatic; they were always in the audience and I felt so self-conscious that I'd slip up and couldn't be my usual obnoxious self.

When we'd first started there was no MTV, but all that had changed and our profiles went skywards. The celebrity culture hadn't yet enveloped every aspect of modern life and I actually thought I could remain low-key and avoid the fuss. It just wasn't going to work out that way.

There was more touring: I was thrilled every time we got to a new place, my ambition to see the world coming to pass, but when a band is rolling out of a bus or airport and into a van, it's not with the same wide-eyed delight as that of a backpacking reveller. I'd always thought traveling meant having no agenda, and that to see the world you had to be free to roam, as in my old Beat-informed romantic view of the hobo. The regimented routine of touring seemed unimaginative, and I would refer to it disparagingly as "the Boy Scouts." Days off were more often than not spent in a hotel room with the curtains drawn, trying to recover from alcohol excess and the fraught attempts to sleep.

There is simply nothing worse than a band member bringing a "significant other" into the fold. It's even more destructive than the general stupidity and absurd egos. When the dreaded outsider shows up, the whole dynamic gets thrown and everybody hates it, no matter what they say. (Remember those pictures of Yoko knitting in the studio and the look on the faces of the other three?)

Ray admired Jimmy and referred to him as "the Hook Man," a veiled compliment meaning that Jimmy provided the hooks that transformed my otherwise ordinary songs into something else. Meanwhile, things were going downhill; the clichés were coming fast and furiously.

Stan Tippins knew more about the pitfalls of touring than any of us, having been in Mott the Hoople, but it must have been quite grotesque and depressing for him to see his young lads becoming depraved drug fiends in front of his eyes. And I was, surely by tour number two, a complete pain in the ass, the likes of which he had no experience of dealing with.

When we arrived at a hotel in LA and I couldn't block the light out of my room, I ran down the corridor, screaming, "Get me out of here!" Stan had to usher me out and find a hotel where I could sit crying on the floor in the dark, surrounded by my notebooks.

Stan couldn't understand the need for us to get so loaded and was often heard to say, "There's nothing better than a nice, juicy pear." We all laughed at him like he was "some dumb farmer" (as my father would say), but the truth was, we were getting worse.

I was a total prick when I was drunk; not a jovial, good-fun type, but a loudmouthed sadist who would taunt anyone before passing out, then wonder why everyone was keeping their distance the next day. Keeping tabs on me was probably as rewarding as stepping into a steaming dog pile, and you just never knew what I might drag home.

Pete was steadily getting worse and I just ignored his heroin shenanigans, regarding them as attention-seeking and pathetic. The guys were also appalled by his excesses and started to keep a wide berth. I discovered that guys never confront each other, preferring to say nothing—the opposite of girls.

Martin remained steady and tried to arbitrate as best he could, but he was chain-smoking, not great for the physical demands of a rock drummer, and he liked a drink too. Because he was thoughtful and a bit of a farmer himself at heart, the other two would habitually walk away from him mid-sentence, which they found hilarious. They could be mean fuckers. Dave would take them aside regularly and tell them, "Back off from Martin; he's getting depressed."

Jimmy was vulnerable to any pretty girl who wanted to latch on. He had an underager on the bus crossing state lines for a while, which could have jeopardized the whole tour. He was even more vulnerable to anyone who had drugs. He abhorred Pete's fascination with smack but liked to get wrecked himself on whatever was going. Like all of us, after a few drinks—and Jimmy was always after a few drinks—he'd take anything offered him.

He was increasingly disgruntled with the tension between Pete and me. Every soundcheck became a battle for dominance, which I usually won. Pete would turn up the volume and I'd shoot him down in humiliating fashion. "Join a fucking heavy-metal band, for fuck's sake!" We were at odds day after day, show after show—a sound-check could leave him in tears.

There's no way to undo things that have been said; time can't heal everything. Jimmy hated it. He hated anything that got in the way of the music.

Everyone was getting out of control, and even our steady-handed leader Stan wasn't impervious to the excesses of the road. He could often be found slumped over in a chair in a hotel foyer after a night of drinking. He'd have to check out the band, corral and get us into the van while brutally hungover, which turned the whole lot of us into sadistic little shits, as if he were headmaster and needed torturing. We even used a photo of him in a terrible state on our access-all-areas laminates.

Another one of the band's favorite catchphrases was Stan's oft-heard explanation: "Must 'ave been summut I 'et." (Must have been something I ate.) But Stan wasn't someone to cross if he was in an ornery mood. I remember him more than once standing at the top of the aisle on a flight, angling for a fight if an Elvis song came on the in-flight entertainment. Stan would be out of his seat faster than a dog, ready to sniff out anyone who might react favorably, because there was only one band you could truly love in Stan's book, and that was Johnny Kidd and the Pirates. He saw Elvis as someone who had usurped Johnny Kidd. It was actually kind of scary to see him standing next to the toilets, foot tapping, just waiting for someone to sing along to Elvis so he could thump them. Jimmy would watch this display with rapturous admiration.

As far as rock bands went, it was all textbook stuff. But the fact that everybody in every band in history had gone through the same things didn't make it any easier to assimilate the horror show of drug addiction. Alcohol was always in the mix too, the lethal ingredient, portal to the dark side, ever-lurking. The only reason we were still standing is that we had youth on our side. But as always, time was running out.

Making a point of never reading the press, I didn't know how the second album was reviewed. I knew people still liked us and we were getting airplay with "Message of Love," "Talk of the Town," "I Go to Sleep"—and we had rockers like "Bad Boys Get Spanked," which were the heart and soul of the band.

Jimmy went from strength to strength, and every guitar player in the world was aware of this new, rare talent. Nils Lofgren came to our shows to hang out with him, and Jimmy loved Nils, another guitar bore to clear a room with. Jimmy attracted them in every town. (It's a shame he never got to meet Billy Gibbons of ZZ Top, because if those two had ever got in the same room together no one would've ever heard from them again and their conversation about string gauges, effect pedals, fret height and valve amps would probably still be in progress.)

We were doing a TV show in Germany and Van Halen was on the same bill. Jimmy and Eddie Van Halen talked guitars all afternoon, boring the pants off anyone still in the room. Jimmy was so excited to have this new guitar-slinging buddy that he insisted Stan get the organizers to arrange a hall—somewhere they could jam later that night. It seemed like Eddie had been guarded by his brother and his band, and didn't get off the leash very often, so he was as excited as Jimmy by the idea of the jam.

We were all hanging around the suite in the hotel when we overheard Eddie on the phone to his wife, saying something that would elevate him in the eyes of the band for its definitive catchphrase content: "No, I'm *not* having a good time!"

The band loved that, and it was referred to endlessly from then on. It was always necessary to play down any merriment when a guy called home to an overworked wife dealing with the domestics on her own.

"No, I'm *not* having a good time!" was a classic.

As evening approached, Stan had it all arranged, a hall secured for the night. Eddie was primed and ready to go in for the historic jam session as promised, but by then Jimmy had passed out in a chair and couldn't be roused, his tooth dangling and mouth gaping, snoring like an old man.

I wasn't in better shape than the rest of them, I must admit. Once, in New York, after crashing a Johnny Thunders show, where I ended up on the floor of the stage crying and calling the audience complacent hippies (which they weren't), Thunders collared me the next day and told me, "Chrissie, man, you'd better do something—get your act together."

Thunders himself had a big purple lip at the time, having fallen down a flight of stairs. I knew I was in trouble if he, of all people, thought I was.

·

After a show in LA, on our final American tour together, the guys went off to party with John McEnroe while I stuck around, talking to John Belushi, the beloved comedian who came backstage to tell me that his mother was from Akron.

I told him I was having trouble dealing with all the attention I was getting, and he tried to convince me that if I wore sunglasses in a photo, the press wouldn't use it. That sounded a little far-fetched to me, because in every picture I'd ever seen of him, he was wearing sunglasses. He asked if I wanted to hang out with him for the night, so we climbed into a white limo together and took off.

Our first stop was in some bar on the Sunset Strip, where he introduced me to Jack Nicholson, who was lovely—exactly the Jack Nicholson you'd expect. It was very low key, not a crazy party, so we had a few drinks and I relaxed. The next stop was up in the Hollywood Hills.

"You gotta meet Tim," said John.

Timothy Leary answered the door naked. Most guys would have reached for a pair of shorts, but not Leary; he ducked into the next room and came back buttoning up a shirt, still *sans* pants. He walked around like that until it just seemed normal. The last thing I remember about that night was swallowing a pill he gave me. C'mon! It was Timothy Leary—to say no would have been out of the question.

I woke up the next morning in my room back in the Sunset Marquis with no recollection of how I got there. I remembered seeing Leary's bare ass but that was all.

The American tour over, we were playing Japan when we heard the very sad news that John Belushi was found dead in his bungalow at the Chateau Marmont: drugs.

Just before we went onstage to do a show in Osaka, I was rummaging through my bag and I found a pair of sunglasses—Belushi must have popped them in there to help me ward off unwanted attention. I walked onstage wearing them as I greeted the Japanese audience and, as far as I know, nobody ever used the picture.

·

The concerts in Japan and Australia were bad. The shows were good, but the vibe wasn't. We were going through the motions—the worst possible thing for a band.

Pete confronted me at the soundcheck in Tokyo: "What are you doing Tuesday?"

"What do you mean, what am I doing?" I asked. "We're doing a show—what do you think I'm doing?"

"Well, I'm getting married."

He said it as if it was a threat, or a cloaked appeal for me to change things, turn back the clock. A few days earlier I had told him that I was planning on doing the same thing.

Pete's girlfriend, Katy, had been on the phone from London to everyone in the band and crew, worried because she hadn't heard from him for days. Why had he not phoned? Nobody knew what to tell her. Who wanted to say he was getting married to a model he'd met in a club the night before? Oh, Pete.

Jimmy was increasingly unamused. I could see that he'd reached his limit with Pete's exaggerated swagger, louche affectations—the Japanese fighter pilot, the kamikaze schtick—skulking onstage for encores, fag dangling from his mouth—the look he had been culti- vating. Jimmy hated it. We all did. It was as if Pete was rubbing our noses in his addiction and how separate from the rest of us he was.

I knew that Jimmy had made a decision during the last night in Australia, when some old-timer, a janitor, told Pete, "You can't smoke onstage here, mate." What did Pete do? Did he flick the offending dog-end to the floor, crushing it underfoot, apologizing like the Pete of days gone by? No. He punched the old guy in the face.

Jimmy watched this pathetic display, incandescent with rage, but said nothing. He looked at me, though; he shook his head and I knew.

Martin, too. He didn't acknowledge it, preferring to have a few moments to recover, get back out there and finish the show. But when he looked up and I managed to catch his eye, yes, Martin too. It was just a matter of time.

Pete's junkie persona had taken over and was inhabiting him, like a demonic possession. His best friends couldn't find him behind the sallow mask; where was the old laughing, joking, fun Pete they'd knocked around Hereford with? Pete was gone.

Jimmy and I had been playing around with some new tunes: quieter stuff, more melodic. It didn't suit Pete's new self-image of junkie hard-ass. As always, Jimmy only had one agenda, the music. The rest was of no use to him. That never changed. Pete was testing the waters, trying to throw his weight around, making a show of his uninterest in our ideas, distancing himself in too obvious a way.

Maybe it was because we didn't big him up enough. Maybe because he thought we didn't rate him. Maybe because of our strained relationship. Maybe because not once did I go over to him and say, "Nice playing tonight—you sounded great." Not once. But he didn't sound great; he sounded like someone who had a problem.

Pete wanted something but none of us cared what anymore. He was vying for attention and it was standing between us and the music. Whatever his problem was, Jimmy was not having it. The tour was almost over. Soon we could go home.

I recalled a day back in Tufnell Park, the house on Dalmeny Road. Pete said to me, "No one will ever love you more than I do."

Maybe it was true. We'd gone our separate ways, all right—the drugs, the alcohol doing their job. And me, I was like a shipwrecked captain trying to direct the crew back to shore. I just couldn't do it.

Pete was burrowing further into his rut, becoming more and more uncommunicative: smack. It's true that some people can't handle success. With fame, even if a person doesn't change, everybody around them does. It becomes a case of mistaken identity; some people just don't know who they are anymore. Pete had got too caught up in the myth of the rock star he was trying to be.

That show at Barbarella's with Johansen's band. He had been too impressed with the New Yorkers—the tailored suits, style and attitude. But Pete was a middle-class public-school boy (private school, in American parlance), not an old-style gang member from the mean streets.

Then when Thunders came over to Dalmeny Road and left blood on the tea towels, Pete was more than impressed: he was hooked.

.

The last show of the tour was in Bangkok. We didn't know it was the last show we would ever play together.

Ray was coming out for it, and Pete suffered to see me with anyone. Martin and Jimmy dreaded it too, especially after Ray and Jimmy had a boisterous dispute after a show in Brighton that no one really recovered from, when Ray wouldn't let him into my dressing room.

Our last show together: enthusiastic Thai punters stormed the stage, the police moved in, broke it up and ended it. It wasn't pretty. Kids got thrown out, people were hurt and I didn't care. The ending wasn't fun.

We were burned out. Another world tour and the fissures had become cracks. We just wanted it to be over. It wasn't the celebratory end-of-tour gig it should have been. How wrong it all was. It's always sad when you start to hate what you love.

.

The Herefordians, Pete, Jimmy and Martin, led by Stan Tippins, their mentor. Night after night at the side of the stage, waiting to go on, a last encore, looking to Stan to give the command.

"Wait. Wait for the build . . ." Stan held us back like terriers trying to get through a hole in a fence.

"Not yet." Only when Stan said so was it time.

Stan had to watch helplessly as his protégés sank into a murky pool of drugs. There was nothing he could do to stop it.

How much did I hate those leeches who would show up backstage with their calling cards—packets of cocaine—wanting to get close to the band. The one thing I hated about drugs was the assholes you had to hang out with to get them.

I always knew I didn't have the guts for the fame game.

We'd got to know each other pretty well by now, two albums under our belts—success. We had futures now. People wanted us. But the incident in Australia with the old duffer at the side of the stage was the last straw for Jimmy. We limped home from the tour and agreed to take some time off from each other.

.

A month passed. My own wedding plan was another event that should have been enacted only onstage in the theater of the absurd. I was wearing a white silk suit I'd had made in Bangkok, with a skirt (so, you see, I really was serious), and white button-up ankle boots custom-made by Anello & Davide for me. We argued all morning about whether to invite anyone as witnesses, with me finally backing down and agreeing to have no one. He wanted to have the ceremony in Guildford, and I wanted to get a cab there—you know, a little bit of luxury on the day, with me all decked out in my suit under a raincoat and all—but he wanted to take a train so we got the train.

The guy in the registry office took one look at us and suggested we come back another time. I guess mascara smeared over my face was the giveaway. Even a total stranger could tell we were making a mistake, but I'd never heard of anyone getting turned away before. Still, there's always the first time.

We got separate trains back to London. I thought I'd never see him again, but when I walked into the flat on Luxborough Street, there he was, as if nothing out of the ordinary had happened.

Jimmy, Martin and I agreed to have a meeting to figure out what we were going to do about Pete.

When the appointed day arrived they came over to my flat, and I suggested the possibility that we could warn him, give him a chance to clean up his act. Jimmy was impatient; this was taking up his time.

"If he stays—I go," he stated flatly.

Martin, the peacemaker, nodded in agreement. Pete was out. They didn't even want to talk to him—let Dave Hill tell him.

Jimmy seemed more inconvenienced than bothered. It was a done deal and now we could get on with more important things. We just needed to find a bass player and go back into the studio to record a new song I had that we'd been messing around with, "Back on the Chain Gang."

I also had a bomb to drop: I was pregnant. I thought this wouldn't go down well, but Martin said, "Congratulations," and Jimmy didn't seem to think it was a problem. He was more excited to tell us about a kid guitar player he'd met, saying that when the time came, he wanted to get him up onstage with us. His name was Robbie McIntosh.

I called Dave Hill and told him to call Pete.

34

THE END

needed time. I couldn't think about auditions—not yet. Not when I knew that Pete was sitting in his flat in Oxford Gardens, feeling betrayed. I didn't know how to handle this. Maybe in a few days we could meet up and talk. No, that probably wouldn't happen. Maybe Martin and I could go together. No, it wasn't going to work. I'd have to let it sink in. Maybe next week. There was too much to think about; I couldn't bear to imagine how Pete was feeling.

He must have thought it was all coming from me. Did he know how angry Jimmy had become with him? Probably not. Jimmy had just stopped talking to him and let him get on with his junkie bullshit. No, he probably hadn't even noticed the effect he was having on the others. Pete had become so insular; he wanted us to notice him but how much could he see himself? That fucking drug destroyed everything.

Those were the thoughts sloshing around my head after Martin and Jimmy left. There was too much to think about. We all had our own problems now, never mind the band: Jimmy had got married and in my opinion, from the way he was talking, it sounded like divorce was already on the cards. I was knocked up. Martin was married now, too. We all had domestic stuff to attend to. Well, I'd see Pete eventually and we'd have it out.

•

I paced around my flat on my own for the next two days, unable to stop thinking about it. I'd see Jimmy and Mart soon, and maybe we could all meet up with Pete next month. It just needed time.

It was morning, about ten o'clock. The phone rang. It was Dave Hill. His voice quiet.

"Something strange has happened: Jimmy died."

•

Jimmy's body was still lying on the sofa in the girl's flat where he'd spent his last night. Dave and Mart were getting a cab over so they could confirm it was our Jimmy.

They'd shared many a room and Martin recognized his sleeping position, so that was one good thing: it looked like he'd died in his sleep.

He'd been at a charity gig to raise money for Ronnie Lane, a big hero of his. He died of "heart failure due to cocaine intolerance." He was twenty-five.

A day later, I called Dave and asked him to get me on the next flight to New York. A *Sun* reporter had called my apartment for a quote. How on earth did he get my number? I had to get out of town. I'd go see Ray, who was on tour.

The next flight going to NYC was on Concorde. "Get me on it, never mind the cost," I said. I grabbed a small bag and ran out the door.

When I arrived at JFK I had to share a cab with a guy into the city, as I only had a few dollars on me. He saw the Concorde tag on my bag and kept looking at it, then at my stony face. Why would someone who could fly Concorde want to share a cab? Oh, never mind. There was no explaining any of this.

The Kinks were playing a huge stadium in Philadelphia. My pal Joan Jett, who was supporting, walked over to say hi. Nobody knew Jimmy had died. I resented anybody talking to me. How dare they? Grief is like that—there is no rationale. I looked at the scaffolding and flight cases in the aircraft-hangar-sized backstage area. Jimmy would never see that again. That was the thing that brought it all home: he would never play guitar again.

They say you always feel better after a good cry, but when does the feeling better start?

•

That was a long trip, the drive to Hereford: the parish church, the little cemetery, the rain, the pretty Hereford countryside—the hole in the ground.

Jimmy's sister got legless with us after the service, and we badly recounted his favorite jokes. We tried hard to laugh—for Jimmy, always irreverent. Lynn was inconsolable, her little brother now in the ground.

That was the last time I saw Pete. He looked over at me and Martin during the service, and his eyes did the talking; Martin heard it too.

"If I'm so fucked up, why is *he* up there in the box?"

I noticed Pete's fiancée (who I'd still never met), wearing four-inch-high heels. I wondered how that was working out for her on the sodden grass. She looked glamorous, as a model should, I guess. The rain pelted down. No, Pete wasn't going to come over and talk to us.

Eight months passed. I had a darling baby girl now and was on my own with her when the phone rang. It was Dave. He only had to say one word: "Farndon."

He'd nodded off after shooting a speedball. His head went under and he drowned in the bathtub, needle in his arm. There's your rock-and-roll ending.

Oh, Pete.

His mum told us to stay away from the funeral. She blamed us— of course she did. She thought we fired him and then he turned to drugs. I met her a few months later, had her come round to see me in London at my flat.

"But why did you do that?" She wanted me to explain why we sacked her son; after all, we were his best friends. So I told her.

"He didn't start taking drugs because we fired him, we fired him because he started taking drugs."

"But why did no one tell *me*?" she pleaded with me to make it make sense.

"Because he adored you. It would have destroyed him if he thought you knew. I just couldn't do that."

There. Now, does it make sense?

EPILOGUE

And so I continued.

I kept the band going, loosely speaking. Different lineups and producers have seen me through and it's always a pleasure to do the old songs.

So be it.

I went on to have a lovely little family and found out that children really are the most joyful thing.

I still live in London, and go to Paris when I can.

I think it's easy to see that the moral of my story is that drugs, including tobacco and alcohol, only cause suffering. I read Allen Carr's *Easy Way to Stop* books and I stopped.

Philosophically, I've kept an ongoing relationship with the Bhagavad Gita, the glory I bask in, always finding answers for everything and solace.

I've had a few more romantic "dalliances," but for the most part have remained single. I enjoy my little meditations and find that humor is everywhere once you strip away the grief.

·

I always said that if one of us left it wouldn't be the Pretenders anymore. But when we ousted Pete, Jimmy and Mart and I never talked about changing our name.

I never got over losing Pete, never talking to him again. I'd taken him into my reckless world and lost him there.

When Jimmy died I was faced with things I hadn't thought about. His love of playing and meeting me and having a direction. And what he did for me. Making me more than I could have ever been on my own. Or with anybody else.

And I thought if I let it all go it would be as if the music died. No, he wouldn't want the music to die with him.

I found that any musical question I had could easily be answered. I just had to imagine what Jimmy would do. I had come to understand him so well that it was as if he was standing next to me talking to me.

So I listened to Jimmy and he always had the answer. That lasted another fifteen years or so, Jimmy in my ear telling me what to do, and then slowly, he seemed to fade away.

ACKNOWLEDGMENTS

Thank you to everyone who encouraged me to write this book, and to those who helped make it happen.

For their advice and encouragement, I'd particularly like to thank Claire Reihill, James Lever and Imogen Parker.

Thank you to Liz Marvin and Jake Lingwood from Ebury in London, and to Gerry Howard from Doubleday in New York.

PHOTOGRAPHIC CREDITS

SECTION 1
Author's own

SECTION 2
Page 1   Author's own
Pages 2–3 © Getty Images
Pages 4–8 Author's own

SECTION 3
Page 1   © Pennie Smith/ Author's own
Page 2   Author's own
Page 3   © Barry Plummer/ © Ray Stevenson/Rex Shutterstock
Page 4   Author's own
Page 5   © Bob Gruen
Page 6   © Joe Stevens/ © Sheila Rock
Page 7   © Sheila Rock/ © Joe Stevens/ © Getty Images
Page 8   © Bob Gruen

SECTION 4
Page 1   © David Corio
Page 2   © Pennie Smith/ © Simon Fowler
Page 3   © Pennie Smith
Page 4   © Tom Sheehan/ Author's own
Page 5   © Jill Furmanovsky/ © Ebet Roberts
Pages 6–7 © Simon Fowler
Page 8   © Tony Mottram